DISCUSSION

THE MACMILLAN COMPANY
NEW YORK · CHICAGO
DALLAS · ATLANTA · SAN FRANCISCO
LONDON · MANILA

DISCUSSION

by

WILLIAM S. HOWELL

Chairman, Department of Speech and Theater Arts
University of Minnesota

and

DONALD K. SMITH

Associate Professor of Speech
University of Minnesota

The Macmillan Company, New York

Library of Congress catalog card number: 56-7308

PREFACE

The importance of skills in leading and participating in discussion is widely recognized. Such skills seem to be an integral part of the workings of a democratic society. Effectively practiced, they strengthen the society which they serve.

It is not suprising, therefore, that systematic teaching of discussion is increasing in America, and that a considerable literature on the nature of discussion has developed. It is our hope that this book will make a significant contribution to that literature. In it we try to answer two questions which we think must be raised by every teacher of discussion: what should be the theoretical content of the discussion course; and what learning experiences are most effective in developing the abilities to apply relevant theory?

We have sought the answer to the first of these questions from an examination of the nature of discussion. As we see it, discussion encompasses the purposeful efforts of a group of people to work, through talk, toward increased understanding of problems, and toward the identification of satisfactory solutions to these problems. Groups make progress toward understanding and good solutions only if their members have the knowledge and skills necessary to investigation, to the selection of relevant information, and to the interpretation of that information. In other words, the basic ingredient of good discussion is the problem solving, or critical thinking, or *combined investigative and dialectical* skills of the members of a group.

We believe that group members who do not devote specific attention to learning and using the known skills of critical thinking cannot hope to improve their ability to participate in productive discussions. Therefore, we suggest that ways of thinking critically, together, should outweigh all other content in the study of discussion. We have emphasized this thesis in our development of the theory of discussion, and we have devoted the greatest single portion of this text to an examination of the skills and procedures of critical thinking in productive group discussion.

v

The thoughtful student will observe other skills useful to discussion. Critical thinking abilities cannot operate effectively in groups except in the climate of good human relations. Persons who speak with clarity, precision, and animation, who listen thoughtfully, and who manifest appreciation for other persons and their ideas all facilitate critical thinking. Hence, we give proportionate emphasis in this text to principles of effective human relations in group discussion, to the discussant's speech, and to his understanding of language. As tools for the planning, production, and evaluating of discussions, a variety of patterns of discussion are described; participation and leadership standards are specified, and evaluative procedures explained. And finally, since problems in ethics and in the relationship of discussion to other forms of public address often trouble the student, we include a treatment of the relationship of discussion to the advocate or persuader, and an analysis of the ethical problems encountered in discussions. This completes what we believe to be the irreducible minimum of theory needed if the student is to understand the process of discussion.

Concerning the second question, about learning experiences, we are certain that the study of discussion proceeds most effectively through early and continuous practice in actual discussion. A beginning student will find discussion apparently—and deceptively—simple. But early confidence will gradually develop into an appreciation of its complexity as he continues his participation. Hence, we provide suggestions for starting first practice almost immediately, and we urge that discussion courses using this book as a text be based upon a series of discussion activities. Occasionally, it will be necessary to devote class time to clearing up theoretical matters, but even this can be accomplished in an appropriate discussion exercise, using student planners and leaders, with the instructor assuming the role of resource authority.

The student should read the book as rapidly as he is able to make application of the materials. Instructors' suggestions for improvement, based on performance, can be keyed to the text. For example, when a failure in interpretation of evidence is identified, the student can be referred to the appropriate section of one of the chapters on critical thinking. In this and in other ways the major responsibility for assimilating the content of the book can rest with the student.

We suggest that the person who uses this book outside the classroom involve himself in discussion as frequently as is possible and practical. Seeing and practicing the application of procedures and principles fix them in the mind. The reader will find critical thinking skills somewhat difficult to develop by himself. But with practice—trial and error at first—and repeated reading he will be able to make most of the described problem-solving techniques habitual.

We hope most fervently that this book will serve to combat the friendly pooling of ignorance that often passes for discussion. We call attention to Goethe's pertinent observation: "There is nothing more frightful than ignorance in action."

W. S. H.
D. K. S.

CONTENTS

PART ONE

Principles of Discussion

CHAPTER I

The Nature of Discussion

Two simple facts suggest why each of us should become an active student of discussion.

The first fact is: we all participate frequently in discussions. We face, in common with others, many problems in living, and in our effort to find satisfactory answers to these problems, no activity other than discussion is likely to be so productive or satisfying.

The second fact is: many of the discussions in which we participate are inefficient, wasteful of time, and less productive than purposeful communication among rational persons ought to be. This is true because few Americans have ever bothered to become students of this important form of discourse. They not only fail to accommodate themselves efficiently to the discussions in which they participate; often they engage in behavior which impedes progress in the deliberations of an entire group. In such situations the discussion which ought to bring people closer to one another simply drives them apart. Or the discussion which ought to lead toward wisdom becomes a verbose pooling of ignorance.

Discussion, then, is a form of discourse necessary to all our lives; but it is a form of discourse which, in the absence of study, we all too often handle badly.

THE OCCASIONS FOR DISCUSSION

Discussion rises out of our need to solve problems. Of course, there are problems which people solve alone—without seeking the counsel, or criticism, or thinking of others. The solitary thinker may engage in a sort of inward discussion—an argument with himself—

as he confronts certain problems. But he cannot be said to have engaged in a discussion of the sort we shall consider in this book. Moreover, we salute the self-reliance of the person who settles many of the small decisions of his life without involving others. Thus, legitimate occasions for discussion seldom rise out of such problems as:

Does my suit need pressing?

What should I have for breakfast?

Is it wise for me to play golf this afternoon?

But there are other problems whose solutions seem to call for discussion as inevitably as living plants call for sunshine and moisture. For example, consider these problems which have confronted groups of Americans in our recent past:

1. (June 25, 1950. South Korea has been invaded.) What sort of military action, if any, should the United States take to protect the independence of South Korea?

2. (August, 1953. Russia has successfully exploded a thermonuclear device.) What changes, if any, should be made in the planning and conduct of civilian defense in the United States?

3. (1954. The highway accident rate in America has reached an all-time high.) What are the causes of our increasing accident rate? What action can government (or education, business, religion, the individual, and so forth) take at this time to reduce highway accidents?

4. (1954. Marriage between persons of mixed religious heritage continues to increase in the United States.) What ought to be the attitude of religious leaders (or parents, or young people, and so on) toward mixed religious marriages?

5. (1954. Farm income in the United States is declining.) What changes, if any, should be made in the present agricultural policies of the United States Government?

There is no question that these problems, and thousands of others like them, were and are the subject of important discussions. We can observe, by examining these problems, that they have certain characteristics which make them inevitably "discussable."

1. They are problems concerning which decisions must be made, even though no inevitably "right" solution is possible. In making decisions, the rightness of which must be matters of probability rather than of fact, men wisely turn to discussion. Democratic gov-

ernment has always assumed that group decision-making increases the probability of wise decisions in dealing with the contingencies of man's social and political life. Research on the products of group and individual thinking tends to confirm our faith in the wisdom of using discussion as we seek the answers to the complex problems of living.

2. These are problems concerning which no one person possesses all the relevant knowledge, skills, or right to take action. The complexity of modern society has extended constantly the number of problems which involve knowledge or skill beyond the reach of any one person. When we seek a pooling of wisdom, we inevitably turn to discussion.

3. The solutions to these problems will inevitably affect the interests of the discussants. Democratic society assumes that people should participate in the making of decisions which will affect their lives. Often the "rightness" of a decision is closely involved with the "acceptability" of that decision to the people whose lives are affected. Let us suppose that a group of people are confronted with a problem of malnutrition because they refuse to kill or control the cattle which are ravaging their croplands. There is little point in saying that the "right" solution to their problem is the killing of the cattle. This solution can become a useful one only if it is acceptable to the people whose lives are involved. Can you think of other examples in which the rightness of a decision is involved in its acceptability?

Of course, people may be, and often must be, persuaded to accept the rightness of decisions which were made for them by other persons. But no process of discourse so completely assures the acceptability of a decision as the process of discussion, in which the persons who will be affected by a decision participate in the making of that decision.

DISCUSSION DEFINED

The foregoing paragraphs suggest that we do not consider all conversation or talk among people as discussion. Rather, as we use the term in this book, *discussion is that form of discourse which occurs when two or more persons, recognizing a common problem, exchange and evaluate information and ideas in an effort to solve that problem. Their effort may be directed toward a better under-*

*standing of the problem, or toward the development of a program of
action relative to the problem.* Discussion usually occurs in face-to-
face situations, with the exchange being spoken. And if more than
two persons are involved, it usually occurs under the direction of a
leader.

We have now stipulated a rather specific definition of discussion. We do so in order to give focus and purpose to your thinking
about discussion. Many of the activities in our society which are
often called "discussion" fall outside this definition, and are not the
direct concern of your study.

Notice that we have said that discussion is *purposive.* That is,
the spoken exchange occurs in the effort to solve a problem. Thus,
much of the aimless or undirected social conversation in which we
participate is not discussion. Small talk, with its disconnected clichés,
polite comments about the weather, or impolite comments about
"friends not present," is not discussion. Conversation may develop
into discussion, but it usually begins with a lack of specific purpose,
a lack of a common realized problem, and therefore proceeds without the limitation of an end to be sought.

Notice that we have said that discussion involves the *effort to
understand, or develop a program of action.* By implication, then,
the discussant is one who is *in search* of conclusions, not one "who
has all the answers." The discussant talks because his thinking is not
completed. He talks with the expectation that *development* will
occur in his thinking as the talk proceeds. Talk among persons who
believe that they understand completely, or have solved a problem,
is not discussion. Whatever the form taken by this talk, whatever
the outward resemblance of the activity to discussion, the effort by
persons to persuade one another to particular, preconceived conclusions is not discussion. The activity which results when people seek
to influence others to particular, predetermined actions or beliefs we
shall call *persuasion.* The relationship between the discussant who is
in search of answers, and the advocate who wishes to *sell* answers,
is a complex one, and leads to many misunderstandings about the
part played by argument in discussion.

Notice that we have said that discussion involves *exchange* and
evaluation. Most persons have some skill in exchanging opinions and
such information as they may possess. That is to say, they send
messages which contain information and opinions to other persons,

and these messages are received or understood with varying degrees of accuracy. But an exchange of information, by itself, is not sufficient to discussion. Discussion assumes that the message sent by one person is subjected to immediate, public examination by others. It is this *criticism* of information and opinion which distinguishes discussion from much of conversation.

We have limited our definition of discussion to a particular form of discourse. We shall apply the term to discourse which is or purports to be:

(1) Purposive.

(2) In search of answers: understandings or solutions.

(3) Concerned with *critical evaluation* as well as *exchange* of information.

Discussion, then, is recognizable, not by the outward form of the discourse—by the fact that it involves two or more persons, or that it has a leader—but rather by the purposes and procedures of the persons who talk with one another.

It would be interesting at this point for you to listen to one or two radio or television discussion-type programs. To what extent do these discussions exemplify the sort of discourse which we have defined as discussion? In what respects do they seem to involve sorts of discourse which are not included within the definition here given?

PSEUDO-DISCUSSION

We have already indicated that the activity of many groups which purport to be discussing problems bears only superficial resemblance to discussion as previously defined. Here are two types of pseudo-discussion.

Advocacy cloaked in the discussion form

Audiences are frequently much influenced by the conclusions reached by a group of discussants who, sitting around a table, analyze "impartially" the evidence and opinion relative to a certain problem. It is not surprising, therefore, that enterprising advocates of particular points of view frequently use so-called public discussions for propaganda purposes. An extreme example of this is the discussion organized by a campaign manager during a political campaign to "talk over impartially" the issues of a coming election. The experts, of course, all happened to be of one political persuasion, and they proceeded to bring out their point of view under the guise of impartial, critical examination of the evidence about the campaign.

Akin to this "propaganda discussion" is the discussion instigated by an advocate who conceals the fact that he has a particular program which he wishes to sell to the discussion group. This persuader may have, let us say, a program for rezoning certain areas of his community. But he feels that his ideas would have greater force if they were presented to the community, not as the product of his own thinking, but as the product of the deliberations of a problem-solving group of prominent citizens. He organizes the group for the ostensible purpose of considering zoning problems in his city—but his actual purpose is to sell the group on supporting and recommending the plan he has already worked out.

The discussion form used by a status-dominated group

A common form of pseudo-discussion is found in the deliberations of groups dominated by one person or a small clique. Such groups usually consist of a leader and a group of people who for some reason defer to the leader. The deliberations of the group are a sort of ritual in which the members vie with one another in praising the opinions of the leader. Classroom discussions, in the hands of some teachers, can tend toward this form.

The status-dominated group tends to be most obvious when the members of the group are financially or physically dependent upon a group leader.

Witness the familiar stereotype of the motion picture producer and his claque of "yes-men." In such a group, most of the alleged discussants are simply competing with one another in the task of discovering and giving approval to the opinions of the member who has status.

Although the pseudo-discussions we have described raise ethical problems, it would be a mistake to assume that all pseudo-discussion is an unethical or unworthy form of discourse. Our purpose in calling attention to pseudo-discussion is simply to highlight the unique values of genuine discussion in problem solving, and thus to sharpen the focus of students who study discussion and of teachers who seek to develop discussion skills.

CONFERENCE-TYPE AND SHOW-TYPE DISCUSSION

Further insight into the nature of discussion may be gained from a consideration of two types of discussion, both widely used, which place somewhat different demands upon the participants. Conference-type discussions involve talk among a group of persons with a common problem, but with *no external audience.* Club meetings, committee meetings, business conferences, and small "workshop" groups are examples of situations in which conference-type discussion may take place. Show-type discussions have an external audience. Here a group of "experts" discuss a problem for the benefit of a listening audience. The audience may or may not be invited to participate in the discussion. Radio round-table discussions, public panels, and other public forum situations are examples of this type of discussion.

Conference-type discussion is obviously the basic or primary form of discussion. Here the participating discussants confront no problem other than the primary one of seeking increased understanding or acceptable solutions to some problem. The group has maximum flexibility in developing its thinking. Language may be as technical as is consistent with the membership of the group, without concern for the demands of some outside listener. The group may have to consider time as a factor in its deliberations, but time is a less rigid factor than with, say, a radio round table. Expert testimony may be utilized to its fullest. The member of the conference group who listens analytically, making few comments, may be in a real sense an active and creative participant in the conference group.

We believe it helpful to view show-type discussion as a derived form of discussion. That is, conference discussion is the prototype for the show discussion, in which the discussants try to communicate to an audience the essential characteristics of their reflective deliberations about a problem.

Without pressing the analogy too far, a good show-type discussion resembles a dramatization of cooperative problem solving or reflective group deliberation. It bears a relationship to conference discussion similar to the relationship between drama and life. That is, good drama compresses, heightens, and clarifies for an audience the living experiences of people. In the same sense a good show-type discussion compresses, heightens, and clarifies the discourse of a group which is engaged in the problem-solving process. In its "planning discussions" the show group can discover and eliminate unproductive lines of thinking from its agenda, thus giving its show discussion a clearer and more compressed structure than a "first" discussion might have. The group can discover points of agreement and dispute among its members, and thus be able to clarify these matters for an audience more quickly than it could in a "first" discussion.

This is not to say that the discussants in a show-type discussion memorize and rehearse a script. It is to say that they ordinarily meet at some length prior to their public appearance, to plan an agenda which will enable them to communicate with maximum clarity some limited portion of their thinking about the problem at hand.

By observing differences apparent in the discourse of show-type and conference-type discussion, we may see more clearly the relationship between these two forms. Participants in the show discussion must present to the audience the definitions and limitations they have previously agreed to place on their problem. Discussants must pay particular attention to the simplicity and colorfulness of their language, as the nature of the audience may dictate. All members of the show discussion should participate overtly and frequently, since the audience will worry about the "silent" member of a public panel. Rigid time limitations must often be met. The leader may find it desirable to spend more time in making clear to the audience "where we are going, and where we have been."

Most classroom discussion training must be given through the practice of show-type discussion. The demands for clarity, compression, and demonstration of effective critical thinking placed by the show-type form provide excellent training for the student of discussion. Transfer of the skills learned in such activity to the conference situation should provide no problem, provided:

(1) The student is aware of the differences in these two types.

(2) The show-type discussions emphasize the same purposive exchange and criticism of information and opinion necessary to all productive problem solving.

THE ENDS OF DISCUSSION

We have observed that discussion seeks either the end of *understanding* or of *action*. A closer look at these two general ends of discussion will be productive of additional insight into the nature of the discussion activity.

Discussion seeking understanding

Groups are often drawn into discussion through a common need for knowledge or need to learn. A good example of such a group would be a so-called "Great-Books Study Group." In such groups people may meet to discuss the meaning of some book which is important to their intellectual heritage, and to seek understanding of this book. The members of the group may have varied motives for entering into discussion. Some may have felt a dissatisfaction with their own life, and be in search of self-understanding through an exploration of the works of the great thinkers of history. Some may simply be seeking intellectual companionship. Sociologists have observed that large numbers of people in the crowded society of the modern world are really very lonely. They seek some basis for communicating with their fellow men, and hope to find that basis through discussion of common objects of study. The common denominator of such discussion groups, however, is the book to be studied, and the understanding which is sought through such study. No member of the group need visualize any specific "action" rising out of their discussion, even though the understanding reached *may* affect the way of living or the actions of various members of the group.

Study groups of all sorts are a common source of discussions seeking understanding. Parents groups may meet to discuss matters of child development. Understanding is the end sought, even though that understanding may well be linked to various actions taken by the discussants in their own homes. Radio round tables usually are pointed toward increased "understanding" of a problem, rather than the formulation of an action.

Can you list some of the discussions or conferences with which you have had experience which seem to have understanding as their main end? What relationship do these discusions have to "action"?

Discussion seeking action

Other groups may meet to formulate plans for specific actions which are to be undertaken. Often severe time limits may be imposed on the deliberations of the group. The mayor of a city might appoint a citizens' committee to bring in a recommendation on a proposed new hospital, to be presented to the city council on a specific date. Here the action of the discussion group would take the form of a committee report, and the planning of the discussion procedures would have to be pointed toward that report. Can you list other examples of discussion groups which seek some specific action as the end of their discussion?

It should be observed that discussion groups seeking understanding ordinarily operate under little pressure with regard to the amount of progress which must be achieved in a given period of time. Freed from the pressure of time, such groups may require or desire only the most nominal sort of leadership, designed to give every participant the widest latitude in expressing his own thinking.

Action groups, under pressure in terms of time, may wish and require much more active leadership. Discussion of certain matters may have to be halted before all discussants are thoroughly satisfied, simply because of the insistent pressure of the clock or the calendar.

ARE THERE ALTERNATIVES TO DISCUSSION?

At the outset of this chapter we said that everyone participates in problem-solving discussions. This we believe to be as self-evident as the statement that man is a social being, and that many of his problems rise out of, and must be solved by, social participation.

It would be a mistake, however, to think that all men in all cultures make equal use of discussion. It should be observed that the practice of discussion is most highly regarded in a free, democratic society, and that the theories of discussion which will be considered in this book arise out of the same set of values which gave rise to democracy. Let us state two of the values which are important to our democratic society, so that we may see how these values also underlie the theory of discussion:

1. Democratic societies hold that every person, in and of himself, has worth. That is to say, people are not a means to some end—objects to be used or manipulated for some purpose; rather, each

person is an end in himself, deserving to be so regarded and so valued by all his fellow human beings. From this it follows that in a democratic society there is no one whose opinions, experiences, and purposes are not worthy of consideration. Individuals may vary in their knowledge of events, in their capacity to think and act; but each individual has equal right to be heard. Each person has equal right to participate in the making of decisions which will affect his life. In other words, each person has the right to be a discussant.

2. Democratic societies hold that men have the right to discuss; they also hold that men who exercise this right become more able and useful members of society. Powers of self-direction which are not used tend to atrophy. And persons who do not participate in the discussion of a democratic society tend to lose their capacity for such participation.

It is apparent that these values which we have just considered are not held to be equally important by all persons living in a democratic society, and they are often completely negated in authoritarian or totalitarian societies. Thus, alternatives to discussion do arise. People in groups, facing a problem, may live in a society in which the power to make a decision about that problem has been usurped. Thus, Russian farmers, in the 1920's, did not participate in making the decision which forced them into collective farming groups. People in groups may choose to delegate to someone else the power to make decisions concerning their problems. To some extent all our governmental institutions in the United States represent a delegation of power to representatives. The delegation of power is for a limited time and subject to review by the people making the delegation. In some societies people who seem to have grown weary of the burdens of decision-making may delegate power on a more or less permanent basis. Thus, the German Reichstag in 1932, confronted with a man in the person of Adolf Hitler who wished to usurp power, ultimately voted him the power he wished. The German people ratified this "permanent delegation" of their rights of decision.

A more subtle and less easily identified alternative to discussion is provided by people who wish to avoid the hard work of discussion. One way of avoiding the work of discussion is demonstrated by people who have a "formula" answer to all of the problems which they face. The "formula" may be an answer which has had merit in the solution to some problems, but reliance upon it as a sort of "verbal" solution to any and all problems causes it to lose validity. In this sense the "formula" becomes a means by which discussants avoid the hard intellectual work of coming to grips with the reality they face, and refuge is found in a stereotyped solution.

One formula popular with discussants in the United States is the proposal of "more education" as the answer to any and all social problems. Now it is easy to see how and why Americans should believe strongly in the usefulness of "education." But as the "education formula" appears in discussion, it often becomes a generalized and platitudinous appeal for "more education" without any real consideration of what the nature of this education is to be, how it is to be brought about, or what evidence exists of the probable nature of its effects. In the formula sense "more education" is proposed as the answer to all racial and religious discrimination, to alcoholism, juvenile delinquency, traffic congestion, slum clearance, war, and graft in government.

Can you think of other "formula" solutions to problems which are popular in the nation or among persons with whom you are acquainted?

We may visualize the alternatives to discussion:

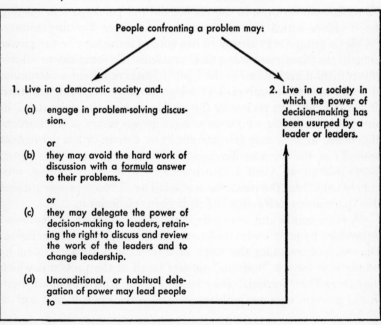

People confronting a problem may:

1. Live in a democratic society and:

(a) engage in problem-solving discussion.

or

(b) they may avoid the hard work of discussion with a _formula_ answer to their problems.

or

(c) they may delegate the power of decision-making to leaders, retaining the right to discuss and review the work of the leaders and to change leadership.

(d) Unconditional, or habitual delegation of power may lead people to

2. Live in a society in which the power of decision-making has been usurped by a leader or leaders.

CHAPTER II

Skills and Attitudes
Basic to Discussion

WHAT SKILLS AND ATTITUDES UNDERLIE EFFECTIVE DISCUSSION?

The basic principles of good discussion were made evident by Socrates more than 2,000 years ago. Plato's dialogues, which dramatize for us the example and teaching of Socrates, reveal conversations characterized by three conditions.

First, they were conversations among friends. These took place in a congenial atmosphere among men whose common concern for wisdom made invective, denunciation, and impatience unnecessary. Not all contemporary discussions can take place among persons with a record of past association and friendship; few of them can take place in an atmosphere as congenial as that of the ancient Greek symposium, which combined the social occasion of a banquet with the form of good conversation. Nevertheless, we can recognize the importance of a friendly climate to productive discussion, and the importance of discussants who have both the desire and the skill necessary to develop good *human relations* among the members of a discussion group.

Can you list examples of discussions which have been unproductive because of a breakdown in human relations?

Second, the Platonic dialogues show us conversation among men who possessed *information* which was relevant to their subject. These men *sought* wisdom through discussion, but they *brought information* to the discussion. It is true that as we read the Platonic dialogues today, we are aware that information per se played a small part in the conversation. The nature of the problems under consideration—problems such as "What is justice?" or "What is virtue?"—disposed against the relevance of positive information. Moreover, these conversations took place in an age in which the importance of investigation and the discovery of information were not as fully recognized as they are in our own age. Nevertheless, we are aware that these philosophic conversations did not proceed among men who were deficient in learning. We can recognize the importance to effective discussion of participants who have both the desire and the skill necessary to *investigate* the problem at hand, and to acquire and exchange relevant *information*.

Can you list examples of discussions which have been unproductive because proper *investigative skills* and *attitudes* were not brought into action by the discussants?

Third, the Platonic dialogues are pre-eminent examples of conversation among men who had a passion for thinking carefully and accurately about the meaning of the statements or hypotheses which came under their consideration. Typically, the discussants would accept an hypothesis as true, and proceed to examine the necessary consequences of that assumed truth. This process might bring into question the truth of an original hypothesis, which would then be examined in its turn. In this way an orderly, thorough analysis of the meaning of verbal statements was carried out; hasty generalizations, vague and imprecise thoughts, and contradictory assertions were all brought into question. The Greeks thought of the knowledge, skills, and attitudes which were brought into action in these extended but friendly arguments as belonging to the study of *dialectic*.

You have probably found it easy to find examples of discussions which were unproductive because of deficiencies in *human relations* or in *investigation*. You may find it more difficult to find examples of discussions which were unproductive because of deficiencies in *dialectical skills* and *attitudes* simply because these skills and attitudes are given less proportionate emphasis in modern education than are skills in *human relations* and in *investigation*. Nevertheless, you may be able to think of discussions in which vague conclusions have been accepted by the discussants without question or exploration, or in which a smattering of information has been made the basis for elaborate and ill-considered conclusions.

We have now identified three groups of skills and attitudes which underlie effective discussion. These are:

(1) Skills and attitudes productive of good human relations.

(2) Investigative skills and attitudes.

(3) Dialectical skills and attitudes.

It is interesting to note that scholars in various historical eras have tended to give emphasis to the analysis and study of one of these groups of skills, sometimes to the neglect of the other two. Thus, as Western civilization developed in Greece and Rome, and during medieval times, tremendous energy was devoted to the study of dialectic. By contrast, higher education in the last three centuries has increasingly come to be dominated by an interest in science; that is, by an interest in the sort of disciplined investigative activity which has resulted in the development of much positive, verifiable knowledge about our physical universe. The energy and enthusiasm which were once given to dialectic have in our own age been poured into the development of attitudes and skills appropriate to investigation or "fact-finding."

And finally, in the last half century, scholars have sought to unlock some of the mysteries of human behavior, and to give to the study of *human relations* the same deliberate, analytical attention which earlier ages gave to the study of linguistic meanings and to the discovery of facts about the physical universe.

It is our conviction that productive discussion is most possible among persons with a balance of dialectical, investigative, and human-relations skills; that preoccupation with any one of these groups of skills has been historically destructive to productive discussion; and that the best discussion training will give to each group of skills its proper emphasis. We can clarify this conviction by a further analysis of the nature of these groups of skills, considering each group now in the order in which study of this group appeared in history.

The use and misuse of dialectical skills and attitudes

We define dialectical skills as those skills exhibited by persons who converse thoughtfully about the meaning of assertions. In this sense, dialectic involves argument about, or critical examination of, ideas.

The term originated with Plato, who made the study of dialectic the concluding phase of the training of the philosopher-king, "the coping stone that lies on top of all the sciences" (*The Republic*). It was widely employed in medieval times to designate the art of logical disputation, the study of which was placed at the heart of the disciplines considered in the medieval university.[1]

We find a high order of dialectical skill in the discussant who evidences: (1) the ability to extrapolate (draw out) from evidence the conclusions warranted by that evidence, (2) the ability to perceive possible alternative interpretations of the same evidence, (3) the ability to supply evaluative standards to the reasoning used by self and others, and (4) the ability to communicate his reasoning clearly and quickly in conversation. In other words, dialectical skill is skill in reasoning *in conversation,* or skill in thinking logically *in conversation.*[2]

The discussant with dialectical skill will characteristically reveal certain attitudes (mental habits) in serious conversation. These include: (1) suspended judgment, or the habit of avoiding hasty or premature conclusions about the meanings of bits of evidence or the worth of particular hypotheses; (2) impartiality, or the habit of giving to all ideas and all evidence the same scrutiny, according to the same standards, which would be given to any idea or any evidence; (3) respect for reason, or the habit of believing that thoroughness, accuracy, and care in reasoning will produce more useful decisions than will the neglect of such processes.

It should be apparent that dialectical skills and attitudes have to do with *words* rather than with *things*; with the meaning of state-

---

[1] The student should not confuse the meaning of dialectic given above with the special use of the term made by the German philosopher Hegel. Hegel used "dialectic" to designate the process by which all thought develops through the stages of "thesis, antithesis, and synthesis." Many other specialized uses have been made of the term, which have tended to extend and sometimes obscure its central meaning.

[2] Our reason for preferring the term "dialectical skills" to possible alternatives, such as "logical skills" or "reasoning skills," rests not merely upon the more ancient tradition associated with the term "dialectic." The essential fact about discussion is that the skills of reasoning are revealed among persons *conversing.* The more ancient term "dialectic" comprehends the way in which productive thinking about matters of probability is not merely facilitated by conversation; it actually originates in conversation. Thus, the solitary thinker, dealing with such problems, has to engage in a sort of internal dialectic—an argument with himself—if he is to make progress.

ments rather than with the facts of the case. For example, the statement that "fourteen boys between the ages of thirteen and seventeen were arrested for armed robbery in the city of X in 1955" is a statement of fact which raises no dialectical problems. On the other hand, the statement that "it would be a good thing if the penalties for juvenile criminals were increased in the city of X" is a statement which raises immediate dialectical problems. What is the meaning of the phrase "good thing" in this latter statement? If the latter statement is derived from the former, what reason has been given for believing that the arrest of fourteen boys was an excessive or alarming fact, calling for a change in community policy? And so on.

It is clear that in any conversation, as we proceed from an exchange of information to an attempt to see what this information means in terms of our beliefs or our actions, we are at once involved in the exercise of dialectical skills and attitudes. The usefulness of such skills and attitudes to productive discussion is not to be doubted.

But preoccupation with the meaning of words to the exclusion of a real concern for facts or things has its potential abuses. It is commonplace to observe today that many of the disputations of medieval universities became mere exercises in "verbal manipulation" in which the discussants exhibited their versatility in prolonging an argument, while at the same time revealing an alarming (to us) lack of interest in the facts about nature. For example, a medieval disputation might take place concerning the question, "Would a donkey, possessed of perfect free will, and tethered equidistantly from two identical bales of hay, starve to death because of its inability to choose one bale of hay as the preferable one?" This "problem" may strike us as foolish ("Everyone knows that a healthy donkey won't starve to death if food is at hand," or "Why not take a donkey and two bales of hay and see what happens? Why argue about it?"). And we may well suspect that such discussion, however fertile a field it provided for the exercise of dialectical skills and attitudes, would have little to contribute to securing a better world.[3]

[3] "Dialectician" has often been used as a term of reproach, calling attention to the ability of persons skilled in verbal manipulation to prolong conversations *ad tedium,* if not *ad nauseam.* The story of two peasants who asked their priest to explain dialectic illustrates this attitude. "Suppose," said the priest, "a clean man and a dirty man came here. I offer them a bath. Which one will take it?"

"The dirty one," the peasants answered.

"No, the clean one," said the priest, "because he is accustomed to bathing. Now tell me who would take the bath?"

Historically, the study and practice of dialectic *separated* from a concern for investigation, for the discovery of facts, and for driving arguments back upon facts led to sterile and unproductive academic exercises. In our own day, discussion among persons who bring only dialectical skills and attitudes to their conversation is likely to be equally unproductive.

The use and misuse of investigative skills and attitudes

The importance of investigation, "getting the facts," is our inheritance from the productivity of science. The great achievements of scientists in solving problems relative to our physical universe suggest that men might well show the same devotion to fact finding in the process of trying to solve problems of social and personal policy and belief. The investigative aspect of problem solving is served by these skills: (1) ability to perceive the kind of information which will be useful or necessary in the discussion of the problem at hand, (2) ability to search out and organize this relevant information, (3) ability to communicate information quickly and accurately through speech. Attitudes contributing to effective investigation are: (1) objective curiosity, (2) thoroughness, (3) accuracy.

The interdependence of dialectical and investigative skills is apparent. We observed that productive dialectical activity must arise out of a concern for evidence, for facts, and that it must remain ever close to the evidence which gives it its proper starting point. We may now observe that facts, in and of themselves, do not solve problems of social or personal belief or action. In the seventeenth and eighteenth centuries many men were carried along by their enthu-

---

"The clean one," answered the peasants.

"No," said the priest, "the dirty one, because he needs it. Now who would take it?"

"The dirty one," replied the peasants.

"No," said the priest, "both of them, for the clean one is accustomed to bathing, and the dirty one needs it. Now which one would take the bath?"

"Both," offered the peasants.

"No, neither one, for the dirty one isn't accustomed to bathing, and the clean one doesn't need it."

By then the peasants were confused. "But, father," they said, "each time you say something different, and each time it is the answer that suits your argument."

"Ah, my son," replied the priest, "now you know what dialectic is."—"Shop Talk," *The Quarterly Journal of Speech,* Vol. 40, 1954, p. 98.

siasm for science to the point of believing that facts, and facts alone, would solve all of man's problems. These men had abandoned the medieval belief in dialectic for the sake of dialectic, only to leap into the equally untenable position of believing in investigation for the sake of investigation; from the worship of *words* to the worship of *facts*.

It is now clear to us that facts do not automatically solve problems. All of the "facts" available to us about highway accidents in this country do not tell us what can be done to reduce the accident rate. These facts are essential, but they become useful only after we have examined their meaning, drawn generalizations about them, and tested these generalizations with critical examination.

We emphasize the inseparability of investigative and dialectical skills in productive discussion. We view the exercise of investigative skills and attitudes as giving a discussion its proper foundation, giving it a starting point. We view the exercise of dialectical skills and attitudes as giving discussion its movement, giving it a possibility of reaching sound conclusions.[4]

[4] The way in which the interaction of investigative and dialectical skills results in the optimal achievement possible to a discussion group is made clear by McKeon's description of four types of group thinking. "We engage in group thinking, on its lowest level, whenever we use someone else's information or ideas; the group need not be assembled for such thinking—a book, a conversation, or a telephone call may provide the needed information. Group thinking assumes a second form when a problem requires for its solution many kinds of competence and many kinds of information: each member of the group then makes his contribution to the common task, and the solution is the composite result. There is a third kind of group thinking in which men of different backgrounds and different disciplines discuss a common problem, and the statement of a difficulty or a conjecture by an expert in one field, who is unaware of the implications of his statement, and unable to develop them by the techniques he has mastered, may start in the mind of another expert a train of thought significant to his experience and adapted to the methods of his discipline which might not otherwise have occurred to him. Strictly speaking, none of these processes is *group* thinking, since in each an individual thinks in the varying contexts and influences the group. There is a fourth stage of group thinking, however, in which the result exceeds, not only what any member of the group has thought, but also what emerges as the sum of their individual thoughts. There are not many clear examples of such thinking, but its nature may be seen in the contrast between philosophical dialogues in which one of the interlocutors is called "master," or "Wisdom," or "Intelligence," and in which the truth is found exclusively in what he says, and philosophic dialogues, like Plato's and Hume's, in which the truth is expressed by no one speaker but it is found in the total development of the discussion. This is a form of thinking that promises new achievements. . . ."—Richard McKeon, *Thought, Action, and Passion*, copyright 1954 by the University of Chicago Press, pp. 51–52.

The use and misuse of human-relations skills and attitudes

The ancient Greek world emphasized the importance of dialectic because of its profound conviction that man is essentially a rational creature. Our own age of science has celebrated the importance of investigation and fact finding from a similar conviction that man can use his reason to better his way of living. But in the last half century scholars have come to realize that any human activity, such as discussion, cannot be completely described or understood if we see man as simply a thinking machine. Students of psychology, sociology, anthropology, and political science have all called our attention to the nonrational dimensions of human behavior.

Skills of human relations have received much emphasis in recent literature about discussion. Many articles and some books encourage us to study the ebb and flow of interpersonal stimulation which occurs when people talk together. We are encouraged to observe, in ourselves as well as others, the ways in which certain verbal behavior seems to produce friction among people seeking to work together. And we are encouraged to try to develop in ourselves the attitudes toward self and others which will make us effective in cooperating with other persons, or skillful in producing the climate of cooperation.

All of this emphasis on the importance of skill in human relations springs from the oft-observed phenomenon of discussions which break down because of personality clashes among some of the discussants. Perhaps you have had the experience of finding yourself arguing violently against the point of view of some other person, not so much because you disagree with him, but because you dislike him and wish to give vent to that dislike. Or perhaps you have witnessed the halting progress of some committee which had as one of its members a person of strong will and indifferent intellect who insisted that his ideas, and his alone, were worthy of consideration. Opinionated, arrogant persons; persons whose voices and manner seem to radiate contempt for others; persons who like to talk, but who seldom really listen—these and many other types of personalities make it difficult for a discussion group to establish the environment within which progress toward the solution to a problem may best be achieved.

We know that many clashes of opinion which seem all but insuperable will simply melt away once the members of a group have

says one committee member, "tells me that if I know that stealing a car tonight might land me in jail for ten years, I won't steal the car."

Despite the expert's repeated explanations of the adequacy of the sampling presented in his data, of the consistency of the results he reports, and of the mathematical reliability of the results he has analyzed, the other discussants persist in relying on their common sense and Main Street logic. A bit of personal tension develops. Finally, the criminologist questions the validity of the personal hunch as evidence in a problem of this sort, and a member of the committee notes that while figures don't lie, liars figure, and hence statistics prove nothing. Permissiveness dwindles, and expressions of appreciation are mutually abandoned.

It seems to us that the personal conflict in this illustration results from deficiencies in dialectical skills, particularly the inability of the committee members to interpret important information properly. Even had the discussants in this case maintained their atmosphere of good will, the group might well have got no further in its discussion than the decision to recommend a course of action contrary to the course which the evidence indicated. We would add the further observation that people with easily offended, obstreperous personalities are often persons who feel insecure in their own capacities to handle evidence and reasoning. Shared skills of critical thinking may well be the most powerful single factor in stabilizing the personal relations of members of a discussion group, for if people were more competent in thinking, they would have less need to be sensitive or defensive in their attitudes toward one another.

Finally, exclusive emphasis on the human-relations aspect of discussion may lead us into the sands of pseudo-agreement, upon pseudo-solutions, by persons who face a serious problem. Pseudo-agreement occurs if certain members of a discussion group suppress their real opinions in the interests of "group harmony." These members will leave the discussion group conceding freely that they did not agree with the conclusions to which they gave verbal assent, but that they thought it best to "go along."

Pseudo-solutions to problems are those solutions which are agreed to, but which can have no practical effect upon the problem at hand. A discussion group considering the traffic problems of a large city reached consensus on the solution that the state legislature should act to grant a greater portion of the state gasoline tax to the city for the building of express routes. The solution—a plausible one—took no account of the fact that the distribution of the gas tax was not determined by the state legislature but by the state constitution. Thus, in the absence of relevant and necessary information, the group achieved a pseudo-solution to a real problem. The human-relations requirements of good discussion had been fulfilled, but the critical thinking requirements had been neglected.

Critical thinking skills

As we see it, useful solutions to problems can be achieved only by groups in which *investigative and dialectical skills* are widely shared. We use the term *critical thinking skills* to include both dialectical and investigative abilities: those *attitudes* useful to the exercise of critical intelligence; the *knowledge* of techniques of reasoning necessary to effective critical thinking; and the skills of discourse needed in the analysis of evidence and reasoning and the communication of reasoned opinion. Moreover, as we see it, the most secure, enduring, and practical basis upon which groups can achieve warm, harmonious human relations is provided by the shared critical thinking skills and attitudes.

The relationship of human-relations skills and critical thinking

Clearly, the most productive discussions are those which take place among persons who have skills in human relations as well as investigative and dialectical facility. We see no incompatibility in these different abilities. People can learn to be pleasant to one another as they think critically together. Moreover, people who share the wish and the capacity to be rigorous and exacting in their use of evidence and reasoning may share the sort of discipline most useful to truly cooperative behavior.

It is our belief that persons studying discussion skills might well devote much of their attention to the cultivation of their capacities to think critically, and to communicate the products of such critical thinking. These skills are not easily achieved. In a sense they are the ultimate objective of all that portion of education which is devoted to the cultivation of the intellect, to the reduction of foolishness, to the development of man's rational capacities. We have repeatedly observed discussion in which persons with critical thinking skill were able to transcend personality clashes and to reach useful solutions to problems—useful bases for cooperative action. We have yet to observe a group, however well-intentioned, which was deficient in critical thinking and was yet able to move toward useful solutions to serious problems of social action.

A simple diagram will serve to clarify our discussion of the nature of human-relations skills and critical thinking skills as they interact in the process of discussion.

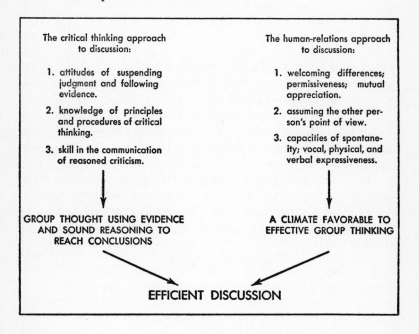

The critical thinking approach to discussion:

1. attitudes of suspending judgment and following evidence.

2. knowledge of principles and procedures of critical thinking.

3. skill in the communication of reasoned criticism.

GROUP THOUGHT USING EVIDENCE AND SOUND REASONING TO REACH CONCLUSIONS

The human-relations approach to discussion:

1. welcoming differences; permissiveness; mutual appreciation.

2. assuming the other person's point of view.

3. capacities of spontaneity; vocal, physical, and verbal expressiveness.

A CLIMATE FAVORABLE TO EFFECTIVE GROUP THINKING

EFFICIENT DISCUSSION

CHAPTER III

Preparing a Discussion

Let us consider briefly the organization of this book. Chapters I and II were designed to orient the student of discussion to his field. But it is our conviction that after brief orientation, the student should continue his study through actual participation. Hence, this chapter will seek to assemble and present the *minimum* information which is needed by a group interested in organizing and conducting a round-table discussion.

The remainder of this book will treat in greater detail the skills, knowledge, attitudes, and procedures which are useful in the development of productive discussions. These matters should be studied with reference to actual practice in the conduct of discussions, so that any insight developed from the study of these subsequent chapters may be instantly tested in action.

The round-table discussion

Consideration of the variety of forms which may be used for discussion is given in Part III, Chapter XI, of this text. At this point we want to consider the procedures in a *round-table discussion*. We recommend this form as useful for the initial experiences of groups studying discussion. Indeed, its versatility may commend its use for the majority of the discussion experiences of study groups.

The round-table form conceives of the discussion activity as taking place through informal but purposive conversation among the members of a small group. Minimum characteristics of such a discussion include the following considerations:

1. The group should be large enough to provide for a variety

of opinion and information, and small enough so that all members can conveniently engage in face-to-face conversation with one another while sitting in an informal circle or around a table. Groups of from four to seven persons tend to have these characteristics.

2. The members of the group should have agreed as to the nature of the problem which they accept as the basis of their discussion.

3. The members of the group will ordinarily have designated one of their number as leader, making him primarily responsible for exercising the leadership functions which will promote real progress.

4. If their round-table discussion is to be public (as will ordinarily be the case in the discussion class) the members of the group will have made considerable advance preparation. They will have prepared an *agenda,* defining the scope and sequence of their public conversation. For the most part, however, they will avoid the use of set speeches by the discussants, or the rehearsal of the exact nature and sequence of the contributions to be made.

Applications of the round-table form

The round-table form is a common one for a number of discussion situations in our society. It is a popular program on radio and television. Typically, small groups are brought together, and after a brief period of common preparation, engage in a conversation concerning their topic before a listening or viewing audience.

It is, in general, the form used in private, conference-type discussion. Groups preparing for a public round table will ordinarily engage in a conference-type round table in the course of preparing for their later public appearance. Labor-management conferences, conferences of educators, scholars, businessmen, salesmen, and study groups all make use of the round-table form.

The round table is also useful for a public discussion before a small audience. Because of its informal, conversational style, it is not a useful means of discussion before a large audience unless radio or television transmission is contemplated, but an audience small enough to "overhear" the conversation readily may find the round table a stimulating program.

Time limitations for public round-table discussions

Round tables presented over radio or television are usually limited to fifteen or thirty minutes. It is doubtful that much less than thirty minutes is sufficient time for a group to make any real progress in the analysis of a serious problem, although the shorter period of time may be sufficient to stimulate further talk among the members of an audience.

Conference-type round tables may, of course, continue for many hours or days—their duration presumably being governed by the endurance of the discussants and the requirements of the problem under consideration.

We suggest that groups studying discussion may find the public round table or the radio round table, of from thirty to fifty minutes' duration, a useful initial discussion experience.

Identifying problems for discussion

Many discussion groups are drawn together by the existence of a problem with which the discussants identify themselves. The board of education, discussing the problem, "Should our community set up a salary schedule for teachers?" finds its problem in a function being performed by the group.

Other groups need to engage in deliberate identification and selection of topics for discussion. Students studying discussion would be an example of such a group. Since poorly chosen or poorly stated problems can prejudice all subsequent activity, it follows that groups making a deliberate selection of a problem for discussion might well give careful attention to the characteristics of a good discussion topic.

Characteristics of a question that makes effective discussion possible

We identify three major characteristics of a discussion question which is likely to be productive of a good discussion:

    (1) The question should raise an issue which is of *real* concern to the discussants.

A good discussion involves hard intellectual labor. Real critical thinking is seldom forthcoming except from people who sense or experience a problem, and who have a genuine, live, immediate concern in working toward a solution to that problem.

(2) The problem should be *limited* to a scope suitable to the time limitations facing the discussion group.

Discussion groups, having identified a problem area for consideration, usually find it advisable to limit their immediate concern to some significant, but limited, aspect of the problem.

Thus, a discussion group might wish to consider: What can be done to reduce traffic accidents? If the group had only thirty minutes for a public discussion of this problem, many proposals doubtless would emerge which would have to go unevaluated—uncriticized—and thus, in a strict sense, undiscussed. The group might well decide to limit its consideration to a single aspect of the traffic accident problem, as:

Should the public schools undertake driver education programs?

or

Should changes be made in present traffic laws, or in traffic law enforcement?

or

Should changes be made in procedures for licensing drivers?

As we begin to list several of the problems which are included in the broad problem area of traffic safety, we realize how superficial and uncritical a discussion of the whole problem area probably would have been.

(3) The problem should be suited to the capacities and resources of the discussion group.

Discussion groups need to consider soberly the question of whether or not the members of their group have, or can get, the sources of information suitable to the discussion of a selected problem. Discussions may be superficial—a pooling of opinion and half-truth—if the problem area is too broad. They may suffer from the same characteristics if the problem area is too far removed from the background of the discussants.

Usually deficiencies in the background of the discussants can be met by adequate research prior to discussion, including consultation with persons who have a good background in the problem to be discussed. Thus, students, who are in no sense "experts" in international politics, may nevertheless have a profitable and informative discussion of a problem such as: Should the United States recognize

Red China? The possibility that their discussion will be useful depends upon the willingness of the discussants to seek, through reading and interviewing, a real understanding of the nature of the problem they have decided to discuss.

In some cases, however, discretion is the better part of valor so far as the selection of a discussion problem is concerned. Should students who have had no direct experience with war and little or no study of clinical psychology or psychiatry attempt to discuss the problem: "What can our armed forces do to prepare American soldiers for the brain-washing techniques of the Communist nations"?

Stating the problem in terms of scope and focus of discussion which is planned

The preliminary analysis of any discussion problem should seek a statement of the problem which will roughly define the scope and focus of the discussion which is anticipated. In this connection it is useful for the discussants to ask whether they intend to deal with a problem of fact, of policy, or of speculation. Each of these problems implies a different discussion emphasis.

The problem of fact   Examples of problems of fact are:
Does cigarette smoking cause cancer?
Do most Americans receive adequate medical care?
What kinds of juvenile delinquency are increasing in America?
Are high school graduates today better educated than were the graduates of twenty years ago?

Note that the question of fact sets sharp limits to the sort of discussion which is implied. In each case the group is seeking to present and analyze the evidence available which will make possible a verifiable answer to the problem of fact. While evidence is available pointing toward an answer to the question stated that evidence is usually not sufficient to permit a *conclusive* answer to the question. A question of fact to which a conclusive answer is known by a member of the discussion group is scarcely suitable for discussion.

Groups discussing questions of fact will ordinarily spend much of their time examining available evidence seeking understanding of how much or how little weight can be placed upon it and combining items of evidence to establish probabilities that some hypothesis is true or false.

The problem of policy Examples of problems of policy are:

Should the federal government subsidize the college education of high-ability students?

Should the lecture method of college instruction be replaced by other methods of teaching?

Should comic books be subjected to censorship by governmental agencies?

Note that the problem of policy in considering a proposed controversial change of the status quo implies a somewhat more extensive discussion than the problem of fact. Policies must be considered in the light of facts, and it is apparent that most problems of policy raise certain problems of fact as necessary to the consideration of the problem. How many problems of fact could you list which might well arise in the course of a discussion of the three foregoing problems of policy?

The problem of speculation Examples of problems of speculation are:

Will there be a general war between Russia and the United States?

Is happiness the goal of living?

Will successful interplanetary travel be achieved in our lifetime?

You will note that we use the term "speculation" to describe those problems which seek the sorts of answers which will necessarily have a low order of verifiability. Problems such as the first and the third deal with matters of "future fact." They may result in an interesting discussion—even in the making of a decision upon which some sorts of action may be based—but any decision reached remains highly speculative. The second problem calls for a discussion dealing with a matter of personal values. Our values are those beliefs we have about the nature of right and wrong and about the relative worth of various purposes and pursuits. Nearly always when we discuss problems of fact or policy, some problems of value arise. That is to say, in a question of fact we may find a conflict between evidence that has been "intuitively" derived by some authority and evidence supplied by the observation of data in a controlled experiment. The weight given to each of these two bits of conflicting evidence will have to rest upon some conviction held by the discussants as to the nature of "good" evidence. Similarly, in a question of policy, such as "should euthanasia be legalized?" the question of the value or worth of human life, per se, is likely to be an important determinant of the attitudes of various discussants.

We would make this observation about discussions which are exclusively speculative considerations of questions of value. Such discussions were a popular pastime in ancient Greece. Plato shows Socrates insisting that the unexamined life is not worth living. In the Platonic dialogues we find a constant effort to reach, through discussion, answers to such questions as "What is virtue?" "What is justice?" "What is the good?" There is little evidence that such discussions resulted in the attainment of secure or usable answers to these questions, however much they stimulated intellectual activity among the discussants. People tend to derive their values from the particular culture in which they live, and to change these values, if at all, only after intensive experiences over a considerable period of time. They may, through discussion, see how their values are related to questions of fact and policy which they confront. But they are not likely to find discussion a profitable way of establishing *values* in the abstract—i.e., values cut off from problems of fact or policy. We would suggest, therefore, that the most productive discussions in our experience are those which seek to establish reasonably verifiable facts and those which seek a choice on matters of policy. This is not to say that purely philosophical discussion does not have its own rewards.

Word your problem clearly

The discussion group will find it worth-while to devote some time to considering the phrasing of the problem which is to serve as the basis for discussion. Three considerations are most important in the matter of phrasing:

1. The problem should be stated as a question. The question tends to suggest the fact that a discussion is an act of *seeking* or of *inquiry* rather than an act of proving or disproving some assertion. It is the most useful form for stating the problem, since the question solicits the sort of activity which should characterize discussion.

2. The question should be as free as possible from ambiguous words. Students who wished to discuss the wisdom of reducing or increasing the amount of required course work in the college cur-

riculum hit upon the following unfortunate wording for their problem: "Should the college curriculum be liberalized?" The word "liberalized" hinted at any number of possible centers for their discussion, such as the addition of more courses to the curriculum, change in the content of existing courses to stress their liberalizing values, and reduction in the amount of prescribed work. Thus, "liberalized" was so ambiguous in this context that it provided a poor basis for discussion.

3. The question should be impartially worded. Some discussion groups word questions in ways which suggest that the answer has already been reached before the group begins its discussion. Do the following questions seem to have been worded by a group which is reserving judgment?

Should the United States adopt the Communist-inspired plan of socialized medicine?

What can be done to improve the outdated methods used by our teachers?

What could be done to make examinations given by the law school fair and equitable?

Evaluate the following discussion topics according to the criteria we have suggested for a "good" discussion topic. In each case think of the topic as one to be used by a round-table group, preparing for a thirty minute public (radio) discussion.

(a) What should be the relationship of church, state, and school in American democracy?

(b) Should public schools teach "facts" about the world's major religions?

(c) How can the present deplorable public taste in literature and the arts be improved?

(d) Is a "great books" education the best approach to liberal education at the college level?

(e) Should the government subsidize the legitimate theatre in the United States?

(f) What level of confidence can we place in the honesty and accuracy of reporting in the American press?

(g) Should restrictions be placed on the publication of comic books emphasizing crime and horror stories?

(h) Should the hearings of Congressional investigating committees be televised?

(i) Should regular sessions of Congress be televised?
(j) Should public employees have the right to strike?
(k) Was it wise to drop the atom bomb on Hiroshima?
(l) How can the educational possibilities of television best be realized?

Classify each of the above topics as problems of (1) fact, (2) policy, or (3) speculation.

STEPS IN PREPARING THE DISCUSSION

Preliminary analysis—the first meeting

Having selected and phrased its problem, the discussion group will find it useful to meet briefly for preliminary planning and analysis of the problem. Typical items of business for the first meeting include: (1) The selection of a chairman for the planning work, who may also serve as moderator for the final discussion. (2) An informal consideration of the present status of knowledge about the problem among members of the discussion group. Such a discussion should reveal items of knowledge in which members of the group are adequately prepared and areas of relevant knowledge which would require extensive research before a productive discussion can be planned. (3) An informal consideration of the present attitudes of the discussion group toward the problem, as well as the extent to which the background of members of the group will help make for a well-rounded discussion. This consideration may suggest particular types of research which will be needed by the group, and ways in which the group will have to be careful to bring out points of view which are not well represented among its membership. What plans could be made to aid in getting a balanced discussion from groups which find themselves in these positions:

(a) A group considering: What attitude and action should the church take toward interfaith marriage? This group finds that all members of the group are of the Protestant faith.

(b) A group considering: Should teachers join labor unions? This group finds that no one in its group is a union member, nor comes from a family in which there are union members. All members of the group concede that they tend to regard labor unions as organizations of doubtful usefulness.

(4) Discussion of available sources of information, including possible library sources, persons who can be interviewed, and organizations from which literature can be obtained. Plans can then be made to share in the task of research, with certain members of the group designated to carry out special interview assignments or other information-gathering assignments. (5) Setting the time and place for a subsequent meeting, to be held after research assignments have been carried out.

Research   It is impossible to place too much emphasis on the importance of adequate research *prior* to making final plans for the organization and presentation of the round-table discussion. We have, in this book, placed great emphasis upon the critical thinking skills which underlie productive discussion—in other words, upon skills in handling evidence and reasoning. But the beginning point for the exercise of such skills is obviously the possession by the discussion group of an adequate supply of evidence relating to the problem at hand. We make three suggestions for the conduct of research prior to the first discussion experience.

First, the research task can best be conducted cooperatively—i.e., with partitioning of the effort so that various members of the group may seek different sources and so that work will not be unnecessarily duplicated. But the research goal to be achieved prior to the round table is that each member of the group should be widely informed about the whole of the problem at hand. This means that *the products of cooperative research should be shared by the members of the group prior to their final discussion.* The object of each member of the group is not to attain knowledge which he will hoard in order to dazzle his fellow discussants at the time of the final discussion. Rather it is to obtain knowledge which can be shared so that the discussion group can make maximum progress in considering the meaning of available evidence.

Second, the group should consider carefully the possible availability of sources of information other than those to be found in the library. Although books and magazine articles may be the most important source of information, special sources are often available which will give to discussants the sort of firsthand or personalized knowledge which may add much to the interest of the final discussion. A group planning to discuss the student counseling services of their college should by all means talk over the counseling services with the persons actually conducting them on their campus. A group considering "the lecture method versus the discussion method of teaching" ought obviously to talk to a number of teachers who use either or both methods, to discover the nature of their experience and their attitudes. A group considering traffic safety programs in X community might well send a member to interview the head of the traffic division of the local police force. A group considering the problem of alcoholism in America might well wish to visit the alcoholic ward of a near-by state hospital; or send a member to interview leaders of the local chapter of Alcoholics Anonymous; or talk to a doctor or psychiatrist specializing in this field.

Third, evidence should be carefully noted, as it is gathered, with a record of its source. Notes on 4 by 6 file cards are a good way of recording evidence. Such cards are readily passed from one member of a discussion group to another; they are usable for reference or quotation at the time of discussion. We recommend heading each file card with a title indicating the general nature of the evidence on the card, and placing at the bottom of the card a careful statement of the source of the evidence.

Fourth, evidence should be evaluated as it is gathered. One of the on-going tasks of any discussion group is the evaluation of the evidence at its disposal. The student doing research is preparing properly for the discussion as he gathers evidence if he asks himself about the reliability of the source from which evidence is obtained, and if he asks about the possible meaning, or limitation of meaning, which can be inferred from particular bits of evidence.

The second meeting

With information at hand, the task of the second meeting of the round-table group may be divided into three steps: (1) the analysis of the problem, (2) the formation of an *agenda,* (3) planning technical details of the final discussion.

The analysis of the problem   Perhaps the most critical preparation time spent by the discussion group is that devoted to the analysis of the problem. Good analysis makes an intellectually adequate discussion possible. That is to say, good analysis brings members of the group to see, in common, the essential questions relating to their problem which need to be dealt with by a group seeking a real solution. It brings the members of the group to a common appreciation of the questions which are likely to create division of opinion among intelligent people. And it brings the members of the group to perceive some sort of orderly progression which may be established by a group seeking to discuss the particular problem.

There is no single "formula" which can be applied which will result in "good" analysis. But there is a plan for attacking problems which has been widely followed by discussion or problem-solving groups with generally good results. This *plan* is derived from the analysis made some years ago of the problem-solving thinking process by the philosopher and educator, John Dewey. Dewey divided the act of thinking into six steps.[1] These steps may be thought of as the reaction of an orderly mind to a problem situation:

(1) A difficulty (problem) is experienced.

(2) It is located and defined.

(3) Possible solutions are suggested.

(4) These possible solutions are examined and compared.

(5) Further observation and experiment lead to acceptance or rejection of each.

(6) The solution regarded as most tenable is subjected to further verification.

Since discussion groups considering social issues often fall short of agreeing upon a single solution, and since their opportunity for further verification of a selected solution is often limited, a slight modification of the Dewey steps results in a plan which we think has maximum utility for a group analyzing a problem. This plan consists of four consecutive operations.

Step 1: Definition of the problem.

The group seeks through discussion to remove any ambiguity or controversy from the statement of the problem. It looks for terms that may need definition, and for operational definitions for these terms which will free the discussion from ambiguity. If necessary, definitions are "stipulated" for purposes of the discussion.

Step 2: Exploration of the problem.

The group explores certain relationships which may be implicit in the problem selected which need to be brought to light, as

(a) Out of what facts does discussion of this problem rise?

[1] John Dewey, *How We Think*, Boston, D. C. Heath, 1933, p. 107.

(b) What are alleged to be some of the causes of this problem and the important consequences of its existence?

(c) What interest groups in our society have been concerned with this problem? Do they have attitudes toward it?

(d) By what criteria may we judge the adequacy of a proposed solution to this problem?

Step 3: Stating possible solutions.

As far as possible the group should consider in its analysis the variety of solutions which have been seriously proposed as an answer to this problem. By grouping or arranging various selected solutions, the major differences in proposed solutions may be brought to light.

Step 4: Criticism and comparison of proposed solutions.

The group should proceed to the examination of proposed solutions in the light of evidence as to the practicality and desirability of the proposals. This discussion may or may not lead as far as group preference for a particular line of action.

The formation of an agenda   For the group planning a public discussion, the immediate objective of analysis is the formation of an agenda for the discussion. At its best, this agenda will select a series of related questions which may be asked and suitably considered in the time available for the public performance. A good agenda should:

(1) Give the audience the background information which the members of the discussion group believe necessary to adequate thinking about their problem.

(2) Acquaint the audience with the exact nature of the problem being considered.

(3) Bring out into the open the essential conflicts of evidence, or of values which give rise to differences of opinion concerning the problem.

(4) Raise the questions which will make clear to the audience, as far as possible, the nature of the thinking done by the members of the discussion group about the problem at hand.

Good agendas are usually quite brief. They are not the analytical outline of a problem, but the working outline of the discussion group. Only three or four major questions can be raised by the members of a round-table group for consideration in a thirty min-

(1) What do we mean by "drunken driving"? *I'll lead off. Mention "scientific tests" as commonly accepted legal evidence.*

(2) Does drunken driving constitute a present problem in our city?

   (a) What is the present rate of arrest and con-

      viction? *Figures for last year. Stress number who got off.*

   (b) Is drunken driving increasing or decreasing?

   (c) Are the present control measures adequate? *No! Evidence: quotation criticizing present laws as weak.*

(3) What further control measures have been proposed?

   (a) Compulsory use of "drunkometer" tests. *Experience in Illinois.*

   (b) Increased penalties for conviction. *Quotation from criminologist. Experience in state of Iowa.*

   (c) Increased educational campaigns. *What is now being spent?*

(4) What is our judgment as to the practicality and desirability of these proposals? *Change in state laws needed for (3a) above; (3b): present laws not always used; we need more severe laws.*

ute period—i.e., only this number can be raised if there is to be any real critical thinking done about them. A practical suggestion for members of the discussion group is for each member to make notes on his copy of the agenda as a reminder of important bits of evidence or important points of view which he wants to make certain are brought out at each stage of the discussion.

On the preceding page is an agenda used by a group discussing the problem: Should the city of Minneapolis take further action to curb drunken driving? (The marginal notes of one of the discussants are also reproduced.)

Technical plans for the final discussion   The final public discussion is likely to be much more efficient if certain technical plans are thought through by the discussion group. Some of these are:

1. When, and by whom, are the members of the group to be introduced?

In a radio discussion it is often good practice to have the members of the group introduce themselves, to establish the relationship of voices with names. This same plan may be followed in face-to-face discussion, although it is more common to find the chairman handling all introductions in the latter circumstance.

2. How can the problem be introduced so as to gain quick attention and interest in the listening audience?

The chairman of the group discussing drunken driving read a short news story of a tragic auto accident, involving a drunken driving charge, as a way of getting attention to the problem of the group.

3. Who will "lead off" the discussion after the posing of the key questions on the agenda?

While the order of speaking is informal and conversational, it is often desirable for the inexperienced discussion group to agree that a particular member of the group will "lead off" the discussion for each of the major sections of the agenda. By "lead off" we do not mean that this person makes an extended statement or speech, but only that he offers the initial reaction to the posing of the question.

4. How are summaries to be handled?

The chairman of the discussion group has the responsibility of keeping the discussion clear and of seeing to it that needed summaries are made. The chairman may do the summarizing himself, or he may from time to time ask members of the group to summarize either their own position or the position of the group as they see it. If the latter plan is to be followed, it is well that the group decide on it in advance so that the "call" for a summary does not fall on surprised ears.

Some "helpful hints" prior to your first discussion

Certain recurrent questions are asked by students about to take part in their first carefully prepared public discussion. Following is a listing of some of the questions which seem to cause the most trouble, together with a brief answer to each question. Doubtless after a few experiences with discussion you will have other questions to ask, and you may well wish to modify or elaborate your first understanding of the answers given here.

Question 1: Should I write out and rehearse what I am to say?

The general answer to this question may be found from a careful reading of the definition of discussion given in Chapter I. Good discussion, of the conference or round-table variety, is a form of conversation, not a form of individual speech making. Certain sensible modifications of this general answer ought to be observed. The chairman of a public discussion ought, certainly, to rehearse very carefully his opening remarks so that the discussion may be opened in an efficient, interesting manner. Discussants planning to cite statistical data, or to quote directly from authorities, should have their evidence on cards and read it to assure accuracy and efficiency. Students planning to open the response to specific, prearranged questions from the chairman might well think through carefully the nature of their remarks.

Question 2: Is there any rule to follow concerning the length of my contributions to the discussion?

There is no rule governing the length of a contribution. Obviously, the speaker should take enough time to make clear the point he is seeking to contribute. Certain general principles concerning the length of contributions may be of help, however. Since it is desirable to have participation by, and interaction among, all members of the group, each discussant should keep his contributions as short as possible. For this reason it is good practice for each discussant to make *one, and only one* point each time he contributes. The tendency among discussants which destroys the flow of discussion and turns the round table into a series of speeches is that of "unloading" everything each time a discussant "gets the floor." The "one-point-at-a-time" method of contributing keeps contributions short, makes for maximum clarity of discussion, promotes interaction among discussants, and leads usually to a more interesting, more productive group effort.

Question 3: What are the major responsibilities of the leader or chairman?

Discussion leadership is an important enough problem so that the whole of Chapter XVI is devoted to a consideration of leadership. In brief, however, the leader is responsible for the introduction of the discussants and the discussion question. As the discussion proceeds, he serves best if he views himself as a clarifier, organizer, moderator, and summarizer. That is: (a) He tries to see to it that all contributions are clear to the members of the group or the audience. He may do this by asking for restatement or illustrations of contributions which seem vague or ambiguous, or by making his own restatements. (b) He keeps the discussion moving in terms of the agreed-upon agenda. Since the agenda is, or should be, the work of the group, the chairman serves the group by keeping discussion relevant to the question at issue and moving in the direction sought. An overly rigid chairman, of course, can spoil the spontaneity of a discussion by ruling too autocratically on the relevance of various contributions. But an overly lax or indifferent chairman can permit a discussion to become hopelessly disorganized. (c) He tries to reduce personal conflicts among members when these conflicts threaten the orderly processes of critical thinking which are desired in discussion. This does not mean that the chairman minimizes or discounts real conflicts of opinion, but that by restatement, or an example of personal good humor, he may seek to reduce personal animosities which interfere with the progress of the group. (d) He may wish to make periodic summaries of the progress of the group, to remind discussants of the situation in which they find themselves. The "what-have-we-done-and-where-are-we-now-headed" sort of summary helps to clarify the progress of the discussion both to the participants and to the audience. The chairman may also wish to make the final summary for the discussion group, or he may wish to call for this from members of the group.

Question 4: Should the chairman participate in the discussion, offering evidence and opinion of his own?

In general, a chairman has enough to do without making contributions to the discussion in the nature of evidence or argument. He operates most effectively as a clarifier, moderator, organizer, and summarizer if he is conspicuously impartial in his relationship to the substance of the discussion. Sensible exceptions to this general rule should be observed. If the chairman, and the chairman alone, seems to have some relevant evidence at hand, he ought to contribute this rather than letting the other discussants proceed in a state of ignorance. If it seems to him that the discussant is ignoring a relevant opinion or argument, he may offer this as an "object" for their consideration. It is reasonable to observe that the discussion group with well-prepared, able members makes it possible for the discussion leader to confine himself to leadership functions, and thus concentrate on his most important role.

Question 5: What are the major responsibilities of members?

Chapter XV considers participation standards in some detail. In brief, we suggest here that each discussant has the responsibility (a) of preparing himself thoroughly; (b) of supporting the leader by keeping his own contributions short, clear, and relevant; (c) of maintaining good personal relationships with fellow discussants; (d) of listening carefully to all contributions by fellow discussants; and (e) of carrying his reasonable share of the task of contributing evidence and critical examination to the discussion.

Question 6: Can a group of discussants do justice to a problem-involving controversy if the members are all initially biased in favor of one point of view toward the problem?

Discussion groups tend to handle controversial issues more adequately if the real attitudes of the discussants represent different points of view toward the controversy. However, good discussion is possible when this is not the case. Discussants ought to see to it that all relevant viewpoints in a controversy are stated as fairly and completely as possible. The members should be able to recognize, and make explicit for an audience, the possible influence of their bias or preconceived attitudes on the direction taken by their discussion.

Question 7: Must our discussion group agree to a solution of the problem in order to have a successful discussion?

We have referred to this question previously. Consensus is an admirable goal for discussion groups, but it is not a practical goal for groups dealing with complex problems. Dishonest or uncritical consensus is certainly not the goal of any discussion. A discussion group ought to go as far as it can in the time available, clearing away disagreement when this is possible, and clarifying important disagreements when these cannot be resolved.

Evaluation of discussions

There are many useful procedures which can be followed in evaluating discussion activity. These are considered in some detail in Chapter XIV. We suggest that initial discussion activity might well be evaluated through a postdiscussion of the group experience. Members of the discussion group probably profit most from a recording of their initial discussion, to which they can listen and from which they can identify successes and shortcomings. The initial experience should form a good basis for clarifying many of the concepts about discussion presented in these first three chapters.

PART TWO

Critical Thinking in Discussion

CHAPTER IV

A System of Problem Solving

Discussion is a problem-solving process and, as in the case of individual problem solving, the methods used are the rather definite techniques of *reasoning*. It follows that an individual who would be an efficient leader or participant in discussion should not only know *about* the reasoning activity but should also be skilled in the application of particular methods of reasoning to various kinds of problems for which we seek solutions through discussion. To the extent that the members of a discussion group are deficient in skills of reasoning, the group will be inefficient, and the probability of agreement upon an unwise solution will increase.

Reasoning is a systematic procedure of using known facts or accepted beliefs to develop or support other beliefs. Explicit or revealed reasoning supplies all the links in the chain of thought: the factual information involved and its interpretation, and detailed exposition of the way in which that interpretation increases the "believability" of the conclusion (belief) which emerges. Implied or concealed reasoning tells only part of the problem-solving story directly. Information is hinted at or implied, and gaps in the reasoning process must be filled by assumptions supplied by reader or listener. Both implied or explicit reasoning may be *sound,* but there is less likelihood of error in discussion or any other communication when care is taken to present reasoning as explicitly as is possible and practicable. Some writers dramatize the importance of this fact to discussion by advocating the "empirical method" of contributing to discussion.[1] In essence, the "empirical" speaker takes pains to explain rather meticulously the "reasons" for the belief he expresses. Advantages of improved understanding and more objective and critical thinking result.

Good reasoning in discussion differs little from good reasoning in any other form of communication. If a persuader chooses to rely upon reasoned discourse, his treatment of a problem will follow the same general pattern and be tested by the same criteria as would the consideration of the same problem in discussion. The persuader's conclusion may have been determined before the act of communicating, while a final belief usually evolves from discussion, but the logical operations are the same, the same evidence has the same importance, and the conclusions have the same degree of probability, i.e., chances that they are really true.

Students of discussion, argumentation, and public speaking have always had difficulty in seeing relationships among the techniques of critical thinking, owing to the fragmentary and superficial treatment of reasoning in their textbooks. In the interest of gaining understanding of probem solving as a complete and highly integrated process, we present a "system" of reasoning (or problem solving, for they are the same) which lends itself equally well to exposition, argumentation, and discussion. The remainder of this chapter explains the rationale (the "reasoning") or theory of our particular arrangement of the familiar ingredients of critical thought. The purpose is to help the reader to "see" the complete act of tackling and solving a single problem *as a unit*. If all steps are clear and their interdependence is understood, the later chapters applying the system to discussion in some detail will be more meaningful.[2]

---

[1] J. H. McBurney and K. G. Hance, *Discussion in Human Affairs*, New York, Harper & Brothers, 1950, pp. 203–208.

[2] The stages in a complete act of reasoning, as presented here, are not simply an idealized schema of how people *ought* to think together. Rather, they seem to describe the way in which people *do* think together. Formal analysis of actual conference or discussion situations has shown that the first third of a discussion is often dominated by the presentation of information and authoritative evidence (opinion). With the progress of the conference, the presentation of information will ordinarily decline, as the processes of generalizing from information and working from generalizations to proposals for specific action begin. For an interesting report on the analysis of conference groups, see Robert F. Bales, "How People Interact in Conferences," *Scientific American*, 192, 31–35, March, 1953.

STAGES IN A COMPLETE ACT OF REASONING

Stage 1: Inductive analysis of evidence.

Definition of problem and exploration
{
  (1) Authoritative analysis
  (2) Comparison analysis
  (3) Analogical analysis
  (4) Circumstantial detail analysis
    (a) Reasoning from sign
    (b) Reasoning from concomitant variation
    (c) Reasoning from causal relation

Location of possible solutions; comparison of possible solutions
{
Stage 2: Generalization.

Stage 3: Deductive application of generalization(s).

Comparison of possible solutions; selection of best solution
{
  (1) Implication
  (2) Alternation
  (3) Syllogism

THE THREE STAGES IN REASONING

Perhaps the "stages" of problem solving and their interdependence will be best understood if we first explain them briefly, then apply the explanation to a specific problem. Remember as we proceed that reasoning always uses facts or beliefs as a foundation upon which to erect a structure of implied beliefs, which in turn eventuate in final conclusions.

When we begin to reason about a problem we cannot avoid two essential operations: (1) deciding just exactly *what* the problem is and (2) investigating the circumstances which lead to and surround the problem. This problem definition and exploration amount to "inductive analysis of evidence." The factual information we need is the evidence, and its interpretation is the analysis.

The reasoning done in Stage 1 is labeled *inductive* because induction is the inspection of particular instances, circumstances, and opinions in an effort to determine whether statements can be made about similarities and differences. Precisely this effort is typical of Stage 1. Here we collect facts to be sure that we know the important facets of the problem (i.e., become able to make statements interpreting the facts and thus define the problem). The forms of inductive analysis in Stage 1 are particular *methods* of deriving reasonable and accurate statements about all available items of information concerning the problem.

The problem-solving individual or group passes from Stage 1 into Stage 2 when what is arbitrarily judged to be a sufficient amount of information about the problem has been examined thoroughly enough so that its significance seems to be understood. Forms of inductive analysis applied to the substantially complete body of information no longer yield different and revealing statements of interpretation. The time has come to consolidate and reorganize, a process of *generalization*, which is Stage 2.

Generalization is the summarization of any probabilities which emerge from the various forms of inductive analysis. Similar statements interpreting information are combined, irrelevant material is discarded. Stage 2 refines and combines the statements developed in Stage 1, and rather carefully arranges them so that they are accurate, mutually exclusive, and as precisely oriented to the solving of the problem as possible. At the end of Stage 2 only a capsule may remain, but it includes what is vital to the solving of the problem learned through analysis of all information considered.

Stage 3 is a further consolidation of a special sort, for its purpose is to make the outcomes of the act of problem solving conclusive, or as highly probable (certain) as possible. The method here is to apply valid patterns of deductive reasoning to the generalizations evolved in Stage 2. Deduction moves from statements of belief to their application to particular instances. Statements (premises) known or assumed to be true are combined with the products of inductive analysis (Stage 2 generalizations), and all are oriented to the particular problem situation under discussion. Stage 3 is orderly and predictable, for there are a limited number of deductive forms. The nature of the generalizations to be used determines which forms are suitable, and once a generalization is fitted into a deductive pattern a fixed series of operations leads to a conclusion. Only after we have exhausted the possibilities of deductive application can we decide that the act of problem solving is, for the time being, complete.

The above exposition of the sequence of events in the thinking through of a problem is necessarily abstract. But if the reader will refer back to the theory of each stage as that stage is developed in the following example, we promise that most, if not all, of the preceding description will become clear.

An example of the three stages of solving a problem through discussion

In one of our state universities recently, an innovation in student government was introduced. For the first time students were appointed to regular faculty committees of the liberal arts division of the university. Our example of discussion occurs at the end of the first year of the new program.

Discussants are members of the Student Council, the top student group overseeing all student activities. Council officers and committee chairmen, a group of nine people, have decided to investigate the new program and meet to discuss it and other matters under the topic, "How can students contribute more to the determination of policy within the Arts College?"

The group is dedicated to the cause of student government. They are motivated to gather information before the meeting because they see in student representation on faculty committees an entering wedge that holds open the door to real student participation in running the university. By interview and library study the nine students have collected most available information on the new experiment by the day of the discussion.

The meeting occurs in the Student Council room in the Union building, a small and bare but pleasant room, with a table large enough to seat a dozen people and with a blackboard on the wall toward the corridor. The group meets on time at 1:00 P.M., and the Student Council president serves as chairman.

Preliminary discussion reveals that the process of collecting information has resulted in a consensus that the problem should be narrowed to a specific difficulty. Briefly, investigation has uncovered so much student and faculty dissatisfaction with the new system of student representation on faculty committees that the program appears to be in danger of being abolished. Yet the Council views the new representation as the first step forward in student government for several decades! Quickly the group agrees to limit the discussion to "How can student members on faculty committees become more effective?" It is their common opinion that the future of meaningful student government on their campus depends upon making a success of the committee work done by student representatives.

With a meeting of minds on problem definition (understanding of precisely what is to be discussed) the group proceeds to exploration of the present status of student representation on faculty committees. Authoritative analysis is plentiful. The college dean made a guarded statement to the effect that ". . . the system has yet to prove itself of value to the college." Faculty committee members testified in two ways, first, that the system is a success because the purpose of student representation is for the students to become informed and the students sit and listen quietly as they should; second, that the student members are failing because their rare contributions have been naive and they repeatedly violate committee protocol. All faculty interviewed noted that student representatives' attendance leaves much to be desired, particularly when the weather becomes pleasant in the spring of the year.

The student committee members made authoritative statements to these effects: that they felt unprepared for the committee experience when they began it; that the faculty committee members tolerate their presence but obviously do not expect them to exert influence on the course run by the committee; that the majority of committee business is concerned with highly technical curricular and administrative problems on which the students are literally unable to have an opinion; that the committee sessions are as a rule unbelievably long and boring; and that because the student members are unable to make their presence on the committees further the cause of student government, they become discouraged and admit that their attendance record at committee meetings is less than perfect.

These reactions are compared with authoritative comments on similar ventures on other campuses. Published authority opinion is of little help because it ranges from condemnation of the student representation on faculty committees to enthusiastic endorsement, with little evidence cited to support conclusions given. There is agreement that it would be a good thing if students could take a more active part in running our colleges and universities. Beyond this statement of principle, agreement vanishes.

One of the discussants mentions that he has studied the mimeographed minutes of all the faculty committees in the Arts College on which there were student representatives for the past year, and has been unable to find any committee action which suggested student influence, or would not have been expected had student members not been present. "This isn't conclusive proof that the students were ineffective," he notes, "but it is at least a *sign* that they weren't initiating changes successfully." Another member comments that this conclusion is reinforced by the apparent *causes* which render the students ineffective, particularly their lack of information and being outnumbered by faculty members. Attendance of students at committee meetings might be expected to vary with the amount of success experienced in those sessions, says another, and the steadily decreasing attendance toward the end of the year probably indicates a *concomitant variation*.

"The present situation is like appointing a lay citizen to a committee of doctors who are to decide what equipment is to be bought for a new hospital," summarizes a member of the group who is sure he now sees the problem clearly. "Students are like the patients, they want good service but don't know enough about the technical side to be helpful in defining and procuring it." This *analogy* is immediately challenged on the ground that students are better able to define their needs in terms of goods and services than are hospital patients, and that Arts College committees deal not only with what might be compared to "equipment" (the curriculum), but also determine policies which are of vital concern to the student. "This last fact alone makes a voice for students mandatory if any democracy is to be claimed for a system of administration." The chair asks for disagreement on this issue, and none is volunteered.

Further evidence is contributed and evaluated, but since it all supports the general findings above we will not report it. Apparently, *inductive analysis* is complete and the chairman guides the discussion into Stage 2 by saying, "It seems that the facts of the problem are clearly understood. Now, let's summarize our interpretation of this information as simply and directly as we can. The chair requests statements which describe accurately the fix we're in."

Only a few minutes of discussion are needed to come to agreement upon these *generalizations*:

1. The present program of student representation on Arts College committees is failing.

2. Student members are handicapped mainly by ignorance of college affairs and committee functions.

3. Faculty attitude toward the program is bad, apparently because the role of students on faculty committees is not understood.

4. Student members last year were easily discouraged.

5. Productive student participation on faculty committees seems a worth-while objective for student government.

6. Hence, if at all possible, the program of student representatives on Arts College committees should be made to succeed.

Head-nodding and expressions of agreement make any voting on the generalizations superfluous. "If these statements are all true, and we apparently believe that they are," says the chairman, "what about next year?"

Here is a summary of the *deductive* application of the generalizations which evolve in the attempts of the group to answer that highly pertinent and critical question:

If student representatives are failing primarily because they are not informed on college matters, then it follows that as long as they continue to be uninformed they will continue to be ineffective.

In order for students to become informed on matters of college business, they must either instruct themselves or be taught by others. They cannot possibly instruct themselves, for there are no printed materials which at all cover the needed information.

Hence, if they are to become effective, they must first of all be instructed in the essential knowledge. If they are to be so instructed, the teaching must be done by people expert in these matters; and if the teaching is to be done by subject-matter experts, then the teachers will be faculty or administrative personnel, or both, since no students have comprehensive knowledge of this sort, and the only groups from which teachers can be drawn are students, faculty, and administration. If student committee members are to become effective, it follows that a faculty-administration-instructed training program for them must be established.

If faculty members are impressed by knowledge and ability, then the selection of strong student representatives and their thorough training can be expected to improve faculty attitude.

If student members last year were easily discouraged, the Student Council next year should supplement the training program with detailed orientation and encouragement to guarantee that the student representatives appreciate the importance of their jobs and develop a firm resolution to make the program a success.

Present efforts of the student government to gain access to policy-making activities in the university are being supported by the administration. Certainly, student government projects with administrative support should be given every aid and assistance possible. This program deserves all-out, continued sponsorship of the Student Council.

Because the key to solving the problem is the establishment of an adequate training program, a Council Committee is appointed to carry to the Dean of the College the proposal that they appear before the Dean's Advisory Committee to present their plan for increasing the effectiveness of student representatives' participation in the work of faculty committees in the Arts College.

The meeting is then adjourned.

Reread the above example of problem solving in discussion slowly, checking back to the "stages in a complete act of reasoning" to identify the parts of the process. Reread also the exposition of each stage as given under "The Three Stages in Reasoning" to help you to see the functions and boundaries of each stage in the Student Council discussion. Locate each implication and alternation in Stage 3. Try to find the one complete syllogism and look ahead to Chapter X to see how its validity may be tested.

How conscious use of the three stages in problem solving can help discussion

Without conscious application of a complete pattern to group thinking, there is always a probability that loose ends will be forgotten. In the example just given, the Student Council might very well have stopped with Stage 2, after generalizations had been formulated. At this point, a group develops a feeling that something has been completed. Adjournment might have taken place amid a flurry of mutual congratulations and the discussants would have disbanded with a pretty good idea of what was wrong with the present program but *with no knowledge of what should be done, specifically, to improve it.* Fortunately, the chairman realized that without Stage 3, the deductive application of generalizations, no real and definite solution to the problem can be developed. Typically, the many discussions which terminate with Stage 2 leave the participants exhilarated, full of the conviction that progress has been made, but without a plan of action.

It is quite possible that our Student Council group, if no member had been experienced in methods of discussion, might have stopped with Stage 1 of the problem. At this point many significant items of information were common property, and their significance in isolation had been tentatively explored. Had no one demanded or suggested consolidation of this knowledge (and often in discussion groups this is overlooked) the session would have terminated *without any general, over-all conclusions about the significance of the facts discussed.*

Untrained discussants are often satisfied with discussions which end with Stage 2, but discussions which end with Stage 1 are usually unsatisfying to all who take part. Typical comments are that "there is nothing to take away" or that "we didn't get anywhere." These are diagnostic responses, indicating that *generalization* was not attempted or was poorly done.

Conscious application of the stages should go beyond the attempt *just* to complete all of them. Within Stage 1 the discussants may well seek purposively to apply *as many of the forms of inductive analysis as possible.* The search for evidence that will be suited to comparison, analogy, reasoning from sign, concomitant variation, and causal relation often results in more thorough analysis and interpretation of the problem than might otherwise have taken place. As we shall see later, these standard forms have known criteria which help in turn to assess the significance of information used. In Stage 3, groups typically become preoccupied with one deductive application, usually in the form of an implication (an "if-then" statement). The alternation or syllogism which might better serve the purpose of the group, or might supplement the implication already discovered, will never be considered unless someone is attempting to fit generalizations into these other deductive forms.

Effective application of the stages of reasoning demands thorough understanding not only of each stage and its function but also working knowledge of each of the forms of inductive analysis, of the process of generalization, and of each of the forms of deductive application. The quality of group thinking is determined by the extent to which members of the group have developed these abilities. Because skill in critical thinking is all-important to discussion, we devote the next six chapters to the specific techniques of logical thinking which comprise the stages in a complete act of reasoning.

CHAPTER V

Inductive Analysis of Evidence—Part 1

Discussion ideally begins with a meeting of minds as to the precise extent of the problem to be discussed on a particular occasion. It then proceeds to assembling and interpreting of information pertinent to the problem as defined. This chapter studies the early steps of problem solving in detail. General considerations of definition and possible applications of evidence are covered, as well as one form of inductive analysis, that based upon evidence from authority. Stage 1 of problem solving is completed in Chapters VI and VII by study of comparison, analogy, and circumstantial detail.

DEFINING THE PROBLEM

Why should every discussion group spend at least some time in thinking together about the limits of the topic and the meanings of its key terms? Because what seems at first to be a fortunate wording often later turns out to be quite impossible, or at least inadequate, and because the same words mean different things to different people—even to educated, intelligent people like ourselves! The least we can do is to repeat what we think the words mean to each other. If we see eye to eye at once, fine! If we don't, fine too, for we can immediately remove a potential cause of subsequent confusion.

Pitfalls in definition

The chairman or discussant who says, "Now, we all know what the topic means, don't we?" is achieving the top error possible in definition, the *failure to define at all*! Such a remark makes a request for clarification an admission of stupidity. When this happens with respect to a topic that is in itself vague—though admittedly challenging—like "Is it a woman's world?" results can be chaotic. The authors heard a radio round-table discussion of this question which proceeded without benefit of any limitation or definition. Each participant apparently had his own idea of what constituted possession of the world—and no two were alike. The chairman's final summary was, "The only point on which we agree is that we don't know what is meant by a 'woman's world' "!

The other common error in definition, more frequent and only slightly less serious than omitting all definitions, is *unwillingness to reword a topic that needs clarification or limitation*. A group should feel free to violate the integrity of a topic in any way which would seem to speed collective thinking toward problem solution. The attitude here as elsewhere in discussion should be brutally *dialectical*. Nothing can be gained by tolerating a general term in a topic when a more specific word can be substituted for it, or by "going along with" a wording that misses the target even slightly. Let's look at some typical situations in which topic rewording becomes a necessity.

Very frequently an assigned topic encompasses too much. As a group gathers information and thinks about the problem, it may become obvious that in the time available for the discussion the entire topic cannot be treated comprehensively. Two choices are possible, to attempt a survey treatment of the whole topic, or to agree to discuss the subdivision of the original which will be of most interest and value to the group. Usually, greater progress toward a solution is made if a fundamental subtopic is discussed, although this depends on problem and attendant circumstances. A group whose original intention was to discuss "What are Minnesota's problems in educational television?" decided to limit the actual discussion to "How can Minnesota pay for educational TV?" This illustrates limitation by group consensus based upon this criterion: "What is the most vital of the many subtopics under the original question?" A survey interpretation of the original topic would have been entirely possible, in which case the goal of the group would have been to list and come to understand all of the subproblems, something this particular group thought it had already accomplished by individual study.

Rewording is mandatory when a group discovers that a topic

"begs the question," i.e., assumes part of the answer that it apparently is seeking. "Why are juvenile delinquents getting younger?" is a stimulating problem, but it assumes that they are, and until proof is available, we can't *know* that to be true. "How can we eliminate communism from our colleges?" and "What can be done to return public utilities to private ownership?" are as "loaded" as "Have you stopped beating your wife?" These are good examples of topics that need conversion to impartial inquiry with no axe to grind. Can you reword each one so that it is "unloaded," yet so that the essential "focus point" of the possible discussion is not lost?

Unusual, difficult, and unnecessarily technical terms in a topic need to be replaced with accurate synonyms that will be generally understood. "What can be done for the vocational and social welfare of the indigent aged?" became "How can we help our aging poor?" "Can the use of 'black' propaganda by the United States be justified?" was more generally understandable when worded "Should the United States use propaganda which appears to originate within the country against which it is directed?" How can you improve the wording of this topic: "Can the principles of group ownership be applied to the media of public transportation in our city?"

Sometimes technical terms should not be changed, certainly not when doing so would create a cumbersome topic. The "black" propaganda illustration above is a borderline case. The questions "Is the Marshall Plan succeeding?" and "Is the Fifth Amendment an aid to communism?" contain technical terms that should not be changed. However, they impose upon the discussion group the necessity of defining fairly completely what *is* the subject in each instance.

Generally, the use of a single term as a discussion topic is unsatisfactory. While "Preventive War," "Creeping Socialism," or "UMT" may be good titles for speeches because they arouse curiosity by a sort of "chase" technique, it is desirable that a discussion question be so worded as to make abundantly clear the approach being taken to a particular aspect of the problem. Dozens of excellent discussion topics are possible under each of the three single-term topics above. A group with a single-term topic must select one of many possible approaches to the central problem well in advance of the actual discussion if efficient preparation is to be made possible.

Incomplete discussion questions are best reworded a long time before the discussion, but if that is not possible the completion of the wording is much better late than never and should be done early in the actual discussion. Often a topic takes on increased significance when it is "localized" for a group, and the completing is in itself a valuable limitation. The topic, "Would fair employment legislation work?" is more concrete and meaningful as "Would fair employment legislation work in Minnesota?" For a college group, "Do fraternities discriminate?" is better worded "Are fraternities discriminating on bases of race, color, or creed on our campus?"; and "Should we change our grading system?" would be sharper if it read "Should we replace our grading system with a system of 'S' ('satisfactory') and 'U' ('unsatisfactory')?"

"Fuzzy" terms often need to be replaced by clearer ones. There is value in so wording a topic that it is unusual and compels attention, but the hazard is loss of precision in the meaning communicated. At the time of the signing of the armistice in the Korean War an interesting topic discussed was: "Syngman Rhee: hero or heel?" Chairman and discussants recognized the dangers of ambiguity in this "fuzzy" wording, but decided the phrase was so "catchy" they would keep it as a title. The result was an interesting discussion that bore little relation to the topic. It turned out that they wanted to, in fact did, discuss "Why does Syngman Rhee oppose the signing of an armistice?" After the discussion the group agreed that a tricky but inaccurate or confusing title is of more damage than help to a discussion.

Typically, "fuzzy" terms are discovered only after much study and thinking about a problem. Suddenly a member of the group realizes that a term has at least two acceptable meanings and that confusion has set in or is impending. This insight should be shared with the group at the beginning of the discussion if it dawns early enough. But should it come any time before the final summary, the group can still benefit from it, for an unspoken confusion in the mind of a participant may be resolved by even a very late semantic clarification. A discussion of "Should we educate for propaganda?" resolved itself like magic into a meeting of minds about halfway through when a participant observed that some of the members apparently thought that "educate for propaganda" meant the training of professional propagandists, while others seemed to think it meant teaching people to understand and analyze propaganda. They agreed to use the latter definition, and most of the conflict which had previously prevailed evaporated.

Principles of successful definition of the problem

From the preceding list of difficulties in definition we can derive two positive principles to guide us in defining terms and concepts in discussion. First, we should expect people to differ on what they think the topic and the key words in it mean. With this attitude of realistic skepticism we will be motivated to check our interpretations against theirs, explicitly and in detail. Second, we should feel no hesitation in changing any part or all of the topic wording if it thereby becomes clearer and better suited to the purposes of the group concerned. This includes agreement upon arbitrary definitions in which you, for purposes of the discussion, assume that a term means "thus and so" without worrying very much about whether this interpretation would satisfy an expert authority. If such a definition increases understanding and facilitates solving the problem, it is unimportant whether this interpretation is authoritative or is ever used again.

Carefully worked out "special" definitions are most helpful to discussion, and while we would like to preserve the freedom of groups to define words as they see fit, we don't want to encourage people to define "black" as "white." In evolving an arbitrary definition, then:

(1) Restrict the term as much as is logically sound.

(2) Conform to current usage of the term as much as possible.

Arbitrary definitions are often unique. The people who were preparing a panel discussion presentation on "Is there suppression of news at the source?" agreed, for purposes of the discussion, to define "suppression of news" as:

(1) Limited to newspapers only, within the United States.

(2) Limited to news of a political and economic nature.

(3) To mean unreasonable selection of facts revealing an identifiable bias on the part of the selecting agent.

With these matters accepted by all, the investigation into this question of fact appeared to penetrate more deeply than it might otherwise have done.

Can you think of any dangers inherent in exercising the privileges of arbitrary definition?

THE THREE WAYS OF TREATING EVIDENCE IN COMMUNICATION

By now you know that the authors of this book believe *evidence* to be extremely important to discussion. Many people agree with this generalization without facing the fact that using different kinds of evidence for different purposes is difficult and complicated. One result is that they confuse the several types of communication which transmit the significance of evidence. It is important that the student of discussion understand these different ways of talking about factual information and know which is appropriate to a specific situation in discussion. Other modes of communication can become more precise and efficient also if these fundamental distinctions can be made by communicator and/or communicatee.

Three ways of communicating information are:

(1) Recitation.
(2) Explanation.
(3) Interpretation.

Recitation is the simplest possible communication of items of information, a listing of the facts to be transmitted to others. The speaker or writer says, "Let me call to your attention some events that are related to the subject being discussed." He makes no attempt to influence the reaction of his hearers or readers to the facts presented. He *recites* the facts, and once reported they are left to shift for themselves.

Explanation is recitation of evidence plus an added expediter, clarification. The question, "What do we need to know to understand these facts?" is answered by "Something that is necessary whenever their meaning is not readily apparent." Suppose that in a discussion of "How can the President act to control inflation?" the fact is introduced that living costs have gone steadily upward for the past three months, but only to a total rise of two-tenths of one per cent. What does this mean? The discussant who introduced the information might well cite data for comparable periods over the past several years. Such supplementary knowledge would clarify the picture by establishing the relative size of an otherwise abstract quantity, two-tenths of one per cent.

Explanation supplies just enough carefully selected supplementary information and paraphrasing to guarantee that the facts transmitted are intelligible to all. No attempt is made through explanation to assess their over-all importance as evidence related to a problem.

Interpretation says that "these facts are significant to the problem we are discussing because—" The communicator who interprets shows how the information he advances supports or denies some contention. Interpretation is a matter of revealing or constructing connections between specific information and a statement of opinion, an hypothesis that the speaker or writer is attempting to establish or disprove. While explanation or recitation leaves the recipient of the communication free to relate information to issues as he sees fit, interpretation attempts to show him a preferred pattern for this relation.

Interpretation includes evaluation, a judgment of badness or goodness, of relative worth, a qualitative estimate of the intrinsic values of the evidence itself. Evaluation attempts to conclude either (1) that the evidence in itself is enough reason for holding the belief it supports, or (2) that it is more significant than contradictory information. Interpretation embraces all statements which suggest *how* the evidence reinforces a conclusion, while evaluation is that type of interpretation which answers the question, "*How much* is this evidence worth?"

Our example of the rise in living cost would have been an interpretative communication had the discussant added, "Obviously, two-tenths of one per cent is so much less than previous advances in the cost of living that it may be considered insignificant. Actually, it indicates that the present administration has stopped inflation."

Is there evaluation in this example of interpretation? If so, what part of the example is evaluation, and why?

The necessity for discriminating among the three ways of communicating evidence

A classic example of confusion resulting from a misuse of the ways of communicating evidence occurred in the summer of 1953, when the Kinsey report on sexual activity of the human female was widely discussed in newspaper and magazine articles three weeks before it was released. People who wrote about the book relied upon *interpretation* with a high percentage of evaluation; and understandably so, for the limited space assigned to an article permitted inclusion of only fragments of Kinsey's complex and extensive data. Because the reviewers didn't agree, the reflective reader needed the facts to "check up on" the thinking of the reviewers. But the facts weren't there, and until publication time judgment on many key issues had to be suspended. The numerous articles thus contributed to the sale of the book but probably generated more misunderstandings than clarifications.

This situation parallels the one which often arises in discussion when interpretation is attempted with an inadequate foundation of recitation and explanation. A group working on a problem is ready or unready to begin interpreting evidence depending upon the thoroughness of recitation and explanation of that information.

We mentioned that solutions should be listed only after the topic had been explored. Listing and comparing solutions are types of interpretation. There is always danger that discussion of solutions will come too early, as there is that discussants will attempt to interpret each bit of evidence they advance. Careful formulation of recitation, explanation, and interpretation-type statements is an insurance against half-baked opinions in discussion. Even overt cautioning ("We aren't ready to interpret that evidence until we know more about it") is sobering and helpful. Individuals who are all too ready to propose solutions early in a discussion may be compared to the trigger-happy hunter who shoots before he has clearly identified his target. Such hunters, looking for deer, have taken an unfortunate toll of cows, horses, and fellow hunters.

Early in a discussion there should be a great many more statements of recitation and explanation than statements of interpretation. Even in the solution stages contributions of recitation and explanation should outnumber interpretations and evaluations, although the process of interpretation becomes appropriate here. Knowing when and when not to interpret is a great asset to leader and participant in discussion.

AUTHORITATIVE ANALYSIS OF EVIDENCE

The nature of authority evidence

Factual information and opinions, or combinations of the two are *authority evidence* if revelation of the source increases or decreases their significance. The source can be an individual, groups of individuals, or an organization speaking for a group. Authoritative information may range from recited facts (e.g., uninterpreted statistics) to sweeping value judgments. However, authoritative evidence is always factual in the sense that someone said the particular thing that is being quoted—that it was *said* is a fact.

Documentation makes much information authoritative that would otherwise weigh less. Identification of sources becomes more important as the problem becomes more complicated and extensive. When discussants can't "check up on" information first hand, they are forced to rely on printed and other second-hand versions of the facts. This necessitates estimating the relative trustworthiness of various sources of authoritative evidence.

Classification of authority evidence is by source—*lay* or *prestige*, *expert* or *nonexpert, individual* or *group*—and by the character of the information: *simple value judgment, judgment with supporting reasons,* and *factual information with implied or explicit interpretation.* Examples of varied sources and types of authoritative materials will reveal the use of these classifications in estimating their significance.

Levels of authority evidence

Let's look at some uses of authority from real and hypothetical discussions.

1. "A critical point at issue is whether profits of industry are related to wage-paying potential. We know that most of the investment that expands an industry comes from the surplus capital it generates. Well, Dr. Carl Snyder, in his book, *Capitalism the Creator*, has proved statistically that wages go up in direct proportion to the increasing investment of new capital. Doesn't this indicate that higher profits for management mean highest possible wages for labor?"

2. "How can we doubt the wisdom of this expanded youth program for our state? As the great man who originated it, our former governor, Luther Youngdahl, said, 'Our youth are our most precious asset.' He ended the era of slot machines and we should be willing to spend a fraction of the money saved by that reform on increasing opportunities for boys and girls."

3. "Why even discuss the possibility that the tax on oleomar-

garine will not be removed? As Senator Jones put it a week ago, facts have a negligible chance against a multimillion dollar lobby."

4. "The press of the state backs Senator Smith for re-election. One editor was so impressed with the Senator's integrity that he wrote, 'Senator Smith places his country first, his job second.' Said another editor, 'He puts the country's future above political disputes. We couldn't vote against him and go to bed that night with a clear conscience.' Tributes of this type from leaders of public opinion can't be shrugged off !"

Examples 1 through 4 have one common element: the authoritative quotations are all simple value judgments. Authoritative opinion is used to reinforce a conclusion of value in each. Each authority cited is an individual, but there are lay and prestige, expert and nonexpert sources. How would you classify each, and why? Remember that *expert* means qualified in the subject under discussion.

Note that the simple value judgments above differ greatly in specificity. The first asserts a definite relationship between wages and investment, allegedly established by statistical evidence. This is the most specific and hence probably the most helpful of the group, for, if we wish, we can look up Dr. Snyder's figures and the details of his interpretation.

Try to rank the other three examples on a scale of specificity.

An authoritative judgment with supporting reasons would seem to be always preferable to the simple value judgment because it conveys more information. This is in general true, although specious and vague supporting reasons occasionally cause so much confusion that problem solving would proceed more efficiently without them. The following examples of this category should be compared to our simple value judgment for probable usefulness in a discussion.

1. "But the question arises, can the Communist movement be effectively outlawed? Congressman Doe doubts that this is practicable or even possible. In a speech last Saturday he said, 'To convict a person or group of being Communist we would need proof that specific actions are a result of direction from Moscow. Most of us believe that some people are following the party line because of their associations and of the pattern of their actions. But proving this in court is a different thing. Since orders from Moscow are usually by word of mouth, our only evidence would be something that is hardly

the best evidence in court, the word of ex-Communists. Except for a few known leaders of the Communist party, court action against people suspected of Communist-dominated activities would probably fail.' Is there something that Congressman Doe has overlooked which might make court action against suspected Communists effective?"

2. "The suggestion has been made that the present railway strike might be ended by bringing it under the Taft-Hartley Act. The answer of the railway unions to this proposal is that the railroads have already gone through fact-finding and mediation procedures for from 90 to 150 days. To add a further 80 day injunction period seems to them to be unfair. They allege it would place more restraints on railway employees than on employees of other industries."

3. "The present plight of our public schools has caught the attention of many influential groups. The McGraw-Hill Publishing Company, in a series of advertisements, has appealed to business to help relieve pressures on our schools. These advertisements predict two disastrous results of the fact that teachers are taking an economic beating, namely, that 'the more competent teachers will continue to desert our schools in droves,' and that the organization of teachers into economic pressure groups will result in increasingly frequent strikes. These predictions are disturbing. Does other information indicate that they are justified?"

4. "Mayor Humphrey has a lot of backing from thoughtful citizens in this campaign. Rita O'Brien, a stenographer who owns her own secretarial service, says, 'As a small business owner, I stand to gain most with Humphrey in the Senate.' Dr. Hedin, prominent surgeon and mayor of Red Wing, says, 'He's outstanding in the fields of housing, law enforcement, and social welfare. He has a great future as a statesman.' Oscar Erickson of Madison, a farmer, says, 'Humphrey's been a good mayor of Minneapolis, and farmers can bank on him for laws that will help them.' Bob Mussman, a veteran of Iwo Jima, says, 'Humphrey knows the needs of the veterans.' Many other citizens are standing for Humphrey, and their statements can be found in this folder and other literature circulated by the Humphrey-for-Senator All-Party Volunteer Committee. He must be highly qualified for the Senate of the United States."

By now you have probably discovered that only part of the

significance of an authoritative judgment with supporting reasons rests in the reputation of the authority. Much of its worth as evidence is dependent upon the quality of the reasoning presented. Our examples of reasoning range from the quite sound and fairly conclusive to the relatively worthless. Using the criteria of sound critical thinking, arrange the above examples on a continuum from strongest to weakest. Explain your reasons for assigning to them this particular rank order.

Interpretation of factual information by an authority is a potentially strong form of support. Of course, the nature of the evidence cited and the cogency of the reasoning in its interpretation are critical items, but if they meet acceptable standards and the authority is a reputable expert, then the contribution of this type of material to the thinking of a group may be considerable. Here is a sampling of instances in which authoritative interpretation of facts is used to further problem solving in discussion. Again, the range of significance is from strong to severely limited. As you read them, compare their relative weight as units of support.

1. "But we have nothing to fear from lowering our tariffs. As *Time* Magazine points out, '. . . wherever or whatever we buy from abroad, our money comes home to roost.' *Time* tells of the $7,000,000 we spent for Dutch tulip bulbs last year, with the result that more people were employed in all forty-eight states. Spending money abroad helps us, for as *Time* points out further, telephones require eighteen imported materials, electric lights use tungsten from China, Bolivia, and Argentina, and American automobiles use 300 different materials from fifty-five countries. *Time* concludes that the more international trade we have, the more we profit. Since lowering tariffs increases international trade, it must be to our advantage to steadily—and rapidly—reduce our present tariffs."

2. "We seem to be assuming that valuable inventions are suppressed by individuals and industrial concerns. The National Association of Manufacturers doubts that this is true. As proof they report Thomas Edison's statement to a Congressional investigating committee that he did not know of a single case of a corporation buying up the patent of a valuable invention to suppress it. They note that three Commissioners of Patents have testified before Congressional hearings that they did not know of a single case of a

suppressed invention. The NAM cites also the fact that Thomas Midgley, Jr., President of the American Chemical Society, a few years ago published in *Industrial and Engineering Chemistry* an invitation to all chemists to report cases of suppressed patents. Five alleged instances were reported, and not one of these was later substantiated. The 1945 NAM study from which I have taken this information seems to cast some doubt on our assumption that any significant number of important inventions are suppressed."

3. "Senator Jones believes that if the tax on colored oleomargarine is removed, the result will *not* be cheaper oleo for the average housewife. Since less than 8 per cent of oleo sold is colored and pays the ten cents a pound tax, over 92 per cent pays only a nominal tax of ¼ cent a pound, and prices on this preponderant part of oleo will be unchanged by killing the tax on colored oleomargarine. Jones says that the oleo lobby would like to have us believe that removing the colored oleo tax would lower the price of oleo, but that their effort is revealed as just another propaganda trick by these figures."

4. "A great deal of the taxpayers' money is being wasted on government publications. Senator Styles Bridges once asked all government agencies to send him a copy of each of their current publications. Among the 83,000 plus he received, were booklets on bats in belfries, how to trap cats, a report on the status of the Cuban frog-leg industry, and a study of North America's fleas."

Where in the examples immediately above is the interpretation of the authority *implied* and where is it *explicit*? Classify these authorities as "expert" or "nonexpert," and as "individual" or "group." Should we consider example 2 (dealing with suppression of inventions) as use of a single authority or the citation of several authorities?

Select from all our examples of use of authority in discussion those in which the authority is a lay person or persons. Does this fact detract from the significance of the evidence as support?

Our samples identify authorities with varying degrees of definiteness, and document sources with varying precision. Examine them to determine where identification and documentation are sufficiently accurate for the purposes served, and where more information on these matters would probably increase the importance of the authoritative information as evidence.

Prejudiced authority

Even when an authority presents facts and reasoning to support his opinion, we must remember that he has selected the information. The basis of that selection may be unintentionally—or intentionally —less than completely fair. The slanting of information can be countered by collecting similar facts from other sources and observing how well these fit in with the facts given to us by the authority. In addition, we are justified in scrutinizing the authority as an individual to determine whether he is subjected to obvious influences which might be expected to color his opinions.

Financial and political affiliations often reveal these influences. A record of public utterances favoring a single point of view is another cue. Association with biased sources, such as magazines with a political and social "line" and sponsors who have an axe to grind, is worthy of mention. The protection against too much reliance upon prejudiced authority is found in seeking sources of differing persuasions and attempting to include some which have a vested interest in being unprejudiced, for example, academic sources.

Prejudiced authority can be most damaging when its generalizations are sweeping, for vague statements are hard to disprove. Statements which impute motives are similarly difficult to attack. Remember that such opinions are as difficult to support as to destroy, and that the burden is on the originator of the statement to prove that it is so. Logically, it cannot be accepted until proved, hence simple challenge is all that is needed to counter a sweeping but unfounded assertion. General statements of authorities should always meet challenge in discussion.

Campaign literature furnishes excellent examples of prejudiced authority. Let us see how Republicans and Democrats characterized some of each other's policies before a recent Presidential election.

1. "Russia has grown strong and ugly from the secret deals and foolish concessions given her at Yalta, Teheran, and Potsdam.

"These deals were made by a Democratic administration.

"Now the Democrats are seeking to regain control of the Senate with the power to dictate our future relations with Soviet Russia."

2. "They [the Republicans] believe in international trade—so much that they crippled our reciprocal trade program and killed our international wheat agreement.

"They condemn 'cruelly high prices'—but fight every effort to bring them down.

"And they admire the government of the United States so much that they would like to buy it."

Regardless of the prestige of an authority as prejudiced as those above (the second example is from a speech by a President of the United States) such statements are worthless as evidence. You might attempt to work out criteria to be met by an admittedly prejudiced authority if his contribution is to become significant to a critical discussant.

The concept of "levels" of authority evidence is useful because, as we have illustrated, competing authoritative statements frequently differ widely in their intrinsic worth. The attempt to use only high level authority (conforming to the characteristics we have found to be desirable) is rewarding to a discussion group.

CHAPTER VI

Inductive Analysis of Evidence—Part 2

The basic operations of defining terms and collecting and communicating evidence make possible logical analysis in terms of the problem being discussed. In this chapter we proceed to inductive methods and the reasonably objective criteria governing their use.

COMPARISON ANALYSIS OF EVIDENCE

The nature of the process of comparison

Comparison of instances (cases) for purposes of evaluation and prediction is a substantial segment of all critical thinking. When we decide what college or university to attend we do so by comparing what the available institutions have to offer. Buying a car is a many-sided comparison. How do different brands of automobiles differ in past performance records as well as present characteristics, and what is their comparative cost? "Dates" for dances and wives are often, not always, selected by comparing possible candidates according to criteria established by the person making the choice. Note that these examples of comparison yield both *evaluation* and *prediction*. The problem solver concludes that one is better than another (school, car, or girl) in terms of his unique needs, and concludes further that his selection will stand the test of time and in the long run will be more satisfactory than another possibility.

Often comparisons are for purposes of prediction, with evaluation incidental or implicit. A village board is discussing municipal ownership and operation of the local electric power plant. They turn to the experiences of two other small towns wherein municipal ownership has been tried for several years, and compare the circumstances there with their own situation. They decide that the three sets of circumstances are alike *in all factors which would affect the ownership and operation of a power plant.* Then they feel safe in predicting results in their village similar to results of municipal ownership in the other two communities. There is some evaluation in the survey of the two test cases, but primarily the comparison is to uncover probable consequences of their contemplated action, in other words, to make reasonable predictions.

An example is an incomplete comparison. Sometimes from the study of a single case we can draw conclusions that will enable us to predict what will happen *under similar circumstances.* These are not specified but the implication is clear. When we make the similar circumstances explicit, the comparison is completed.

The samples above suggest that the process of comparison is not limited to relating *two* cases or instances. The number of sets of circumstances considered is limited only by practicality—availability, purpose to be served, time, and resources. When we must include many examples in our analysis, we usually resort to statistics, often called a shorthand method of dealing with individual instances. Statistics select out relevant details and by quantification add a further objective dimension to the process of comparison.

Good comparisons are thought to yield significant similarities. But a special application yields significant differences. This is comparison for contrast. When two examples might be normally similar but in certain vital respects turn out to be strikingly different, the differences are often instructive. Comparison for contrast is standard procedure when a business concern studies the operations of a competitor. Warehousing and shipping *similarities* may be interesting, but the *differences* between two companies in these operations is of real concern to both. We should get used to the idea that the reasoning associated with comparison frequently aims at differences rather than similarities.

It is helpful to separate the process of comparison from analogies and figures of speech. The term "literal analogy" is often used interchangeably with "comparison." In the interest of avoiding confusion we will use the term "comparison." Figurative analogies resemble comparisons with one exception—the cases compared are in sharply differing contexts. Where the comparison stresses identity of detail, the analogy seeks to establish identity of principle. We might show the need for hospitalization insurance through discussion of cases in which it saved the day (positive comparison) or by citing instances in which not having this protection caused tragedy (comparison for contrast) or by stating that the person who does not have hospitalization insurance must be like an ostrich, which at least in legend tries to avoid danger by ignoring it. The cases assumed to be analogical obviously have little detailed identity. The analogy has weight to the extent that the asserted common principle is shared by the instances related. Is the principle of "ignoring danger as a poor way of avoiding it" common to case 1, that of the ostrich with his head in the sand, and to case 2, that of the adult head of a family who refuses to consider the purchase of hospital insurance? If so, the conclusion that the person in question should consider the purchase of hospitalization insurance has been reinforced by analogy.

Analogies are vivid and colorful dramatizations of issues, and in this respect resemble figures of speech. In fact, only stress, extended development, and careful definition of the principles common to the analogical cases distinguish analogies used as logical support for an argument from the similes and metaphors common to literature.

Statistical comparison analysis

Numerical summarizations of factual information (statistics) are important to all forms of reasoning at one time or another. "Reasoning from statistics," then, is not a basic technique of problem solving. Rather, we use statistics to support all sorts of inductive reasoning. We may find statistical data highly important to authority, comparison, analogy, and the three varieties of circumstantial detail. Each type of reasoning imposes particular requirements upon statistics used with it. Many comparisons are basically statistical, so let us examine first the general theory of reasoning from statistical evidence, then techniques of analysis through statistical comparison.

General methodology of reasoning from statistical information Why statistics? Briefly, they are needed whenever the number of instances with which we would like to deal becomes unwieldy. Statistics are a shorthand method of making comparisons. Selected characteristics are counted (or measured, one variety of counting) and summary statements are made about a group of cases using numbers to facilitate the process of summarization. Conversion to numbers expands the horizons of evidence tremendously. Here is the main reason why the discussion participant will find that an understanding of the frequently used statistical procedures is necessary to efficient analysis of most problems.

Statistical descriptions are always simplifications, although at the moment to some people they seem to make the situation very complicated indeed! They consolidate a number of items of information into one or more of a number of standard and accepted statistical concepts. If we know the rather definite potentials and limitations of these standard concepts, we can interpret the information that is in numerical form with greater definiteness and certainty than we can most nonstatistical bits of information.

One basic question is used to test any evidence in the form of a statistical description, "Is this simplification an oversimplification?" All the information and suggestions following are intended to help you answer this key question.

In statistical treatment of data something is lost and something is gained. Details are left out, as in any process of summarizing. Often, omitted details may be as important as what is counted and recorded, for the purposes of a particular application. One gain is in a new dimension, the addition of *quantification*. Answers to questions such as "How regularly . . . ?" "How frequently . . . ?" "How many . . . ?" and "How much . . . ?" are most helpful to our thinking and can be found only in statistical summaries of one sort or another. If the goal of a comparison is prediction, then statistics may make it possible for us not only to agree that, in our opinion, something will probably happen, but *how likely* it is to come about. In other words, statistics make possible estimates of relative probability. Other methods of handling information cannot yield this type of conclusion.

Some general cautions apply to all reasoning from statistical information. Because statistical methods are based on grouping multiple cases, the resulting generalizations apply only to similar groups, and rarely can be applied to individual cases. Normative statements should not be applied to single instances. If the average student at Pogo University has an IQ of 110 we can conclude nothing about the IQ of the next person who enters the freshman class. Many errors in interpreting statistics come from such fallacious attempts to apply group generalizations of central tendency to single members of a similar population. Even a generalization of a perfect induction that all students at Pogo are over five feet tall may not apply to the next applicant and is useless for individual case prediction.

Another caution is always to evaluate the *source* of statistical data. Items dealt with statistically are generally beyond the reach of personal verification. Hence, we have no choice but to trust the people who collect, summarize, and publish the information. A prejudiced source may present a partial presentation as one that is complete and impartial. An incompetent source may apply certain statistical procedures to data for which these are inappropriate. We can investigate the reputation of the source for reliability and accuracy. We can study the source in quest of monetary or other influential connections that might contribute to a vested interest in a particular outcome. We can compare the statistics from one source to those from other sources. These operations ought always to enter into any use of statistical materials in discussion.

Statistical consolidations and generalizations often appear to be far more precise than they are. A "mean" (arithmetic average) may be carried out to as many as three decimal places when the items in the data averaged are meaningful only as whole numbers. Numbers are frequently assigned to subjective factors or poorly quantified objective items in arbitrary fashion and the grouped data treated with great precision. These are examples of many kinds of meaningless statistics that confuse more than they enlighten, and should be eliminated from the problem-solving process.

Our final general caution is repetitious: every unit of statistical information must be interpreted with full understanding of the purposes and limitations of the particular statistical procedure used. Perfectly valid and potentially valuable statistical summaries, misapplied, lead to the said observation:

"Floods of figures carry with them no assurance of an advance in understanding." [1]

Techniques of statistical comparison analysis Statistical comparisons are of central tendencies or of measures of variability, or of a combination of both. The *mean* is the most used index of central

---

[1] H. A. Larrabee, *Reliable Knowledge,* Boston, Houghton Mifflin Co., Copyright 1945 by H. A. Larrabee, p. 379.

tendency: "Our present minimum cannery wage is $1.65 per hour while the average Japanese cannery wage is 35–50¢ per day. Our raw tuna costs us $310 a ton and in Japan it costs approximately $100 a ton." The concept of *range* is a frequent measure of variability: "Although many tariffs have been lowered under the Reciprocal Trade Agreements Act, many United States imports have tariffs of 25 per cent or more. Lace, embroideries, and imitation pearls have a tariff of 90 per cent. On coal products, such as perfume, the tariff is over 100 per cent. On most toys the rate is 70 per cent. Hundreds of items have a tariff rate that exceeds 60 per cent." Frequently range and mean are combined to give a more valid cross-section of the instances summarized statistically. This appears in the above example.

The simple mean is based upon the assumption that all items in a group are of equal importance. In many situations this is not a desirable assumption. If you are computing your college grade point average for purposes of estimating your chances of succeeding in medical school, certain courses will be more important than others. Because chemistry, mathematics, and physiology are more closely related to the work you will do in medical school, grades in these have greater predictive value than have grades in freshman composion, art appreciation and English literature. So, for this particular purpose you may decide to distort the mean by *weighting* certain course grades that seem to be more important than others. You might arbitrarily double or triple the weight given to those courses you have had which are similar to the studies in medical school. The new mean, then, would be heavily influenced by these items in the distribution, while the other unweighted courses would continue to contribute, but not as much as before. In using a statistical average we should try to identify and examine any system of weighting that may have been used, and in case of the unweighted average consider whether we are willing to accept the assumption that all items in the distribution are of equal significance.

A pitfall in the use of the mean comes from the possibility that it may be heavily influenced by a few extreme instances, and may not realistically represent a "central tendency." A small business might pay each of its nineteen employees $3,000 a year and the plant superintendent a salary of $50,000. The average salary of $5,350 has little meaning and may convey quite erroneous impressions. We tend to assume that a mean is in the middle of a range, and that a fairly normal distribution surrounds it. As this instance demonstrates, such may not be the case.

It is easy to "check up on" a mean by comparing it to two other indices of central tendency which are not affected by extreme instances, the *median* and the *mode*. If the items averaged are in rank order, i.e., from high to low or vice versa, the median is that item at the mid-point of the range. The mode is the item which occurs most frequently. In our hypothetical example of the industrial enterprise which pays all workers except the manager the same salary, median and mode would be the same, $3,000. This figure is more representative of the existing salary situation than is the average.

A measure of central tendency has greatest significance when median, mode, and mean are close together. It is helpful to study real and hypothetical distributions of items in the effort to determine why this is true. What conditions in a distribution can cause these three measures to separate widely?

We have seen the necessity of describing the characteristics of a distribution in order better to interpret a measure of central tendency. It would be desirable to quantify variability or dispersion in the interest of more accurate comparisons, since the amount and kind of variability are often the vital considerations. The simplest way this is done is to compute the *range of variation*. By subtraction each item is compared to the mean, and a table of "differences from the mean" is worked out. Inspection will then reveal how many items differ substantially from the mean value, and how much that difference is. If we average the differences from the mean we get the *mean* deviation, a single index of the amount of variability in a distribution. An example will clarify these matters:

A radar device for measuring the speed of automobiles has been used in studying traffic movement on a one-way street during various times of day. From 4:45 to 4:50 P.M. on a Tuesday, 100 cars were picked up by the gadget, a grouping that was assumed to be representative of traffic at that hour on a weekday. Because a table of 100 items is cumbersome, we have selected from the rank-order tabulation eleven instances that include the fastest and the slowest and nine others selected at equal intervals covering the range of the group. By "equal intervals" we mean "numbers of items" not "numbers of miles per hour." Hence, from top to bottom of the rank order we have selected cases numbered 1, 10, 20, 30, 40, 50, 60, 70, 80, 90, and 100. Obviously, the 100 motorists were not distributed evenly over the speed range.

Speed Survey Table

Speed (MPH)	Differences from Mean (x)	x^2
50	17	289
46	13	169
42	9	81
36	3	9
33	0	0
32	1	1
30	3	9
26	7	49
25	8	64
23	10	100
20	13	169
Total 363	84	940
Mean 33		

Mean
deviation 7.6

$$\text{Standard deviation } (\sigma) = \sqrt{\frac{\epsilon x^2}{n}} = \sqrt{\frac{940}{11}}$$

$$\sigma = \sqrt{85.45}$$

$$\sigma = 9.3$$

For the moment, consider only the first two columns in the preceding table. The mean is calculated by totaling the individual speeds and dividing by the number of cases, here eleven. This tells us that the average speed of the checked cars was 33 miles per hour. Since the speed limit at this point is 35 miles per hour, this seems to be eminently law-abiding. But when we tabulate the differences from the mean (column 2), we see that four of the eleven motorists exceeded both average and legal speeds, and that in terms of the average the range of variability was from 17 miles per hour on the fast side to 13 miles below the mean, or 30 miles per hour dispersion. Traffic here doesn't seem to be moving at a uniform rate of speed!

To simplify the estimate of variability further, we can say that the mean deviation from the average speed is 7.6 miles per hour. Note that in computing mean deviation the algebraic signs are ignored, since we are interested here in *amount* rather than *direction* of deviations. What does the "mean deviation" signify? In normal distributions (this one is fairly close to a "normal" distribution although it is "skewed" slightly to the low end) something over half the cases will be included in a range of the mean deviation above and below the average. Here we can say that a majority of motorists at this time and place were driving at 33 miles per hour plus or minus 7.6. Or, that the majority were driving between 25.4 and 40.6 miles per hour.

Standard deviation (σ or sigma) is a similar index of variation, one which is more precise and which is used in the calculation of other statistical measures such as coefficient of correlation (explained in the next chapter). The "x^2" column in our table illustrates the basic manipulation of data that yields this measure, the squaring and adding of the items of differences from the mean. The resultant total (the sum of x^2) is divided by the number of items, and the square root of this quotient obtained as indicated by the formula. The range of one standard deviation above and one standard deviation below the mean in a substantially normal distribution includes about two-thirds of the cases in the group. Here we might apply it by saying that at most a third of the motorists drove slower than 23.7 or faster than 42.3 miles per hour.

The usefulness of mean and standard deviations increases with the complexity and extent of the data they summarize. With increased numbers of properly selected cases, prediction becomes more accurate. Then it becomes very important that we know what to expect of a majority or of two-thirds of the population in terms of how much they will vary from the average.

Mean and standard deviations of similar sets of data can be compared directly. For example, two one-way streets might be found to differ greatly in the uniformity of speed of traffic at the same time of day by such comparison. Variability in prices charged for certain commodities in different cities, and temperature changes in the month of July in selected years or places, can be compared quantitatively through mean and standard deviations.

As suggested above, many statistical concepts are in terms of a "normal" distribution or "the normal curve." This is the sort of distribution that results from measurement of a very large number of some kind of natural phenomenon, such as the weight of bumblebees. A few are relatively heavy, a few are light (relative to the others), and as we approach the average weight the numbers increase. If we weigh enough bumblebees, perhaps 100,000, and graph the result, we will achieve a bell-shaped normal curve like this one:

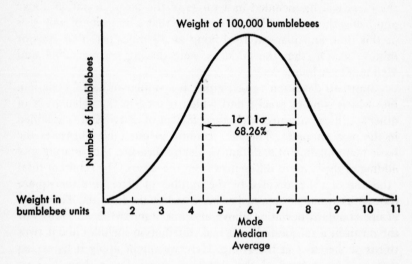

More bumblees weigh six units than weigh any other amount. As we approach the limits of the range, the numbers of bumblebees in each weight interval decrease uniformly. The curve tapers down to the lightest and the heaviest bee at the two extremes.

In this ideal or perfect distribution the mean, mode, and median are the same. Two standard deviations in the middle of the rank order include 68.26 per cent of the total number of cases. All real-life collections of data deviate from the normal curve to some degree. The more pronounced the distortion of the distribution from the normal, the less is the significance and the precision of standard and mean deviations. Comparisons of this nature must take into consideration the pattern of rank-ordered items and its general resemblance to the normal curve.

Statistical comparisons are many and complicated. They infiltrate controversial subjects wherein numerical data would seem to be unlikely. In the process of preparing for discussions, it is revealing to record briefly every comparison you encounter that has a statistical base. A composite list of those found by several researchers will be instructive in dramatizing the great variety in applications of the statistical comparison.

Reasoning from nonstatistical comparisons

The nonstatistical examples and other comparisons that authors who write about reasoning use as samples are often in the context of laboratory experimentation. Here a small number of important conditions can be kept constant and all, or nearly all, variables can be known. When the addition of one drop of chemical X to a gallon of motor oil is followed by reduction of friction in the test machine by the same amount in three consecutive experiments, the comparison leads us to suspect that the same friction reduction will come about the next time the procedure is duplicated.

Reasoning via comparison about social problems is less precise, for obvious reasons. Relevant conditions are too numerous to be listed, variables are many and unknown. The result is a "miserably inexact" sort of reasoning. There is much doubt that in the consideration of two instances of a social problem, similarities can ever be shown to outweigh differences. Yet oftentimes they seem to, and some such comparisons make possible productive interpretations. It is important that we recognize the vast chasm separating laboratory and social comparisons and not delude ourselves into thinking that we are applying the scientific method to the analysis of a community problem with the precision achieved by the medical researcher who isolates critical factors associated with breast cancer in mice.

Statistical comparisons are practically always more meaningful than nonstatistical comparisons. When we cannot *quantify* (use numbers), we resort to subjective judgment, and to some extent this enters into every nonstatistical comparison. Good comparisons substitute observable facts for value judgments wherever possible. The indirect inference is always inferior to direct observation in establishing differences and similarities in the things being compared. Statistics are always based upon direct observations.

Let us suppose that you are in the fortunate position of having money enough to buy a new car. You will probably make your choice through reasoning from comparison. It will be either by example (if the comparison is incomplete) or by multiple comparison if you extend your reasoning to several examples.

Let us suppose further that you buy a Buick because your best friend has one, you enjoy riding in and driving it, and he assures you that it is thoroughly satisfactory in every way. Without study of other examples you find this one instance sufficiently convincing to influence your decision.

This example is an *implied* comparison, for although you do not make it explicit, the facts about your friend's Buick are persuasive to you because you are comparing them against the specifications of the ideal automobile you would like to own. If you should list the criteria that you deem important and check the Buick against that list, then you would complete a comparison of an important type, the criteria case study comparison.

Reasoning from example is weak and dangerous because of its incompleteness. It is always desirable to make explicit the criteria or the set of circumstances which give the example significance. Multiple examples clarify and objectify the situation too. You would be a better buyer in the above illustration if you checked a couple of other cars against your criteria to see how they measure up in comparison to Buick.

Examples are more subject to oversimplification than are complete comparisons. We often cite examples of outstandingly good citizens, policemen, ministers, and housewives. Usually there is no criterion list or point-by-point comparison to establish the honored individual's superiority in performances relevant to the recognition bestowed. Selection is by a generalized subjective judgment that the person named is "representative" of a class. The implication is that if a list of standards were agreed upon, and if ratings of candidates were made, our subjectively selected person would get the highest score. True enough, he *might,* but the quick assumption that he *would* represents drastically oversimplified thinking. We can't escape the basic test of a sound comparison: Are vital similarities established and differences accounted for? To meet the tests, observable performance factors must enter in.

Personally conducted comparisons can be excellent sources of evidence. Here as always a systematic procedure is prerequisite to optimum results. Sometimes it is possible to control conditions and variables with close-to-laboratory precision. Selection of record playing equipment can be done in this way if you have access to a large demonstration studio in a department or radio supply store. A preliminary selection of players to be compared can be made by applying the criterion of what you can afford. Then, using different types of records of known quality, you can compare pick-ups, amplifiers, and loud speakers under the same listening conditions, *varying only one element at a time*. This homely example illustrates the necessity of striking a balance between the practical and the ideal in a personally conducted comparison. It would be desirable to try out all the combinations you experimented with in your own living room, since room acoustics determine to some extent the tonal balance of record players. This is usually beyond the merchandising methods of the distributor. A compromise might be to select a player at the store on a tentative basis, final purchase being dependent upon a satisfactory home listening test.

We tend to be careless in making personal comparisons. Few people go to the bother of comprehensive listening tests in buying "high fidelity" equipment, although they will readily admit the desirability of so doing. One substitute for a personal comparison, and a rather satisfactory one, is to hire unprejudiced experts to make the comparison for you. This is done most economically by subscribing to one of the consumer research publications.

The impersonal or remote comparison is well illustrated by an example of the services offered by these organizations. The purchase of a highly competitive product like an electric razor will likely be a shot in the dark if you rely solely on advertising claims. Personal comparison is severely limited by practical considerations. But the research organization can develop criteria of electric razor performance, rent the faces of a couple of dozen men with all types of whiskers, and collect their reports on performance of various brands over a period of several months. When criteria are clearly stated and the user reaction is summarized accurately, the potential razor buyer is helped significantly toward a wise decision. The best use of consumer report data involves not simply the decision to buy the brand at the top of the list, but a study of the criteria that placed it there. Perhaps the circumstances of the use to which you intend to put the article or your personal preference will make another choice a better buy for you.

Comparisons of products seem simple and easy when we turn to comparisons involving people. Yet we must compare stores, schools, fraternities, rooming and eating establishments, political candidates and parties, and corporations. Again, criteria should be listed and performance records compared on listed items. There will be two sorts of items of comparison when people are involved, observable and otherwise verifiable phenomena and generalizations that are your own interpretations or the interpretations of others. The generalizations are inevitably subjective and not only summarize verifiable facts but weigh their significance in terms of predictions that are crude probabilities. These generalizations are a substitute for statistical techniques where statistical measures are impossible.

Comparison of two political candidates illustrates this objective-subjective relationship nicely. First we "rough out" a list of criteria, what we would like to see in terms of specific performance in the man we send to represent us in, say, the United States Senate. This includes "stands" on particular legislation as well as general philosophy of government in its domestic and international roles. Inevitably, we include less concrete items also, such as personal integrity, speaking ability, probable influence among his colleagues. Next, we collect factual information in the form of what the candidates have done and said. The voting record of the incumbent is helpful, as is the record of the other candidate in various positions he has held. Assuming that the individual elected will continue to be the same sort of person he has been up to the present (a fairly safe assumption), we are able to predict with some confidence how he will probably vote on certain bills.

Now, we have shifted from verifiable data to generalizations about them. We proceed to collect other generalizations of this sort from knowledgeable people to test our own judgments. Finally, we toss into the hopper opinions about the great abstractions of political office holding; personal integrity, and probable influence. The primary evidence that would substantiate these sweeping judgments is almost never available. We are now in the realm of hunches and intuition, with tiny incidents triggering mighty opinions that become increasingly firm with repetition.

To keep our feet on the ground at least occasionally in comparing political candidates or other human institutions, the best advice is to keep going back to the record. Clashing generalizations make an exciting but unproductive discussion. The person who generalizes should always be willing to cite incidents to support his opinion. Everybody in the discussion should help everyone else reveal the basis of each assertion. A good question to use in a comparison of political candidates is: "In what measurable characteristics which will affect their discharge of the duties of the office to which they aspire do these candidates differ?" If this stops the discussion, perhaps the discussion should be stopped.

In arguing and discussing, we use a great many pseudo-comparisons, structures that resemble comparisons on the surface but make no serious effort to develop comprehensively similarities and differences and to account for the differences. These are most frequently outsize, foolish comparisons like comparing democracy and dictatorship, or the present with the "good old days," or city living with suburban living. These are hopeless oversimplifications and should be viewed as figurative language phenomena rather than reasoning from comparison.

Comparison for purposes of contrast is often a productive form of reasoning. The objective of this type of comparison is to develop differences which are highly significant and can be accounted for in only one way—the conclusion of the comparison. Insurance companies collect data to contrast safe and accident-prone drivers. One of the authors contrasted two brands of antimosquito spray under similar conditions to verify an important difference. One killed the mosquitoes, the other had little, if any, effect. During the summer of 1954 televised Congressional hearings claimed public attention for weeks as the Army sought to demonstrate that Senator Joseph McCarthy and his staff had brought to bear upon the Army improper influence in behalf of then Private G. David Schine. The stories of the opposing factions were told and documented. The main objective of the hearing was to define points of difference in these stories and explain them. The differences developed quite clearly, but they turned out to be unverifiable differences in the recall of past events, or differences of opinion (generalizations).

Comparison to develop contrast is the same basic method of studying evidence as comparison to bring out similarities. It is subject to the same cautions and misinterpretations. But its conclusion, when a single difference or very few develop, can be sharply limited, hence helpful to the reasoning process.

ANALOGICAL ANALYSIS OF EVIDENCE

Some highly effective argument by analogy is to be found in the Bible:

No man also seweth a piece of new cloth on an old garment: else the new piece that filled it up taketh away from the old, and the rent is made worse.

And no man putteth new wine into old bottles: else the new wine doth burst the bottles and the wine is spilled, and the bottles will be marred, but new wine must be put into new bottles.[2]

No one sews a piece of unshrunk cloth on an old garment, if he does, the patch tears away from it, the new from the old, and a worse tear is made. And no one puts new wine into old wineskins; if he does, the wine will burst the skins, and the wine is lost, and so are the skins; but new wine is for fresh skins.[3]

And the scribes of the Pharisees, when they saw that He was eating with sinners and tax collectors, said to His disciples, "Why does He eat with tax collectors and sinners?" And when Jesus heard it, He said to them, "Those who are well have no need of a physician, but those who are sick; I came not to call the righteous, but sinners."[4]

And He taught them many things in parables, and in His teaching He said to them: "Listen! A sower went out to sow. And as he sowed, some seed fell along the path, and the birds came and devoured it. Other seed fell on rocky ground, where it had not much soil, and immediately it sprang up, since it had no depth of soil, and when the sun rose it was scorched, and since it had no root, it withered away. Other seed fell among thorns and the thorns grew up and choked it, and it yielded no grain. And other seeds fell into good soil and brought forth grain, growing up and increasing and yielding thirtyfold and sixtyfold and a hundredfold." And He said, "He who has ears to hear, let him hear."

[2] *The Holy Bible,* Authorized King James Version, Mark 2:21-22.
[3] *The Holy Bible,* Revised Standard Version, New York, Thomas Nelson and Sons, Copyright 1952 by the National Council of the Churches of Christ in the U.S.A., Mark 2:21-22, p. 41. Reprinted by permission of the copyright owners.
[4] *Ibid.,* Mark 2:16-17, p. 41.

And when He was alone, those who were about Him with the twelve asked Him concerning the parables. And He said to them, "To you has been given the secret of the kingdom of God, but for those outside everything is in parables; so that they may indeed see but not perceive, and may indeed hear but not understand; lest they should turn again and be forgiven." And He said unto them, "Do you not understand this parable? How then will you understand all the parables? The sower sows the word. And these are the ones along the path, where the word is sown; when they hear, Satan immediately comes and takes away the word which is sown in them. And these in like manner are the ones sown upon rocky ground, who, when they hear the word, immediately receive it with joy; and they have no root in themselves, but endure for a while; then, when tribulation or persecution arises on account of the word, immediately they fall away. And others are the ones sown among the thorns; they are those that hear the word, but the cares of the world and the delight in riches, and the desire for other things, enter in and choke the word, and it proves unfruitful. But those that were sown upon the good soil are the ones who hear the word and accept it and bear fruit, thirtyfold and sixtyfold and a hundredfold." [5]

One of the most familiar forms of analysis in reasoning about our problems is the analogy. By "analogy" we mean "figurative analogy" like the parables quoted above. "Literal analogies" are *comparisons*, as was noted earlier in this chapter. Hence we use the term "analogy" to mean "figurative analogy" to describe the use of the procedures of comparison to relate incidents or cases which are in different contexts but are asserted to share common principles. When Jesus argues for his practice of associating with sinners by telling of the duties of the medical doctor he is reasoning by analogy. He establishes an *identity of principle* in saving souls and saving lives.

The mending and wine bottling analogies are repeated in two forms to illustrate some interesting differences between the King James and Revised Standard Versions of the Bible. Since the Revised Standard seems to be written in the language of our times, the other parables quoted are from that version.

The parable of the sower is an illuminating example of a complex analogy, for Jesus explains its meaning—the application of the common principle—in detail. How would you word the principle

[5] *Ibid.*, Mark 4:2-20, pp. 42, 43.

or principles that sum up the main points Jesus was trying to make by this illustration?

The nature of analogical reasoning may be summarized briefly: an analogy is a dramatization of one or more principles via the familiar illustration. It ignores identity of details and strives to establish identity of principle. There are three steps in reasoning by analogy:

(1) Making explicit the central principle(s) to be clarified and dramatized.

(2) Selection of a familiar illustration which shows a clear and vivid application of the principle(s).

(3) Optional explanation of the illustration in terms of the principle(s). If a common principle is obvious, the analogy makes a stronger psychological appeal when the explanation is suppressed. But, as in the parable of the sower, a complex analogy usually requires some explanation if its full significance is to be appreciated.

Some analogies are good and sufficient reasons for the beliefs they support, some are fairly convincing but inconclusive, and a great many are worthless as proof, though they may be vivid and colorful. Because the comparison of the way a principle applies to two cases in different contexts is always subjective, logical evaluation of analogies is not easy. We believe it is helpful to place an analogy on a continuum that classifies the principle illustrated and the amount of detailed development of the illustration.

Analogy Continuum

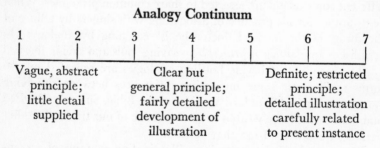

Examples will serve to show how the above scale can help to evaluate reasoning by analogy. The reader is invited to examine and possibly challenge the authors' classification of the following samples.

At the left end of the continuum (at No. 1) analogies shade off into figures of speech, usually metaphors and similes, which add color to communication but are not, in themselves, reasoning. Lots of "smart sayings" are in this category, such as "he has more opportunity than a mosquito in a nudist colony," or "her mind is like concrete, all mixed up and permanently set." To demonstrate the desirability of having confidence in our own judgment we might cite the case of the big league umpire who was complimented for his integrity in "calling 'em the way he saw 'em." He was indignant. "I don't call 'em the way I see them," he said, "I call 'em the way they *are*!" Or we might use as a basis of a discussion about similarities and differences between democracy and communism the statement: "Communism is like a colony of ants."

These borderline analogies contain the suggestion of identity of some generalized, vague principle. But it is elusive because the illustration remains undeveloped, and explanation of its significance is neither obvious nor made explicit. So we believe that the reasoning illustrated is severely incomplete, and that these analogies may be located between Nos. 1 and 2 on the scale.

A somewhat more definite principle was illustrated by the late Senator Vandenburg when he commented upon the role played by Senate Republicans in a Democratic administration's foreign policy: "We are always asked to participate in the crash landings but never in the take-offs." Elmer Wheeler, often termed "America's Number One Salesman," has crystallized his philosophy of salesmanship into an analogy: "Don't sell the steak, sell the sizzle." He reminds us of the experience of walking into a restaurant, hungry and tired, and of passing a waitress carrying a sizzling, aromatic steak. Suddenly, uncritically, we want a steak like the one we saw (and heard), without asking the practical questions concerning price and quality. Wheeler says that every product has some "sizzle" for a particular prospect, a characteristic that may be unrelated to its performance. Find the sizzle, present it attractively, and the prospect can be made to desire the product as a hungry man wants a steak.

During the Army–McCarthy hearings in the summer of 1954, the Army presented a chart to compare the passes granted to Private G. David Schine with those issued to the average G.I. of his rank. On a gray background the average G.I. passes were represented by white lines, those of Private Schine by black lines. Senator McCarthy questioned the Army witness sharply about the significance of representing his staff members' record in *black* while the "average G.I." record appeared in *pure white*. He suggested that this was an effort to smear Private Schine. "Why," asked Senator McCarthy, "is the average G.I. represented in white and Private Schine in black?" The witness replied, "Probably for the same reason that one prize fighter wears white trunks and the other black, so people can tell them apart."

A standard analogy is used frequently in political rhetoric to demonstrate the interdependence of different economic groups in this country. Probably it occurs most often to demonstrate the need for safeguarding the prosperity of agriculture. We are told that labor, management, and agriculture may be thought of as sharing a boat that represents national prosperity. They occupy different sections of the vessel and tend to forget that an even keel depends upon their mutual welfare. If agriculture experiences hard times, management and labor will suffer just as surely as a boat with a serious leak in one end will sink as a unit, totally.

The principles that are held to have identity in the above illustrations are more accessible and definite than were those in the first group. Some are explicit and some are suppressed. Try to isolate and word the principle or principles that must apply in each instance, if the analogy is to have weight as logical proof. In the authors' opinion, the preceding group of four analogies falls in the range between Nos. 3 and 5 on our analogy continuum.

Analogies can be close and precise without being elaborate. The case for studying communism in our schools has been developed by a brief analogy, one reminding us that the prize fighter who failed to study the style and record of his probable opponent would be considered exceptionally stupid. Just as the boxer can't have too much reliable information about the person he will encounter in the ring, we as a nation can't know too much about our major potential enemy.

Earlier in this chapter we mentioned the ostrich analogy, used to support the contention that one of the authors should continue his hospital insurance payments. Dropping this protection was by implication as futile as the ostrich practice (alleged) of hiding its head when frightened. The principle that ignoring danger is a poor way of avoiding it comes out clearly.

The "study communism" and "ostrich" analogies seem to be reasonable enough to amount to substantial proof. They might be placed between Nos. 5 and 6 on our scale.

An analogy which has been tremendously helpful in the early stages of instruction in radio engineering is the "water analogy." The flow of electrons in a circuit is likened to a familiar hydraulic system. Resistors operate to slow this flow, like constrictions in a pipe, and vacuum tubes control it, like water valves or faucets. Batteries furnish electricity under pressure, like a pump and pressure tank in a water system. Some principles of electronics can be taught through this identity. Later the advancing student breaks with the analogy by identifying principles of electronics which are not analogous to the functioning of hydraulic devices.

In the previously mentioned Army–McCarthy hearings, while Secretary of the Army Stevens was testifying, Senator McCarthy was exploring his attitude toward investigations at Fort Monmouth that had been conducted earlier by the McCarthy Committee. "Did you oppose these investigations?" asked McCarthy. "No," answered Secretary Stevens. "Did you, personally, want them to continue?" "No." "But that is inconsistent," said Senator McCarthy, "for if you didn't want them carried on, you must have opposed them." And Stevens never successfully resolved this alleged inconsistency. What he might have said, reasoning analogically, was, "I felt toward those hearings at Fort Monmouth the way you feel when your dentist is drilling out a cavity. You don't *want* the drilling to continue, but you wouldn't oppose it for you know it is necessary to the proper treatment of the tooth."

An argument for periodic overhaul of TV sets is appearing in advertisements in the form of a rather carefully developed analogy. The reader is reminded that he, like most motorists, has come to know that it pays to have his automobile checked over and "tuned up" at regular intervals. Why is this necessary? Because the modern car is a complex machine with many interacting operations going on at the same time, and with wear and aging affecting different parts at different rates. As the functioning of one part changes, the balance of all interacting operations is affected. With passing of time the maladjustment increases until much efficiency is lost. The only way the car's efficiency can be restored is to replace worn parts, clean out accumulations of dirt, and readjust all the delicately timed operations, using expensive measuring instruments so that the coordinated synchronization of a new car is again achieved. Hence, the periodic check and tune-up.

A television receiver is at least as complicated as a car. Tubes change characteristics with use, condensers dry out and age, the precise balance of interacting circuits is affected. Picture detail, stability, and contrast are lost. To get full enjoyment from your TV set and to protect yourself against its breakdown, you should have it checked over and aligned ("tuned up") each autumn as you do your automobile.

While these analogies are not in themselves completely conclusive reasons, they are clear-cut arguments based on identifiable principles and have a reasonableness that justifies our calling them "proof." They fall toward the right-hand end of our analogy scale, probably between Nos. 6 and 7.

A good test of the soundness of an analogy is this: Can you answer it with a counteranalogy that shows a more relevant identity of principle? If you can, the original analogy is conclusively refuted. Here is an analogy used to help prove that columnist Westbrook Pegler was attacking President Eisenhower because he would attack any man who was President of the United States.

You can't teach an old dog to give up tricks that have been bringing in the Ken-L-Ration since he was a pup, and I suspect Pegler is like one of the dogs the Army trains to attack anyone they see wearing an enemy uniform. It is apparently not so much Mr. Eisenhower of whom Mr. Pegler disapproves as it is the very office of President. Any man of any party who didn't begin his term by abdicating all his powers to the state legislatures would hear that brutish snarl and feel those huge paws on his chest before long.[6]

The creation of a counteranalogy involves reinterpreting the same basic ingredients. It frequently begins, "But you might as well say . . ." Thus, a proponent of Pegler's, wishing to refute Bingham, could argue as follows: "Bingham might as well have said that Pegler is as consistent as an Army-trained dog in sniffing out the enemy, no matter how thoroughly he is camouflaged. This was a difficult case because the disguise was professional and complete, so getting the scent took a little time. But it was sure to happen.

[6] Robert K. Bingham, "Westbrook Pegler and 'That Man in the White House,'" *The Reporter,* Vol. 11, No. 3, Aug. 17, 1954, p. 36.

Even Pegler's respect for the Republican label and the office of President didn't prevent him from detecting and exposing the internationalist New Dealer in Ike."

Is the counteranalogy more reasonable than the original? It is if it clearly represents a more relevant application of a common principle. This has to be a subjective judgment. We leave the relative evaluation of these examples to the reader. In practice even a fairly good counteranalogy effectively reduces the convincingness of the analogy it attempts to refute. It accomplishes this by reminding us that conflicting interpretations are possible.

Reasoning by analogy has been the most overused and underrated rhetorical device. Most writers on rhetoric and logic have asserted that analogies have no logical significance. We disagree, believing that the better, closer analogies have an intrinsic reasonableness that justifies admitting them to the category of "proof."

CHAPTER VII

Inductive Analysis of Evidence – Part 3

Circumstantial-detail thinking occurs wherever the conclusion sought is an explanation of a unique relationship among the parts of a pattern of events. The conclusion is an hypothesis that "reasonably" relates phenomena which together are alleged to make up a system with some degree of order and coherence. Without the conclusion the significance of individual events in the supposed pattern is unclear.

The name "circumstantial detail" comes from the court procedure which furnishes the classic illustration of this basic method of problem solving. As a murder trial develops, let us say that the following evidence has been verified: (1) the defendant was seen entering the house where the corpse was found a half-hour before the shot was heard; (2) his fingerprints were found on the doorknob of the murdered man's room; (3) the defendant's topcoat is shy a button; (4) a button matching those on this topcoat was found clutched in the murdered man's hand; (5) the defendant was admittedly very jealous of the murdered man, who was friendly to the defendant's wife; (6) a gun of the same calibre as the murder weapon (unfound) was registered in the name of the defendant; (7) the defendant does not have the registered pistol in his possession, claiming it had recently been stolen; and (8) the defendant is unable to produce evidence that he was at a place other than the scene of the crime at the time it was committed. In his summation the prosecuting attorney may well allege that in the absence of contradictory evidence the only sensible interpretation of this pattern of isolated bits of information is the conclusion that the defendant is guilty. This conclusion completes a meaningful story in which each event can be understood and each becomes significant. The defense then has the opportunity of reinterpreting the list of items by reasoning toward a different conclusion that will create another, more probable, pattern than that hypothesized by the prosecution. The contest refereed by the jury is one of circumstantial-detail analysis, or interpretation of a list of circumstances in an effort to discover how they are related. "Further knowledge" necessary is a great fund of information concerning the ways of human behavior, probabilities of coincidental happenings, other laws governing natural phe-

Reproduced by permission © 1946 The New Yorker Magazine, Inc.

nomena, and so forth. This further knowledge makes possible evaluation of particular circumstantial details.

Items in a circumstantial-detail pattern form an incomplete picture of what happened. Typically, there is no close connection between items, except for possible cause-and-effect linkages. Consequently, the chance for error in reasoning from a list of circumstances is great, and legal procedure provides many limitations upon the use of circumstantial deail. A single incompatible element which cannot be assimilated into the pattern can destroy an entire unit of reasoning. For example, the case of the prosecution in our hypothetical murder trial would be severely crippled by the introduction of a witness who admitted to stealing the murder weapon and committing the crime! The major test of circumstantial-detail reasoning is whether all other discoverable relevant factors are consistent with the asserted pattern of events.

REASONING FROM SIGN

The simplest and usually the weakest form of circumstantial-detail analysis is reasoning from sign. When two phenomena are conceded to happen together reliably, some use may be made of this knowledge to predict what will happen, or understand what has happened. The connection between the events need not be made clear. The essential element in sign reasoning is the consistency with which the elements go together. If one is found not to occur without the other, then the verified presence of one will enable us to conclude the probable occurrence of the other. At present it is raining. I know from long experience that when it rains on a school day the flag over the armory is lowered and taken in. The rain is a sign that the flag is not flying, and if I look at the armory in midforenoon on a school day the absence of the flag might be construed as a sign of rain. What human and other elements link the armory flag and precipitation I do not know or need to know. But I would be confident enough in the probability that "rain-flag-lowering" and "clearing-flag-raising" go together to place a small wager that at the moment the flag is not flying over the armory. I might lose, but nine years of fairly regular observation have caused me to have faith in the regularity of this sign relationship.

There is increasing interest in argument from sign and greater awareness of its productive possibilities. In science it was once considered greatly inferior to cause-effect analysis. The medical researcher once was not encouraged to publish even a fairly established sign relationship. He might have discovered for example, that administering a drug was reliably followed by relief of a certain symptom of a particular disease. Until recently he was expected to trace the cause-and-effect linkages that explained the action of the drug before presenting information about it to his colleagues. This frequently took years of research beyond that needed to establish the drug-administration-symptom-relief relationship and the absence of harmful side-effects.

Today the reliable concurrence of phenomena in research of many kinds is conceded to be of great significance, even though the *why* of an observed relationship may not be understood. Prediction becomes possible. Many applications can be evolved while the study of causal relationships is continued. There is no need to wait for the discovery of a cause-effect chain before putting the established, reliable, coincidence information to work. This revolution in method leads to the observation that sign and concomitant variation reasoning have to a significant extent replaced causal analysis in laboratory research.

The same shift in emphasis is found in the social sciences. Sign relationships are frequently quantified through statistics, and the addition of definite probability makes sign reasoning about social phenomena increasingly precise. Discussion is often concerned with "signs of the times," for important trends are usually detected and plotted in terms of signs that have been found to be reliable concomitants.

A typical use of reasoning from sign is found in discussion of the possible interrelation of international cordiality or lack of it and trade between nations. Signs of this interaction may be discovered by noting trade figures between two nations such as Russia and the United States in times of friendship and times of discord. A sampling of three years of trade statistics is worth discussing:

Obviously, this is only part of the story. Factors other than accord between the two nations undoubtedly enter into determination of these differences in volume of trade. But the signs that go together, cordiality-high-trade, mistrust-low-trade, certainly are significant and need to be investigated. What conclusions can we draw from

U.S. Trade with the U.S.S.R.

1935	Imports	$17,800,000
	Exports	24,700,000
1946	Imports	100,600,000
	Exports	1,836,400,000
1951	Imports	27,400,000
	Exports	55,000

this information? What further information and what other types of reasoning are needed to estimate the worth of this sign analysis? These are typical questions used to evaluate argument from sign.

As in the case of any circumstantial-detail pattern, a single bit of evidence that is inconsistent with it will challenge an entire argument from sign. During the search for causes of polio some investigations indicated high consumption of dairy products wherever polio epidemics broke out. A relationship between the two was hypothesized until another section of the country with epidemic polio was surveyed and the use of dairy products there was found to be extremely low. In our international friendship-trade discussion the discovery of a case in which trade between two countries went up as their relations deteriorated would make the first sign analysis shaky indeed.

Sign analyses furnish significant clues to stimulate discussion along productive lines. As sign relationships are explored and elaborated they tend to mature into concomitant variations and the establishing of causal relations. Seldom is a bit of reasoning from sign of sufficient weight to settle the social issue involved.

REASONING FROM CONCOMITANT VARIATION

Concomitant variation may be thought of as sign reasoning plus an added element of quantification. Sign analysis asserts that things do or do not go together (are present or absent) and concomitant variation adds the *extent* to which they vary together, answering the question, "How much?" Is it true that the volume of department store sales in Minneapolis is a reliable index of the amount of city-wide employment? Is reducing tariff on a product by varying amounts followed by corresponding fluctuations in quantities of this product imported? Will doubling the amount of radio time devoted to campaigning by my candidate be followed by a proportionate increase in the votes cast for him on election day? These are problems that demand factual data for study to determine to what extent the quantities involved are related by *concomitant variation*.

The sciences, physical and social, produce tremendous amounts of concomitant-variation knowledge. Voltage and the length of a spark that can be produced, wattage and the amount of heat that can be dissipated with a certain type of heating element, the economic status of a community and the amount of juvenile delinquency that can be expected, fluoridation of the community water supply and the extent of reduction of tooth decay—understanding of these much studied covariations is essential to the solving of a variety of problems.

The quantitative aspect of concomitant variation dictates that the great majority of such reasoning must rely upon statistics. Numbers cannot be avoided if we would compare amounts. So let us turn our attention to the typical uses of statistical concomitant variation that we need to understand for the purposes of using them in discussion.

STATISTICAL ELEMENTS IN REASONING FROM CONCOMITANT VARIATION

Basic concepts

Correlation   The basic principle of concomitant variation is embodied in the single term: correlation. In everyday language any covariation is termed a correlation. If two variables, such as outdoor temperature and numbers of people patronizing a golf course, are closely related we say they are "highly correlated." When two elements tend to vary together as a general rule but with many exceptions, such as time spent on studying and grades achieved in college, we say that these phenomena are "loosely correlated," or that there is a "low correlation" between them. If two variables change with no apparent relationship, as might be the case with physical height and interest in classical music in the population of a community, we say that no correlation exists, or that there is "zero correlation." And in the situation wherein one element increases reliably as another decreases, such as amount of church attendance and incidence of crime, there is said to exist a "negative correlation," i.e., the two elements vary inversely.

Obviously, the above descriptive terms are inexact. Correlation is commonly made more precise by the calculation of the *extent* of the covariation in the form of a "coefficient of correlation." This is a widely accepted statistical concept that needs to be understood if errors in the interpretation of correlation information are to be avoided.

The coefficient of correlation, symbolized as r, may be any positive or negative number in the range from -1 to $+1$. The size of the number indicates the closeness of the covariation, and the sign indicates positive or negative (inverse) correlation. If our two quantities vary together without exception, the coefficient of correlation will be $+1$. If they vary inversely without exception, with one always getting smaller as the other becomes larger, r will be -1. With no relationship between the two, r will be zero, and a less than perfect positive covariation will vield a coefficient of correlation between 0 and $+1$.

Intelligent use of the coefficient of correlation in discussion or other problem solving does not require the ability to calculate it. However, the concept "closeness of covariation" is difficult to grasp without an example of a complete correlation computation. So we shall first explain the idea of covariation of two elements and then work out an r to illustrate it.

Covariation as expressed by the coefficient of correlation is a numerical index of the way items in one distribution cluster about its mean as compared to the way the same items group about the mean of a different distribution. If the grades of twenty high school pupils in mathematics and geography are to be correlated, then r will indicate the tendency for one pupil's grade to be above the mean in mathematics *if it were above the mean in geography*. Also, it would indicate the same tendency for any student who was below the mean in geography to be below the mean in his mathematics score. The coefficient of correlation, r, in itself is not a percentage of anything, but its size is simply a rough indicator of the relationship of items in two distributions with respect to their means.

To make this concrete, let us create a group of twenty hypothetical high school students, award each arbitrary achievements in mathematics and geography, then compute and interpret r. We will use the Pearson short formula to determine the coefficient of correlation. Sigma (σ) is the symbol for standard deviation, as explained in Chapter VI.

It is difficult to estimate whether the relationship between the columns of mathematics and geography scores is close or remote by

Computation of Coefficient of Correlation between Mathematics and Geography Grades

Pupil	Math Grade	Geog. Grade	x	y	x^2	y^2	xy
1	100	83	+18	+17	324	289	+206
2	98	90	+16	+24	256	576	+384
3	97	89	+15	+23	225	529	+345
4	95	80	+13	+14	169	196	+182
5	93	75	+11	+ 9	121	81	+ 99
6	90	76	+ 8	+10	64	100	+ 80
7	88	73	+ 6	+ 7	36	49	+ 42
8	87	69	+ 5	+ 3	25	9	+ 15
9	86	68	+ 4	+ 2	16	4	+ 8
10	83	71	+ 1	+ 5	1	25	+ 5
11	81	72	− 1	+ 6	1	36	− 6
12	80	70	− 2	+ 4	4	16	− 8
13	79	65	− 3	− 1	9	1	+ 4
14	77	55	− 5	−11	25	121	+ 55
15	75	63	− 7	− 3	49	9	+ 21
16	74	50	− 8	−16	64	256	+128
17	72	40	−10	−26	100	676	+260
18	70	44	−12	−22	144	484	+264
19	62	46	−20	−20	400	400	+400
20	53	41	−29	−25	841	625	+725

20)1,640   20)1,320   20)2,874   20)4,482 +3,223

82   66   143.7   224.1   −14

Mean   Mean   +3,209

$$\sigma x = \sqrt{143.7} \quad \sigma y = \sqrt{224.1}$$

$$\sigma x = 12 \qquad \sigma y = 15$$

$$r = \frac{\Sigma xy}{N \sigma x \sigma y} = \frac{+3,209}{20 \times 12 \times 15} = \frac{+3,209}{3,600}$$

$$r = .89$$

casual inspection. The r of .89, however, gives us confidence that these two measure are closely related. We can't say from this figure that it is certain that a person high in mathematics will be above average in geography; we can say only that very likely this will be so. For group prediction r's of .60 to .80 are considered significant, and a coefficient of .85 or higher normally becomes useful for individual prediction. The subjects and circumstances surrounding various correlation coefficients influence to a marked degree their particular interpretations.

The major fallacy in "interpreting" coefficients of correlation is to "read in" causal relationships. Pure coincidence or a common third element that is unaccounted for may underlie a high correlation figure. Fluctuations of coffee prices in Brazil might be shown to have varied as did attendance at prize fights in New York City over a limited period. Here no common cause can be assumed. Heavy smoking in a group might correlate highly with reckless driving, but that does not indicate that one is the cause or effect of the other. A neurological or physiological condition may be the hidden third element which predisposes people to both. Supplementary evidence is needed to develop a coefficient of correlation into an explanation of causes and effects.

Generally, the larger the group the more significant the coefficient of correlation. Strictly speaking, r is meaningful only when applied to members of the group from which it was computed. However, the better the sample the more legitimate is generalization of r beyond the original population. Our conclusion about close relations between grades in mathematics and geography might not hold for another group of twenty with more varied abilities. Twenty is a small group and we know nothing about its representative characteristics.

The coefficient of correlation becomes rapidly more significant as it approaches unity. Small differences between r's are ordinarily not significant. Correlations are useful supplements to other statistical measures, but do not usually present a complete picture in and of themselves.

Percentages The most deceptive and probably the most common statistical measure used to support alleged concomitant variation is the percentage. Its great source of misuse and misunderstanding comes from failure to specify "percentage of *what*." A retailer may make a profit of 50 per cent or 100 per cent, depending upon selection of wholesale or retail price as base for the percentage. To offset a pay cut of 50 per cent the worker must get a 100 per cent increase. Why? Because of the unspecified shifting of the percentage base. Small base numbers lead to amazing percentage statistics—"Fifty per cent of the students in Math 107 received a grade of A" seems to indicate the grading millennium until we learn that this class contained two students. Unrepresentative samples may produce misleading percentages: of twelve small groups of ten people each, one group had six people who selected a well known brand of cigarettes in a blindfold test. The resulting statistic—"in an impartial test, 60 per cent chose ———." A survey of cigarette smoking among students and faculty in a college was carried on through a spot check of discarded wrappers. Not mentioned was the fact that samples of brand X had been given away widespread on that campus for several days preceding the survey. A famous poll came to grief in predicting a Presidential election because it presented the people who had telephones in their homes as representative of *all* the American voting public.

We exhibit no undue skepticism when we advise the reader to mistrust any percentage when its base is not clearly specified. Percentages in isolation are attractive oversimplifications and tend to fix themselves in the mind. We must remember that alone they have no meaning. They can be helpful only when they are used *with reference to* something that is clearly understood. The concept of percentage is analogous to the concept of voltage in electricity. A point in a circuit cannot be said to have a potential of $+50$ volts. It can be said to have a potential of $+50$ volts with respect to another particular point. With respect to still another arbitrarily chosen point, this same connection might have a voltage of -250 volts. Similarly with percentages, an increase or decrease means nothing until we understand the arbitrarily chosen quantity that served in determining a particular figure. The obvious precaution is to insist always upon revealed and clarified bases for important percentage statistics.

Sampling   Correlations, percentages, and many other statistical manipulations are, as we have noted, frequently generalized beyond the information sources that originally yielded the data. Whenever conclusions are drawn that go beyond the group which figured in a computation, the adequacy of the sample should be questioned: Is this group a fair sample (a representative cross-section) of the entire population to which the conclusion is applied?

The ultimate test of a fair sample is found in this criterion: "Does every unit in the whole population have an equal chance to get into the sample?" This question is deceptively simple. Add to this requirement the factor of size, "Is the sample big enough to justify statistical treatment?" and you will have challenged most conclusions based on samples. Careful examination of the process of selecting a sample will usually reveal sources of substantial doubt that it represents faithfully the entire group.

Many statistics are based on sampling that escapes critical examination. An index of retail prices comes from a few selected "representative" items, not from all products in retail markets. What are those selected, and why are they alleged to be a cross-section of the retail market? These questions need to be answered if this price index is to be used intelligently in discussion. Cost of living figures, so prominent in discussion of our domestic economic problems, represent heavy reliance on a most difficult type of sampling.

The habit of always reviewing any sampling involved in statistics adds a new dimension to critical evaluation of evidence. When sales of General Motors cars are cited to show the vigor of the automotive industry, check to make sure that G-M is representative of the auto business. The safety record of one airline may seem to argue powerfully for the conclusion that air travel is the safest form of transportation, but we need to verify the sample by study of other airlines, scheduled and unscheduled, and by surveying the safety record of private aviation. Most statistical information is fragmentary, and we can usually ask with profit, Does it fairly sample what it purports to represent?

Sampling difficulties are great in opinion polls. Because these have become prominent in the discussion of social issues, we are devoting a few paragraphs to polling procedures in a following section which deals with applications of statistical methods to co-variation reasoning.

Application of statistical concepts to discussion in reasoning from concomitant variation

Graphs Graphical representation of data is a vivid visual oversimplification. It is a form of percentage manipulation, subject to all the pitfalls of distortion common to percentages plus a few visual gimmicks that often make what is not, seem to be. We suggest that in the use of charts, graphs, and pictorial representations of numerical quantities you remember to look for the following possible sources of error.

A coordinate graph is always drawn on an arbitrary horizontal and vertical scale. By expanding or compressing one or the other or both, a change in the quantity represented can be made to appear great or small, and the resultant trend serious or insignificant. For example, let us suppose that in 1950, the Little Giant Can Opener Company sold 100,000 can openers; in 1951, it sold 105,000; and in 1952, 110,000. If we place these data on a graph in which the sales units are set at units of 50,000, the increase in can opener sales doesn't seem very impressive. Thus:

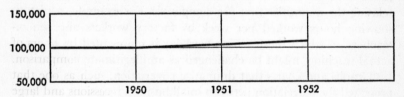

But a manager of the Little Giant Company, anxious to impress the stockholders, might wisely set the sales unit at 5,000 can openers, with the result that his graph would look as follows:

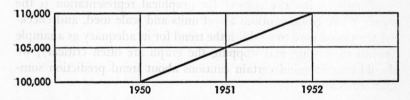

Pictorials conventionally represent double quantities by figures of double height. If drawings of soldiers are used to show a 100 per cent increase in the number drafted into the Army in two successive years, the second figure will be twice as tall, but drawn to proportion, hence will cover four times the area of the first. If the figures are drawn in perspective, they will appear three-dimensional and the second one will seem to have sixteen times the volume of the first. No wonder this visual translation of doubling the number drafted seems so striking! Now, if the draft were started in the middle of the first year, during which only a few men actually were taken into the Army, then the misleading percentage based upon only a few cases further contributes to the misleading quality of the pictorial.

Selection of the units to be graphed is a further arbitrary decision. Whether each tiny TV receiver represents 1,000 or 100,000 sets in the state of Minnesota makes a difference in the visual impression created. And sometimes different parts of the graph use different scales or units, which may contribute to false interpretations. Heavy and light bars and thin and fat lines may give definite visual loading to a chart. Where comparison and contrast are the function of the chart or pictorial, is there a logical justification for relating the quantities that are compared? For example, a picture showing hours worked per week by factory workers and schoolteachers, in which the teaching workday is represented by hours of actual teaching, might be challenged as an illegitimate comparison.

Graphs and charts that dramatize covariation, such as one that presented the correlation between small business recessions and large drops in imports, often imply a cause-and-effect connection. Remember that the only information presented is that of concomitant variation, and that cause-effect relations will have to be established separately through examination of further evidence.

Finally, a favorite subject for graphical representation is the *trend*. While being cautious about units and scale used, and checking the period used to establish the trend for its adequacy as a sample (points of starting and stopping the graph are often critical), we should bear in mind certain cautions about trend prediction summarized below.

Trends   Trends are future statistics. Nothing is more nebulous while giving the appearance of precision than USSR "facts" about its industrial progress. "At the end of the next Five-Year Plan we will have constructed 10,341 new power-producing dams, 1,472,000 new homes, 10,847,221 new tractors, and 976,499 large self-propelled combines." For a people, however, who are jeeringly critical of the Russian tendency to project trends into the future, we are amazingly gullible concerning our own "experts' " speculations about things to come.

In the 1920's and 1930's American sociologists were preoccupied with the future implications of birth control for national population. Trends were computed, plotted, and projected. A substantial agreement on the part of many scholars evolved—the national birth rate was certain to decrease steadily until about 1950 or so, at which time our national population would have reached its peak, and from that point onward the number of people in the United States would slowly but steadily decrease.

Birth control information and equipment continued to be disseminated and used as predicted. But now, in the mid-1950's, an outstanding social phenomenon is the great and increasing popularity of large families! Something, in all probability many things, happened to change the motivations that lead to determining family size. The trend which seemed so well established in 1930 was reversed.

The great fallacy in trend prediction is the assumption that all determining factors will continue unchanged. Most of the time such uniformity is unlikely. To treat a trend prediction as a *fact* in discussion is practically always unwise. Treat it as a *possibility,* and study its context in search of determiners that might well be altered by time and circumstances.

Ranking   In a competitive society rank order is considered important. Not only do we want the largest, the best, the most expensive, and the most powerful, but we like to know the places occupied by competing products in a list of decreasing merit. It is a source of satisfaction in present-day America to be able to rank products, schools, stores, ideas, and people on scales of particular qualifications. Feminine beauty, for example, is ranked and reranked, until we not only locate the first, second, third, and fourth most beautiful girls in America, but in a final glorious comparison select the highest ranking beauty of them all, Miss Universe.

In discussion of relative merit, rank orders should be scrutinized to determine whether (1) the qualities serving as a basis for the ranking are pertinent to the issue under discussion, (2) these characteristics are objectively and reliably measured, and (3) the intervals between ranks are big enough to be significant.

To illustrate, a consumer research organization ranks automobiles according to the requirements of an urban family of restricted income that makes few, if any, long trips. Their rank order is not helpful to the salesman covering North and South Dakota, Iowa, and Montana, who travels alone. Criteria important to him would yield a totally different rank order.

Objective and reliable measurement of the qualities that yield a rank order is in some instances easy and in some practically impossible. Frequency response in a record player can be measured precisely under specified and control conditions, but judgment of the quality of its reproduction of symphony music is inevitably subjective and will vary to a substantial extent with different listeners.

Some years ago a federal government testing agency measured amounts of irritants in smoke from popular brands of cigarettes. The differences were so slight as to be insignificant. The cigarette company whose product had been found to have least irritants immediately launched an advertising campaign based upon the information that by United States Government tests brand X had been found to be least irritating. Not mentioned was the important knowledge that as far as any smoker was concerned, this measured but slight advantage could not possibly be of any significance.

Sound rank orders are designed to guarantee significant steps or intervals. The consumer research agency mentioned above used to follow the practice of assigning a 1, 2, 3, . . . order to all products rated. Now it groups products that are not significantly different into the same quality ranking, a practice which is somewhat frustrating to the reader until he realizes that no purpose is served by a rank order unless there is a real and reliable interval separating the ranks.

Polls Discussions of current social issues cannot ignore what the people are thinking concerning these problems. Public opinion is assessed usually by some form or other of poll. Consequently, we use as material for discussion the results of various opinion polls.

Regrettably, the term "poll" is applied to all sorts of projects, from fragmentary straw votes or small-scale questionnaire surveys to scientifically designed and controlled efforts that cover a large, carefully selected sample of people. The first step in evaluating poll results is to inquire as to the nature of a particular poll. The following description of one rather good polling structure will serve to set standards you can apply to other polling procedures.

Here's how our Minnesota Poll studies are made:

The information is collected by trained, paid interviewers—approximately 65 of them—living in all parts of the state. They call at homes, personally question the respondents, and record their answers on printed questionnaire forms.

All studies are confined to the state of Minnesota. What the Minnesota Poll findings reveal can't be expected to be equally applicable to other states in the Upper Midwest.

Rigid controls are exercised over the types of persons interviewed. To be eligible for questioning, they must be voting-age adults residing in Minnesota. The types of persons interviewed are properly apportioned as to sex, age, place of residence, social and economic status, and other factors. Collectively, they represent an accurate cross-section of Minnesota's adult population.

The sampling plan followed is one worked out and maintained in consultation with the research division of the University of Minnesota's School of Journalism.

Six hundred to 1,000 persons are interviewed by the Minnesota Poll in each of its surveys. (When the annual surveys of consumer finances are conducted for the board of governors of the Federal Reserve System, the national samples involve only about 3,000 persons.) In 99 out of 100 cases, the difference in results obtained from sampling 600 to 1,000 persons—as compared with what the results would be if a complete census were made—will not, statisticians say, exceed 5 to 6 percentage points, if that much.

To be sure that Minnesota Poll questions are impartial and easily understood, they are first examined by the Poll's advisory board of 20 leading Minnesota citizens; then they are "pre-tested" by trial interviews with a small group of adults; then they are re-examined and, if necessary, rewritten to improve them, before questionnaires are printed and sent to the interviewers.

Information obtained through interviews throughout the state is transferred by the Minnesota Poll to punch cards, and machine tabulations are made as a basis for Poll reports.

Scores and hundreds of research organizations in the United States, governmental and private, employ just such methods in their survey work. . . .[1]

We should remember that all public opinion polling rests upon the questionable assumption that all identical responses have the same *intensity* (strength or permanence). A whimsical or uninformed answer is as significant in a poll as one which is the result of years of scholarly study. One which may change tomorrow counts the same as one which will withstand criticism for a lifetime. Another questionable assumption is that everyone *has* an opinion on every poll question. It is probably true that many subjects of poll interviews have not previously formulated pro or con judgments on at least some matters at issue. Does a "yes" or "no" answer, made up on the spur of a moment, provide any valid indication of present belief or potential action? Polls must assume that it does. Interpretation of poll findings should include consideration of the knowledge and probable involvement of the subjects in the topics polled. If a topic is important to their welfare they probably have previously formed opinions to express. If a topic is one remote from the people polled, and if they have had no general access to recent information on it, we may well suspect that a substantial number of the recorded opinions lack intensity and permanence.

As we suggested in the section on "Sampling," polls furnish classical illustrations of perplexing sampling difficulties. Here is a vivid description of some "sample" problems confronting the pollster.

. . . how do you get a random sample within the stratification? The obvious thing is to start with a list of everybody and go after names chosen from it at random; but that is too expensive. So you go into the streets—and bias your sample against stay-at-homes. You go from door-to-door by day—and miss most of the employed people. You switch to evening interviews—and neglect the movie-goers and night-clubbers.

The operation of a poll comes down in the end to a running battle against sources of bias, and this battle is conducted all the time by the reputable polling organizations. What the reader of the reports must remember is that the battle is never won. No conclusion that sixty-seven per cent of the American people are against something or other should

---

[1] "How the Minnesota Poll Is Conducted," reprinted from an editorial in the Minneapolis *Sunday Tribune*, July 25, 1954, p. 2.

be read without the lingering question, Sixty-seven per cent of which American people? [2]

The extent of a particular poll and its methodology should be considered a part of its results in discussion. Look up two or three reports of public opinion polls in newspapers and magazines. What information is included with each about the conduct of the poll? Select one of the polls for investigation and try to rate it on a scale from inadequate to excellent.

While it is important in reasoning from concomitant variation to avoid any unwarranted assumptions of causal relation, it is equally important not to overlook cause-effect connections. If a causal relationship can be definitely established, it is the strongest and most reliable sort of circumstantial detail. Requirements of cause-effect reasoning are exacting, and for many reasons it is deceptive as practiced; hence we devote the final section of this chapter to techniques of using causal relations in discussion.

REASONING FROM CAUSAL RELATION

The cause-effect relationship may be thought of as a "push" or a "pull." In other words, a cause is something that contributes energy to another event. In this direct way a cause is a determiner of an effect; presumably, if the cause were different the effect would not be the same.

Establishing this sort of intimate connection between two events in a complex social system is difficult. In recent years we have come increasingly to appreciate the fact of *multiple causation,* that an effect is contributed to, or collects energy from, a multiplicity of events. Vilfredo Pareto illustrates a perplexing picture of multiple causation by the story of a man who had drunk too much the night before, shaving shakily the morning after with a razor he had neglected to clean when he had previously used it. Our unfortunate drops the razor and cuts his toe. Medical attention comes too late and he dies of blood poisoning. "What," asks Pareto, "is the *cause* of his death?"

We might be tempted to select one of the mentioned events as *the* cause, but more reflection reveals a probability that several items

[2] Darrell Huff, *How to Lie with Statistics,* New York, W. W. Norton & Co., Inc., copyright 1954 by Darrell Huff and Irving Geis, p. 22.

contributed to the drinker's untimely demise. Unknown factors probably contributed, too—ill health, a nagging wife, bad liquor, a truck backfiring outside the bathroom window. The moral of this little story is that most of the time in discussing human events we are wise to speak of *a* cause rather than *the* cause. And we should recognize any apparently simple causation as potentially deceptive.

An interesting case study of an effort to establish a "single cause" for an event involving multiple causation started in 1954 when a group of Japanese fishermen were caught by the fall-out of radioactive ash from an American experiment with atomic weapons. The fishermen were some eighty miles from the center of the explosion, on a boat without radio communication, and were without information as to the potential dangers of fall-out. By the time they had returned to Japan, they were sick men. The event was something of an international incident, and when one of the fishermen eventually died, his death was reported in the Japanese press as "caused by" the American bomb test. By 1955 it was established that this fisherman, the only one of the affected fishermen who failed to recover from his radioactive sickness, had been also stricken with infectious hepatitis (jaundice) which he had caught from infected blood used in the blood transfusions given during the treatment of his atomic sickness. One American newspaper hailed these new facts with the headline "Bomb Fall-Out Absolved in Death of Fisherman." In this case some elements of the Japanese press seemed anxious to have the fisherman "killed by atom test," while some elements of the American press seemed anxious that he "die from jaundice."

The language we use in talking about causes and effects contributes to our unrealistic simplifications of complex matters. We say, "What is the cause of World War II?" "What will be the effect of reducing income taxes?" "What is the reason that Prohibition failed?" This language implies in each case that a single cause or a single effect is an adequate explanation. In good discussion the use of such misleading language is carefully avoided, and the facts of multiple causation and multiple effects are recognized.

The classic mistake of causal reasoning—the *post hoc* fallacy—derives its label from *post hoc, ergo propter hoc* ("after this, therefore, because of this.") It amounts to the assumption of a causal connection because of a time sequence relationship. When some event follows another, the first is said to be the cause of the second. A crusading Senator issues a blast at a government worker and the next week the worker is suspended. Many people who should be more perceptive will believe that the charge caused the suspension. Any alleged time-sequence causal reasoning should be supported by further information. In this instance discovery that suspension proceedings had been started before the Senator held his much-publicized press conference would convincingly deny any cause-effect relationship.

Three types of causal reasoning should be understood: cause to effect, which moves forward in time, effect to cause, which moves backward in time, and effect to effect, which shows the connection of two events through a common causation. *Post hoc* thinking is a threat to all of these, and multiple causation and effects should be remembered and emphasized in using any of the three.

Analysis of causal relations is usually unproductive in discussion. Once in a great while a cause and an effect can be linked together meaningfully and unmistakably. But most of the time a group of people conversing about causation as related to a social problem use the language of causal relation when the circumstances are those of sign or concomitant variation. For this reason we suggest that the terminology associated with causal reasoning be used sparingly and precisely.

Our treatment of causal reasoning has been brief because its application to discussion is relatively unimportant. The facts of multiple causes and multiple effects in matters of human relations prevent effectively our isolating causes or results. Under these circumstances we should turn to other more suitable techniques of analysis, and frequently the productive alternatives are the methods of reasoning from sign and from concomitant variation.

CHAPTER VIII

Generalization

A great deal of pertinent information essential to productive discussion does not in and of itself produce understanding of or a solution to the problem. Somehow, facts must be made to impinge upon the felt difficulty. Deductive forms of reasoning accomplish this interaction. But deductive reasoning is the manipulation of propositions. These come from information, but not spontaneously. The intermediate process that yields propositions for deductive application, that bridges the gap between the inductive analysis of particular evidence and the process of developing conclusions about the central issue of the discussion, is *generalization*.

Simply, generalizing may be thought of as making statements about the interrelations of items of evidence. It is a type of integration, more comprehensive than the single operation of an inductive analysis. In light of the problem being discussed, it pulls together related analyses and summarizes their significance in one or more positive, direct statements. These are the propositions we reason with. The data and preliminary thinking about them are cumbersome. The generalization is a compact consolidation that presents the essence of previous complexity.

An example of generalization (Stage 2 in problem solving) was supplied in Chapter IV in the story of a student discussion. This might well be reread before continuing, since it clarifies the process of generalizing and illustrates the impossibility of leaping from fragmentary data to deductive application.

120

THE PROCESS OF GENERALIZING

We want to emphasize the generalization stage because it is commonly slighted. Discussions are often filled with facts that remain undigested. Attention to generalization can counter a tendency to pile up unselected information. In effect the cautious generalizer is injecting a thoughtful "So what?" into the discussion from time to time, and is highlighting irrelevancies and omissions in facts available. He keeps group activity oriented to the central problem. He inspires caution in interpreting facts, for he is alert to any statement that outstrips its visible means of support. Yet he contributes daring and imagination, too, for he is a leader in projecting probabilities into the unknown as long as the hypothetical nature of such speculation is understood and explicit.

Careful generalizing exploits evidence, wringing from it maximum significance, and highlighting inadequacies in factual information. It alone can guarantee that a group will not either ignore significant facts before it or proceed blithely to conclusions that would be obviously impossible if unmentioned facts were known.

Here are some fairly typical examples of hasty generalizations taken from a college classroom practice discussion.

In a discussion of highway safety one participant noted that in the state of Minnesota so far this year, 242 people had died in traffic accidents as compared to 146 at this date last year. She generalized, "So we can see that the number of fatalities on our highways is increasing constantly." This generalization is premature as well as inadequately supported. Any statement as to the over-all trend in fatal accidents should be made only after all the evidence relating to the trend is entered into the record. Then it would be appropriate for the group to attempt a consensus on a statement that expresses the probable rate of increase of highway fatalities in the United States (or in one state or in a group of states, depending upon the evidence submitted). Should such early generalization occur in discussion, the chairman or any participant should ask that other facts be studied before we suggest such a sweeping conclusion.

Later in the same discussion a substantial amount of inductive analysis was thrown together in an effort to locate some major causes of traffic accidents. Some items considered were (1) a study of 175 fatal accidents in which 88 involved excessive speed, 33 improper passing, 25 disregard of signs or signals, and 13 failure to grant the right of way; (2) an extensive survey which concluded that 96 per cent of vehicles in fatal accidents were in good condition; (3) the experiences of the state of Washington in reducing traffic deaths 45 per cent over three months by intensive law enforcement; (4) the experience of Detroit in reducing accidents by a traffic clinic to analyze and educate offenders; and (5) the statement of an expert that most accidents occur on straight highways in clear weather. The group concluded from this and similar information that the greatest cause of automobile accidents is "driver error."

This generalization is attractive but unclear. What, exactly, is "driver error"? Is there a realistic threshold of driving skill and/or judgment which if attained would have prevented this "majority" of accidents? Or would accident avoidance have demanded unusual abilities? Either situation could be labeled "driver error." And is driver error considered as a primary cause or one heavily influenced by other causes? Road hazards certainly make it more difficult to drive without making mistakes; do they contribute to driver error? Driver error might well mean inability to surmount great difficulties caused by roads, weather, and other drivers. Similarly, airplane accidents are often credited to "pilot error" in cases as extreme as the instance of hitting a tree while flying blind in a storm after engine failure. How? The pilot should have avoided flying into the bad weather. Obviously, "driver error" as a possible cause embraces more than it would seem to at first glance, and illustrates a type of catch-all term that is too imprecise to be part of a useful generalization.

A subordinate generalization came from several bits of information that dealt with accident occurrence and age of the driver. One item was a statistic from a survey to the effect that in a large number of fatal accidents (unspecified), 25 per cent of the drivers were under twenty-five years of age, while in the general driving population 15 per cent of licensed drivers are under twenty-five. The quick generalization was worded: "Youthful drivers are a greater hazard than more mature drivers."

If by "greater hazard" is meant that on the average a youthful driver will cause more than his share of accidents, then this generalization can be challenged by a request for the missing essential fact: What are the relative amounts of driving done by the "under twenty-five" and "over twenty-five" age groups? Until we have this knowledge we can only assume that any difference in accident involvement might be due to the fact that the younger people drive more, hence have more accident opportunity.

The most frequent shortcoming of a generalization is its over-extension, often because a term in it is imprecise, as was "driver error," or because of failure to include needed limitations, as in the statement of generally increasing highway fatalities that might be somewhere, anywhere, sometime, anytime. Vagueness and ambiguity always overextend a generalization. A second unrewarding type of generalization is one which simply restates data. The productive generalization interprets certain evidence in light of other knowledge of the topic and in the context of all the experiences and resultant common sense accumulated by group members. Generalizations are refined by questioning them, to improve accuracy and remove misleading elements. A final check is to estimate a generalization's intrinsic reasonableness. If it is sound, the critic will review the evidence and its inductive analysis, will reread the generalization, and find himself saying the equivalent of, "Well, I guess that this statement is the most accurate summation that it is possible to write at this time."

Three kinds of generalization

Depending upon the nature of the evidence and the relative certainty of the statement that can be made about its meaning, generalizations take three forms: implication, alternation, and relationship between categories. We will illustrate these by reasoning about information concerning the Radio Moscow broadcasts in the English language directed to the North American continent. Moscow Radio terms this part of its broadcast activities the "North American Service of Radio Moscow."

The "North American Service" is an extensive effort involving a varying number of powerful short-wave stations, usually from seven to fourteen. These broadcast concurrently from late afternoon to after midnight and seem to be "beamed" in such a way as to cover the United States quite uniformly. A person monitoring these broadcasts is impressed by the great amount of apparently up-to-date information about what is going on in the United States. Evening programs will include extended quotations from half-a-dozen morning newspapers of the same day from as many widely spread United States cities. Many local items from various United States communities are mentioned, and these, too, seem to be surprisingly fresh. How does all this information reach Radio Moscow? The cautious listener is not sure of the accuracy of the quoted material, so he must generalize *conditionally*: "If the quoted and reported items about the United States are accurate, then there must be some fairly large communication network piping information from the United States to the USSR." Notice that a key assumption is part of the generalization; if something is true, something else follows. This form is called "implication" for obvious reasons.

What is Radio Moscow "up to" with its expensive North American Service? Speculating about intent of those who originate the broadcasts yields a different sort of generalization. All these broadcasts are on short wave, and successful short-wave listening demands not only special and fairly expensive radio equipment, but skill and persistence. Owing to distance, atmospheric conditions, and sharply noncooperative activities of the United States Government, Radio Moscow is easy listening on the best equipment only about one night out of three. Program content seems dull to most casual listeners, though it is crammed with "information" about the United States and the USSR, and interpretations of that information. The general public does not have access to good short-wave receivers. The adequately equipped, ready-made audience are America's radio hams, and they have at least a reputation for being uninterested in politics and international affairs. Some confirmation of this last opinion can be had by eavesdropping for a while on amateur voice transmissions and noting the popular topics of conversation. Yet there is no survey of Radio Moscow listening in America and probably none is possible. So, to summarize what may well be the intent or purpose of those who plan Radio Moscow's North American Service, we must recognize two possible alternatives: Either Radio Moscow is primarily interested in influencing those who listen to it directly, or it aims mainly to supply "information" and ideas to friendly crusaders who will spread the word to others. This is a fairly typical "alternation" form of generalization.

Further reasoning may compare these alternative possibilities. If substantial attitude changes are to come about from exposure to

Radio Moscow programs, then there must be repeated listening over some considerable period of time. We are probably safe in assuming that the Radio Moscow personnel are familiar with the facts about influencing opinion and changing attitudes. What can we assume about the regular listeners to the North American Service? Because of the above mentioned reception problems we know that any regular listener spends time and effort on the project. He really must work at it. So we can formulate a generalization relating two categories or classes of individuals: those who listen regularly to Radio Moscow and those who have strong motivations to hear the USSR point of view on affairs of the day. The generalization follows that the great majority of people who listen regularly to the North American Service of Radio Moscow are people who are strongly motivated to hear what the USSR has to say on current issues.

Note that this generalized statement of a *relationship between categories* specifies a central tendency ("the great majority—") rather than a universality ("each and every one"). This admits of rare exceptions that are not significant to the main line of reasoning, such as the DX fan who is tabulating the number of days in the year when he can "pull in" a readable signal from Moscow.

The next two chapters will present techniques of applying generalizations of these three types in deductive reasoning, the final stage of interpreting and evaluating information in progress toward solving a problem. Implications will be used in hypothetical syllogisms, while alternations and statements about class relationships will be applied in disjunctive and categorical syllogisms, respectively.

CHAPTER IX

Deductive Application of
Generalizations — Part 1

Much in Chapters IX and X will be familiar to readers who have studied logic, as deductive forms of reasoning usually constitute the main content of logic courses and textbooks. Here we select from formal logic what seems to be most useful to problem-solving discussion. We omit and adapt freely to encourage the use of deductive methods in discussion of contemporary social issues.

While guides to inductive analysis and generalization are in the form of somewhat flexible principles, deductive logic is more severely patterned and its procedures are comparatively fixed. There are definite forms or "shapes" to sound arguments from implication, from alternation, and by category. This requirement, if met, produces a *valid* unit of reasoning, meaning that the form is appropriate and that no error in arrangement of its parts has occurred. To say the same thing another way, a deductive argument is valid when the truth of the premises (component generalizations) means that the conclusion must necessarily be true also. Hence, *validity,* a relationship between premises and conclusion of a deductive pattern, must be distinguished from *truth,* which is a characteristic of each of the premises and of the conclusion independently. Truth may be defined as verifiability, or correspondence to objective reality. Of course, a good argument is both valid and true, i.e., a sound deduction has the proper form and is based upon premises the truth of which cannot be successfully challenged.

We suggest that you remember these concepts as tests of deductive reason. First, study *form* to be sure the argument is valid;

then, if validity is established, estimate the *probable truth* of the premises. If a valid argument includes a possibly false generalization, then the conclusion has at least a possibility of being false, too. But if the premises, to the best of your knowledge, are true and the form is valid, you as a logical reasoner are bound to accept the conclusion as a statement of truth. Inductive analysis and generalization deal primarily with the problems of establishing the truth of premises. Deductive development is concerned primarily with validity, the problems of arranging different elements of knowledge into valid patterns that make possible definite conclusions.

Deductive logic is a kind of mathematics and to become proficient in it we should take advantage of a shorthand of symbols. Fortunately, symbolic representation of deductive operations is simple and easy. We will use symbols in explaining deductive processes and encourage the reader to use them in his practice activities. Many premises are long and complicated. Accurate symbolic representation makes possible the writing of a complex bit of reasoning in a small space and the rapid checking of form or validity.

PROBABILITY AND DEDUCTIVE FORMS

Traditionally, deductive logic deals only in statements that are certain. Such arguments are said to be *conclusive* or without exception. In reasoning about people and their affairs there are few generalizations that can be proved to be absolutely and completely true without exception. The useful generalizations about human behavior have been statements of central tendencies. Frequently our thinking on social issues is best served when we know the main currents of action or opinion and ignore the occasional rare exception. Yet the formal logician has preferred to deal in absolutes, and a highly probable but not absolutely certain premise in a deductive pattern would be discarded by him as worthless.

If we are to take advantage of deductive methodology in social problem solving we must somehow adapt it to statements of strong central tendencies and high probabilities. For if only absolutes are usable in deductions, and if social issues have few if any absolutes to manipulate, then deduction is of small use in consideration of contemporary problems of living.

But we can use the deductive forms if we treat statements of predominant central tendency as though they were absolutes, and remember that a resulting conclusion is not a certainty, but a further and possibly revealing statement of central tendency. This admission of probable truths puts deductive thinking to work. Probably the ivory tower reputation achieved by logic books and courses comes from their insistence that the only statements about people with which one can reason have to be verifiable without exception. Hence the "All men are mortal" and "Socrates was a man" type of premises serves as illustrations. Real and controversial issues have to be let alone—there remain some doubts.

We consider the deductive forms to be suited to the manipulation of generalizations of probability as well as those which are certain. Conclusions are probable to the extent of the probable truth of the premises on which they rest. Hence, after determining the validity and estimating the truth of the premises, we can judge the degree of probable truth of the conclusion. In this way deductive forms of reasoning can be used with generalizations which are statements of probability.

Reasoning by implication

The most used deductive pattern of reasoning is that of implication. Its purpose is the exploration of possibilities, leading to increased understanding of their consequences. The language framework for this is "If *A*, then *B*" in which "*A*" and "*B*" represent propositions. Thus, a simple implication is a statement that if something is true (proposition *A*) then something else (proposition *B*) has to be true also. The "if" proposition is examined to see what follows from it, an exploration of possibilities or consequences. The first part of an implication, the "if" part, is called the *antecedent,* and the possibility examined, the "then" part, is termed the *consequent,* quite reasonably, we think you will agree.

Before we look at examples of statements of implication and attempt to reason from them, let us think together about the basic unit of all deductive forms, the *proposition.* What is a proposition? It is a statement of a relationship or a circumstance which is capable of being true or false. Frequently, it is a complete, declarative sentence with a period at the end. The most useful propositions are single-barreled (i.e., they contain but one idea), they avoid emotive language, and they are free of excess verbiage. Simplicity, clarity, singleness, and brevity are qualities to work toward in the phrasing of propositions.

In the preceding chapter we used propositions to build an implication. One statement about Radio Moscow was "Radio Moscow American news is accurate," a proposition relating truth and content of particular broadcasts. Another statement related to the first presented an hypothesis: "Radio Moscow must have a fairly large communication system transmitting information from the United States to it." This proposition describes a circumstance which does or does not exist, hence is true or false. Both examples are declarative sentences and each contains a single idea. The language in both is quite objective (or unloaded, or free from emotive aspects) and the meaning of each is clear. Let us represent the first proposition by "A" and the second by the symbol "B."

A simple implication, "If A . . . then B," represents these words: "*If* Radio Moscow's quoted and reported items about the United States are accurate, *then* there must be some fairly large communication network piping information from the United States into the USSR." Here our implicative relationship between two propositions yields a *generalization* we developed from inductive analysis in Chapter VIII. We see that a generalization in the form of an implication contains two separate propositions and hypothesizes a particular relationship between them.

The implicative relationship has been symbolized as "If A, then B," but by using an arbitrary connective symbol we can eliminate the words "if" and "then." And by selecting letters other than A and B we can suggest the central idea of each proposition symbolized. Hence, we might write the above implication in logic shorthand like this: "$Q \supset N$." The connecting symbol "$\supset$," a horseshoe on its side, symbolizes the "if-then" relationship, so we can read "$Q \supset N$" in these words, "If proposition Q is true, then proposition N must be true also." Or we can supply the two propositions and read the original implication direct from the symbols. It will be found convenient, once the component propositions are understood, to represent reasoning about them in symbols such as these. Writing "$Q \supset N$" is *so* much easier than putting on paper the thirty words of the complete implication!

Now, granting that we have a meaningful "if-then" relationship, what can we do with it? We can interchange antecedent and consequent, for one thing. $Q \supset N$ might become $N \supset Q$. Read in the words of the revised implication. Does it seem to follow from the original, or does it seem to be untenable?

We can deny or contradict either antecedent or consequent; in other words, if either is stated as true, we can assert it to be false, or if it is stated as false, we can assert it to be true. This gives us an exploration of a total of four possibilities:

$$Q \supset N$$
$$Q' \supset N$$
$$Q' \supset N'$$
$$Q \supset N'$$

Obviously, the prime signifies the process of contradiction:

Q = "Radio Moscow's quoted and reported items about the United States are accurate"

Q' = "Radio Moscow's quoted and reported items about the United States are not accurate"

Finally, we can combine the process of contradiction with an interchange of antecedent and consequent:

$$N' \supset Q$$
$$N \supset Q'$$
$$N' \supset Q'$$

When we interchange antecedent and consequent without contradicting either, the new form is said to be the *converse* of the first. $N \supset Q$ is the *converse* of $Q \supset N$. When we interchange antecedent and consequent and deny (contradict) both, the new form is called the *contrapositive* of the original. $N' \supset Q'$ is the contrapositive of $Q \supset N$.

The above juggling represents all the possibilities of altering an implication by interchange and contradiction. Now we must learn which of these are legitimate in that they do not distort the meaning of the original implication and which are fallacious in that they depend upon something other than the original implication for their truth. Ability to use legitimate substitute forms will increase the flexibility and versatility of our reasoning, and the ability to identify improper forms is essential to analysis of invalid "if-then" patterns.

Common-sense examination of our sample implication will enable us to label each possible alteration valid or invalid. We will simplify the propositions to their basic skeletons:

$Q =$ "Quotations are accurate"
$N =$ "Moscow has a network"

Assuming $Q \supset N$ to be a true relationship—"*If* quotations are accurate, *then* Moscow has a network,"—what is the necessary truth of (1) $Q' \supset N$, (2) $Q' \supset N'$, and (3) $Q \supset N'$? We know that "if quotations are accurate," something else is true also, but "if quotations are not accurate" (Q'), *the condition is not met and we know nothing about any consequents.* Hence (1) and (2) cannot be accepted, since *we know something about* N *only when* Q *is true.* If Q is false (Q'), then we have ventured into the unknown beyond our "given" knowledge and as far as we can tell N may be true or false. (3) $Q \supset N'$ is seen to be impossible, for our original "given" material tells us one thing as a certainty, "If quotations are accurate, then Moscow has a network." Hence it is inconceivable that "quotations are accurate" and that "Moscow does not have a network."

So the original, assumed to be true, relationship $Q \supset N$ *does not imply* $Q' \supset N$, $Q' \supset N'$, or $Q \supset N'$, and of these three, $Q \supset N'$ is known to be impossible, while the other two are possibly true or false.

Now let us apply the common-sense check method to interchanging antecedent and consequent. Does $Q \supset N$ imply $N \supset Q$? We asked the reader his opinion on this a few paragraphs ago. As you probably decided then, it does not. When we accept "If quotations are accurate, then Moscow has a network," we do not necessarily believe that "if Moscow has a network, then quotations are accurate." Obviously, having a network does not guarantee accuracy of transmitted material. In other words, even if we accept an implication we have no knowledge about the truth of its *converse*.

As another possible interchange of antecedent and consequent let us test the *contrapositive*. Here, you will remember, both elements are denied. Does $Q \supset N$ imply $N' \supset Q'$? Since the accuracy of quotations guarantees the existence of a network, then the absence of a network makes it impossible for quotations to be accurate! $Q \supset N$ does, therefore, imply $N' \supset Q'$. Actually these are the same relationships, stated differently.

The reader should construct and examine a few examples of implications to be sure that he thoroughly understands why $Q \supset N$ and $N' \supset Q'$ are the same, hence why one may be substituted for the other. Here are three samples: (1) "If I have a ticket, then I will be admitted." If I am not admitted, then, certainly, I did not have a ticket! (2) If my house burns down, then I will be without a home. But I am not without a home, therefore my house has not burned down. (3) If I get a driver's license, then I must pass a driver's examination. But I cannot pass the driver's examination, hence will not get a driver's license.

Symbolize (1), (2), and (3) above. Be sure that, in terms of common-sense examples, you understand why an implication and its contrapositive are the same. If one is true the other is necessarily true also.

Suppose we interchange antecedent and consequent in our original examples and contradict one or the other. Does the truth of the original implication "carry over" to these variations? The original $Q \supset N$ becomes (1) $N' \supset Q$ and (2) $N \supset Q'$. From the contrapositive form $(N' \supset Q')$ we see that (1) represents an excluded possibility, for if $N' \supset Q'$ is true, then the coincidence of N' and Q cannot be. Supply the propositions that N' and Q represent to see at a common-sense level why (1) is impossible. As for (2), "If Moscow has a network, then quotations are not accurate," it certainly seems unreasonable to assume that the presence of a network would *guarantee* inaccuracy of quotations. Knowing N to be true tells us nothing about Q.

The essential ingredient of an implicative relationship is the "excluded possibility." We noted that $(Q \supset N)$ and $(N' \supset Q')$ are different ways of symbolizing the same state of affairs. Either implication indicates that it is not the case that Q can be true and N false at the same time. In other words, $Q \& N'$ (or the relationship could be written $N' \& Q$) is the excluded possibility. The impossibility of this coincidence is the fragment of knowledge that enables us to advance our thinking through manipulation of implications.

To summarize our experimentation with the various forms of implications, we have discovered two operations that yield useful knowledge:

> If $A \supset B$ is true, $B' \supset A'$ is true also
> If $A \supset B$ is true, $(A \& B')$ is impossible

Simple implication reasoning   We have learned about the operations we can perform upon an implication. Now, how can we use the implication in moving toward a conclusion?

The simplest and most frequent implicative procedure is the *affirmation of the antecedent*. Let us say that we have done further research on the content of Radio Moscow and we find that the quoted materials containing information about the United States are surprisingly accurate. So, "If quoted materials are accurate, then Moscow has a network," and if we decide that these materials are accurate, then we can draw the conclusion that "Moscow has a network." This is called affirming the antecedent, permitting us to state the consequent as a conclusion. It is symbolized:

$$Q \supset N \quad \text{(original implication)}$$
$$\underline{Q} \quad \text{(affirming antecedent)}$$
$$\therefore N$$

The three dots in a triangle ($\therefore$) form a conventional symbol translated as "therefore" and one which often precedes the conclusion of a logical pattern.

Another way to view the process of affirming the antecedent is to see the implication as stating that something is true if a particular condition is met or fulfilled. Affirming the antecedent is meeting the specified condition. Naturally enough, we can then state the consequent as a fact (conclusion).

Suppose that instead of studying the content of Radio Moscow to determine the accuracy of its quotations, we concentrate upon collecting evidence as to the physical existence of a special communication network. Suppose further that we assemble convincing proof that Moscow could not possibly have any special network. Could we conclude anything about the accuracy of quoted materials in the broadcasts?

$$Q \supset N \quad \text{(original implication)}$$
$$\underline{N'} \quad \text{(discovered negation of consequent)}$$
$$\therefore ?$$

Obviously, we have done something to the consequent, and have not affirmed the antecedent. Or—have we? Recall that the contrapositive is the same as the original implication:

$$Q \supset N = N' \supset Q'$$
$$\frac{N'}{\therefore Q'}$$

and we can see that by using the contrapositive form of our implication we can again affirm the antecedent and draw the conclusion that these quoted materials cannot be accurate. Note that when you affirm a denied proposition (N'), you leave it unchanged.

To summarize simple reasoning by implication, the two legitimate operations are:

(1) Affirming the antecedent and stating the consequent, unchanged, as the conclusion.

(2) Denying the consequent and stating the contradictory of the antecedent as the conclusion.

A quick review of the other possible alterations of implications will reveal that we can proceed constructively in affirming or denying antecedent or consequent only when we use an implication or its contrapositive. Can we get anywhere by denying the antecedent or affirming the consequent? The answer is "no." Such operations create two of the forms which we found to yield "no information." A good practice exercise is to work out a demonstration proving that denying an antecedent or affirming a consequent cannot yield a conclusion in a simple unit of reasoning by implication.

Chain arguments   If-then statements are often linked together to make a unit of reasoning of several steps. These arrays of implications are termed "chain" arguments. If the linking is valid, then the consequent of one implication must, unchanged, serve as the antecedent of the one that follows. Let us construct and symbolize a three-link "chain."

If Radio Moscow's quotations are accurate, then Moscow has a special communication network. If Moscow has a special communication network, then the United States ought to expose it, and if the United States ought to expose it, Congress should appropriate funds for the FBI to investigate the Moscow network.

$$Q \supset N$$
$$N \supset E$$
$$\frac{E \supset C}{?}$$

What conclusion can be drawn? Since each consequent is used unchanged as the following antecedent in the chain, the form is appropriate, and the conclusion is an implication correcting the first antecedent and the last consequent: "If Radio Moscow's quotations are accurate, then Congress should appropriate funds for the FBI to investigate the Moscow network."

$$\therefore Q \supset C$$

Note that the conclusion of a chain argument is a new implication. The antecedent of the conclusion may be affirmed or its consequent denied to yield a simple proposition conclusion. The reader should practice reading the complete argument from the following symbols (be sure to include always the "if" and the "then" and to keep the wording of each of the six propositions constant):

$$\begin{array}{c} Q \supset N \\ N \supset E \\ E \supset C \\ \hline \therefore Q \supset C \end{array}$$

$$\begin{array}{c} Q \\ \hline \therefore C \end{array}$$

Frequently, it is necessary to rearrange parts of a chain argument and to use contrapositive forms. Here is an example that dwells upon a familiar theme. Chain reasoning is used very often to explore financial possibilities.

"If I spend my savings, I can buy a car, but if I pay my tuition, I can't buy a car. If I don't pay my tuition, I can't go to college this term."

A person in this tangle of speculation needs some system to straighten things out, and the chain pattern provides such a system. If we symbolize the three implications as they are stated we get:

$$\begin{array}{c} S \supset B \\ T \supset B' \quad \text{or contrapositive } B \supset T' \\ T' \supset C' \\ \hline \therefore S \supset C' \end{array}$$

$$\begin{array}{c} C \\ \hline \therefore S' \end{array}$$

Using a contrapositive form converts the sequence into a valid chain, and we can conclude that if savings are spent there will be no college this term. Then if we affirm that college is a "must" (C), we can conclude that savings must not be spent, at least not for anything other than tuition.

Indirect argument   One variation of chain reasoning is termed indirect argument because its purpose is to prove that if some proposition is true, then it must be false $(A \supset A')$! This would seem to be sufficiently roundabout to justify the name "indirect." But an example from argument in a court of law will aid a later explanation.

The defense attorney is presenting his case. He says that since the trial is to determine whether or not his client is guilty of a certain bank robbery, he will begin by assuming that the accused *is* guilty and see what said guilt implies.

If he were guilty, he would have entered the bank at 1:00 P.M. If he entered the bank at 1:00 P.M., then he left his home (about two hours away) before 11:15 A.M. But if he left his home before 11:15 A.M., he didn't buy the holdup gun at his neighborhood hardware store at noon. If he didn't buy the gun, he cannot be guilty.

Here are the symbols which represent the defense attorney's indirect argument:

$$G \supset E$$
$$E \supset L$$
$$L \supset B'$$

$$B' \supset G'$$
$$G \supset G'$$
$$\therefore G'$$

Even without an understanding of all the theory underlying indirect argument, the method makes sense as illustrated in our oversimplified defense case. You assume the proposition you are testing to be true, and see what follows. If it implies something that is intrinsically incompatible with the assumed proposition, then you have demonstrated that the proposition cannot be true.

To summarize, a finding in the form $A \supset A'$ yields the conclusion A'. Similarly, an implication $A' \supset A$ yields the conclusion A. Can you explain why this should be so?

For one more example of indirect argument let us explore the humble proposal that one of the present writers attend the football game next Saturday. If he attends the game, he must do it for a cost of less than five dollars. If he can spend only five dollars, he can't buy tickets and pay for a baby sitter. If he can't buy tickets and pay for a baby sitter, he can't attend the game. So—. The reader should symbolize this brief but discouraging exploration of an initially attractive proposition.

Reductio ad absurdum   One of the ancient and honorable ways of annihilating an opponent's argument is to reduce it to absurdity, to apply *reductio ad absurdum*. A proposition is shown to be impossible (necessarily false) because it implies contradictories: $A \supset (B \& B')$. So, if you can demonstrate that the truth of a proposition demands that another proposition be both true and false at the same time, then the falsity of the proposition you are challenging is thoroughly established.

We might defend another unfortunate suspect by *reductio ad absurdum*. We assume, again, that he is guilty. "If he is guilty, then he rode in the getaway car. If he rode in the getaway car, then he crossed the toll bridge at 3:50 P.M. If he was at the YMCA at 3:30, then he could not have crossed the toll bridge at 3:50. He was at the YMCA, as we have proved, at 3:30. Hence, he cannot be guilty."

$$G \supset R$$
$$\underline{R \supset T}$$
$$G \supset T$$
$$\therefore G \supset (T \& T')$$
$$\therefore G'$$

$$Y \supset T'$$
$$\underline{Y}$$
$$T'$$

In using simple implications, chains of implications, *reductio ad absurdum,* and indirect arguments, remember that one can legitimately affirm only the antecedent and deny only the consequent, and that the contrapositive may be used always as a substitute for any implication.

Reasoning by alternation   Where two or more possibilities are to be explored, it is often convenient to use an extension of the chain of implications, a method termed "alternation." Here a limited number of alternatives, most frequently two, are listed, and the implications of each examined in turn. Implications are characterized by the "if-then" wording; alternations are identified similarly by "either-or" phraseology.

Alternatives frequently emerge from problem-solving activities, usually at the solution stage. The deductive patterns of alternation are helpful in reaching a decision in the competition among alternative possibilities.

One of the generalizations about Radio Moscow formulated in Chapter VIII was an alternation: Either Radio Moscow is primarily interested in influencing those who listen to it directly, or it aims mainly to supply "information" and ideas to friendly crusaders who will spread the word to others. As we study this proposition with its two possibilities, two questions should come to mind. (1) Are there any more alternatives that should be considered? (2) Are the two alternatives mentioned mutually exclusive?

Concerning (1), let us say that those discussing Radio Moscow have mentioned other possibilities but have agreed upon dismissing them as minor or incidental. They have been able to locate only the two *major* potential audiences, direct listeners who are themselves the target of influence, or converts who use Radio Moscow as a source of help in their efforts. So the group is satisfied with the limitation to two possibilities.

As for (2), the discussants should decide whether or not their limited alternatives could overlap. If this is possible, then we have a *weak alternation,* "Either A or B, or possibly both." If the alternatives could not possibly both be true, then this would be a *strong alternation,* "Either A or B, but not both." Our hypothetical discussion group decides that "converts" and "primary targets of influence" are different groups of people, hence we can consider this alternation *strong.* So, if they establish the truth of one alternative, then the other can be dismissed as false, since both cannot be true at the same time. Or, if they disprove one alternative, the other must then be true.

The symbolic representation of alternation is "$A \lor B$" for the weak form, or "$A \underline{\lor} B$" for the strong form. The capital letters again stand for complete propositions. As in symbolizing implications, a prime may be used to indicate the contradictory of a proposition.

Let us carry on the reasoning of the group as it proceeds to examine the strong alternation, $D \underline{\lor} C$. First, they review the evidence that supports the possibility of a substantial body of unde-cided, direct listeners (proposition D) and decide that it is inade-quate. Short-wave listening is so difficult, equipment for effective listening is so scarce, and the Radio Moscow programs seem to be so uninteresting to casual listeners-in that the group agrees to dismiss alternative D as unlikely. Then they are free to accept alternative C as the most probable hypothesis as to the United States Radio Moscow audience in the light of their present knowledge.

This reasoning can be represented most accurately in a com-bined alternation-implication pattern.

$$D \Ydown C$$
$$D \supset E \quad (E = \text{``Evidence will support } D\text{''})$$
$$\underline{E'}$$
$$\therefore \underline{D'}$$
$$\therefore C$$

The close relationship between "if-thens" and "either-ors" can be seen in the above example. Actually, implications can be con-verted to alternations in this manner:

$$A \vee B = A' \supset B \qquad\qquad A \supset B = A' \vee B$$
$$A \vee B = B' \supset A \qquad\qquad B \supset A = B' \vee A$$

Here are rules to remember in effecting these conversions:

(1) To convert an alternation to an implication, use the contra-dictory of one alternative as antecedent and the other al-ternative, unchanged, as consequent.

(2) To change an implication to an alternation, use the contra-dictory of the antecedent as one alternative and the conse-quent, unchanged, as the other.

If the alternation happens to be strong, then it can be translated into two different implications:

$$A \Ydown B = A' \supset B \text{ and } B \supset A'$$

These implications, which resemble each other in that one is the converse of the other, can be combined with the aid of a new sym-bol ($\equiv$): $A' \equiv B = A' \supset B$ and $B \supset A'$. This is read "If, *and only if*, A is false, then proposition B must be true." It corresponds, obviously, to the strong alternation. So we add to our rules for con-verting implications to alternations and alternations to implications:

(3) If the alternation is strong, the corresponding implication

is an "If and only if" ($\equiv$) form, and "If and only if" implications convert to strong alternations.

In the spring of 1954 Senator Joseph McCarthy of Wisconsin
was criticized by television commentator Edward R. Murrow.
Senator McCarthy used an alternation in his rebuttal: "Either
McCarthy or Murrow is for the Communists, and the other is
against the Communists." Then, by citing his anti-Communist
activities, the Senator implied that through the process of elimination Murrow had to be for the Communists.

McCarthy treated this as a strong alternation, assuming that
both of the men could not either oppose or support Communists.
He made mutually exclusive something that obviously wasn't. As for
exhaustion of possible alternatives, McCarthy or Murrow might
conceivably be neutral toward Communists. McCarthy assumes that
there is no middle ground, one either supports or fights Communists. So McCarthy's alternation flunks our two-question test suggested above. Actually, it is a good example of a popular fallacy, the
black-white alternation. Here the two extreme views are presented
as the only possible, mutually exclusive possibilities. Political rhetoric
abounds in these. "Either I am elected or grass will grow in the
streets." They are easily analyzed, as was the Senator McCarthy
example.

We might symbolize the McCarthy argument for practice in representing analysis of alternations. First, let us rewrite the basic elements in standard form: Either McCarthy is for Communists or
Murrow is for Communists, but not both.

$$Mc \ \underline{\lor} \ Mm = Mc' \equiv Mm$$
$$\underline{Mc'}$$
$$\therefore Mm$$

The dilemma When two alternatives (and only two) are
shown through implication to have either a single or two disagree-
able consequents, and hence both possibilities are rendered undesirable, we term the unit of reasoning a dilemma. It is found in four
related patterns:

(1) $A \lor B$	(2) $A \lor B$	(3) $A \supset B$	(4) $A \supset B$
$A \supset C$	$A \supset E$	$A' \supset C$	$A' \supset B$
$B \supset D$	$B \supset E$	$B \lor C$	$\therefore B$
$C \lor D$	$\therefore E$		

(1) This is sometimes labeled a "black-or-black" alternation. Example: "Either this college will raise tuition or it will lower tuition. If the college raises tuition, fewer students will come. If it lowers tuition, money for instruction will be reduced. Hence we can expect either fewer students or less money for instruction."

(2) This shows that of two alternatives one is really as bad as the other, for they both lead to the same eventuality. "Either I will study harder or expand my program of social activities. If I study harder, I will be unhappy because of the fun I am missing, and if I expand my social life, I will be unhappy because of guilt feelings over my neglected studies. So I am doomed to be unhappy."

In (3) and (4) we see the "you do or you don't" varieties of dilemma in which the alternatives are a proposition and its contradictory. In (3), two possible unpleasant results are developed, in (4) the proposition and its contradictory are shown to yield the same unsatisfactory result. An example of (3): "If Minnesota reduces personal income and property taxes, its deficit financing will increase. If it does not reduce these taxes, many industrial concerns will move to other states. So Minnesota will either operate with increasing deficits or it will lose many industries to other states." An example of (4): "If I argue with my wife, then she will become angry and I shall have to give in. If I don't argue with my wife, then she automatically has her way. So my wife is certain to have her way when we disagree."

While the dilemma is frequently valid, it is seldom true. As in the case of the four examples above, it is usually a deceptive oversimplification of existing circumstances. It is tricky and persuasive because it appears to be conclusive, owing to the language used and its neat, closed structure.

Perhaps the flashiest as well as the least reasonable way of answering a dilemma is to use the method of "rebuttal": the creation of a counterdilemma with an opposing conclusion. Example (2) above might be rebutted in this way: "If I study harder I will be happy because of my better grades, and if I expand my social life I will have more fun. So I am certain to be happy!"

Two suggestions will enable the reader to expose most dilemmas in sounder fashion. First, try "slipping between the horns," in other words, look for a third possible alternative. Usually it can be found. Next, if that fails, "take the dilemma by the horns," i.e., try challenging one of the alternatives. After all, both are assumed to be true, and the critical thinker always challenges such assumptions. Practice "slipping between" and "grasping" the horns of the four sample dilemmas above. No one of them will be found to be impenetrable.

In discussion, attempts to consolidate generalizations in patterns of implication and alternation will contribute to precision in group thinking. The more that individuals in the group know about these methods of proceeding from summarized evidence to conclusions, the more efficient their problem solving will be, particularly as the solution stage is approached.

CHAPTER X

Deductive Application of Generalizations—Part 2

Thus far in the study of deduction we have been concerned with the relationship between propositions. We can also reason about the relationship between categories or classes of similar phenomena. This different kind of proposition *fits one class into another,* as "Schoolteachers are intelligent people." This says that schoolteachers as a group or class fall within the much larger category of intelligent folk. And if we suggest that Jim Smith is a schoolteacher, this category manipulation enables us to conclude that in all probability he is an intelligent person.

This form of deduction is called a syllogism or, more precisely, a categorical syllogism. It has two premises and a conclusion, three classes (no more) are dealt with, and the conclusion develops a relationship between the two classes which are not connected to each other directly in the premises.

Syllogistic propositions are always written in a standard form which states that either all or part of the first class is either included in or excluded from the second category. This leads to four possibilities:

All _____ are included in _____.
All _____ are excluded from _____.
Some _____ are included in _____.
Some _____ are excluded from _____.

The basic theory of reasoning by syllogism may be represented visually by a system of overlapping circles. At the moment we can use two circles to show what the above premises mean, and later in a somewhat more complicated system based upon three circles we will learn to check the validity of any syllogism.

When we say, "All schoolteachers are intelligent people," we can represent schoolteachers by one circle and intelligent people by another. Then by use of shading to indicate absence of instances we can graphically represent this premise:

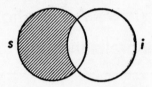

This says that there isn't any schoolteacher that isn't an intelligent person or, phrasing it differently, if there are any schoolteachers, they fall within the class of intelligent people. Let us look at the other possible forms of a syllogistic premise:

All schoolteachers are other than intelligent people.

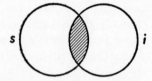

Some of the class of schoolteachers are intelligent people.

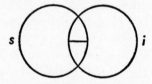

Some of the class of schoolteachers are not intelligent people.

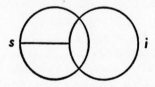

The line or bar in the last two diagrams represents the presence of one or more cases, what we mean when we say "some." Because language used in talking about parts of classes of things is confusing, we will always use the word "some" in place of "a few," "many," "part of," and so on. Thus, each premise in a syllogism begins with "all" or "some." Those beginning with "all" make statements about entire classes and are called *universal* premises, and those beginning with "some" generalize about parts of classes and hence are termed *particular* premises.

Since half the battle of understanding syllogisms is won when you can word premises and represent them by the circle system, the reader should practice converting the following into standard "all" or "some" statements and diagram each with two intersecting circles.

(1) Some college students are the leaders of tomorrow.
(2) A few cats don't make good pets.
(3) Many movie-goers own television sets.
(4) No airplane is lighter than air.
(5) The great majority of people who listen regularly to the North American Service of Radio Moscow are people who are strongly motivated to hear what the USSR has to say on current issues.

Whether to convert the above to "all" or "some" premises should be quite easily decided with the troublesome exception of (5). Here let us recall from the comments on probability of the last chapter that when the statement represents a great central tendency, or deals with practically all of a class, we will treat it as a universal. So we suggest that when you can say "substantially all" at the beginning of a syllogistic premise you use the word "all" and recognize in the conclusion that isolated exceptions may occur. If this is accepted, (5) becomes a *universal* statement.

THE SYLLOGISM

A suitable first syllogism to study is one demonstrating the desirability of outlawing communism as used by Harold Stassen in a historic debate with Thomas E. Dewey. Stassen's central argument, which was presented in stages with supporting materials, may be summarized like this:

Major premise:	**All** attempts directed by a foreign power to overthrow forcibly the government of the United States **are included in** things which should be outlawed.
Minor premise:	**All** the Communist party **is included in** attempts directed by a foreign power to overthrow forcibly the government of the United States.
Conclusion:	**All** the Communist party **is included in** things which should be outlawed.

The boldface elements in the standard syllogism pattern above need explanation. Every premise or conclusion begins with a *quantifier,* in our illustration, "all" because these are *universal* statements embracing entire classes. As previously noted, when we deal with parts of classes (one or more cases in a class of many) the quantifier used is "some."

The two classes in each premise and in the conclusion are connected by a syllogistic element termed the *copula.* All three statements in our illustration fit one class *into* another, hence the copula used is "is (are) included in." Statements of exclusion use the copula "is (are) excluded from."

The *terms* (classes) are frequently cumbersome because many words are used to describe them. We can let simple symbols represent the classes, and once the syllogism is properly and completely worded, as is our illustration, we can move along in analysis of the argument most economically by using these symbols. Let's reduce our Stassen syllogism to a symbolized unit.

$$\begin{array}{l} \text{All } a < o \\ \text{All } c < a \\ \hline \text{All } c < o \end{array}$$

Note that the quantifier is unchanged, that a letter becomes a symbol for each class, and that the copula "is (are) included in" is represented by the symbol $<$. The copula "is (are) excluded from" would be represented by the symbol $\nless$. The horizontal line separates premises from conclusion. And lower case letters are used to represent classes so that we will not confuse them with the capital letters we have been using that stand for propositions.

Symbolization of the syllogism makes diagramming it simpler

because each of the letter symbols can be used to identify an area of the diagram. The three *terms* (classes) of the syllogism are drawn as *three circles of fixed size and unchanging position,* thus:

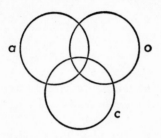

The boundaries of circle *a* therefore enclose "*all* attempts directed by a foreign power to overthrow forcibly the government of the United States." Circle *o* indicates the boundaries of "*all* things which should be outlawed," and the circumference of circle *c* includes the entire Communist party.

We graph the syllogism one premise at a time. Here is the representation of the major premise:

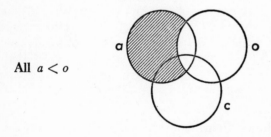

All *a* < *o*

Shading a portion of a circle indicates that it is empty, and that all members of that class therefore lie in the open or unshaded portion. We want to show visually that "all *a* is included in *o*," so we shade all the *a* circle outside the *o* area. Any *a* (attempts to overthrow, and so on) thus are shown to fall within *o* (things to be outlawed). The diagrammatic representation of our major premise is complete.

The minor premise involves classes *c* and *a*, so we deal with the two circles representing them as though the third circle did not exist.

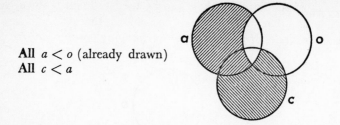

All $a < o$ (already drawn)
All $c < a$

The visualization of the minor premise again consists of showing that the area of one circle outside of an overlapped portion is *empty* by shading it.

We have produced a complete Venn diagram, one of the most useful devices for testing the *validity* (structural soundness) of the syllogism. How does it work? *When the two premises have been graphed we simply inspect the diagram to see if it represents the state of affairs found in the conclusion.* If the diagram corresponds to the conclusion, the syllogism is judged to be *valid*.

Now to test Mr. Stassen's logic. He claims that:

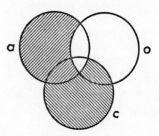

All $a < o$
and **All** $c < a$
lead to the conclusion:
All $c < o$.

The diagram drawn from his premises should show this conclusion.

Inspection of the Venn representation shows that it does! All the c circle is empty except for one compartment which is within the boundaries of o. And that is just exactly what the conclusion says:

All c *is included in* o

Mr. Stassen has completed a *valid* unit of syllogistic reasoning. *If we grant the truth of his premises, then we must accept his con-*

clusion as true. This repeats our definition of a logically valid bit of reasoning, a structure (pattern) such that if the premises are true, the conclusion must necessarily be true also.

Let us analyze a typical "enthymeme" or incomplete syllogism. It was spoken in the heat of Presidential campaigning in 1948, and was designed to fit a group of politicians into a certain category.

"Many people believe these individuals are 'innocent idealists.' I, however, do not believe they are feeble-minded."

When we suspect the presence of a syllogism which is partial and concealed as is this one, we begin by *locating the conclusion.* The speaker seems to be disagreeing with those who believe that the people in question are "innocent idealists," consequently the conclusion of the argument would seem to be that "these people are not innocent idealists." Next we look into the reasoning given to support that conclusion. There is one statement to the effect that the speaker believes the people he is talking about are not feeble-minded. They are not feeble-minded, he says, therefore they cannot be "innocent idealists." Now our syllogism is beginning to emerge. What assumption must we make if we are to conclude that "they" are not innocent idealists from the premise that "they" are not feeble-minded? The assumption obviously relates the characteristics of innocent idealism and feeble-mindedness. A little thought will reveal that in order to complete the syllogism we need the assumption, which will serve as major premise, that "all innocent idealists are feeble-minded." Here is the syllogism.

Major premise:	**All** innocent idealists **are included in** the class of feeble-minded people.
Minor premise:	**All** this group of politicians **are excluded from** the class of feeble-minded people.
Conclusion:	**All** this group of politicians **are excluded from** innocent idealists.

We note that in this enthymeme one suppressed element was the *conclusion.* It was so forcefully implied, however, that it would not be easily overlooked.

Now we will symbolize the syllogism and draw the Venn diagram to check its validity.

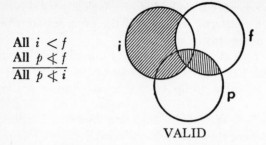

All $i < f$
All $p \nless f$
_____
All $p \nless i$

VALID

The syllogism is *valid* because the diagram resulting from the graphing of the two premises accurately represents the state of affairs in the speaker's conclusion. The politicians in question have been excluded effectively from the class of innocent idealists. If anyone doubts the *truth* of the conclusion he can now inspect the *truth* of the premises. Some would probably doubt that "all innocent idealists are feeble-minded." Should you judge that false, then the validity of the structure has no significance, for the certain truth of the conclusion depends entirely upon the truth of the premises. Given one false premise, the *valid* conclusion may be either true or false; we have no way of knowing which. This is so because the conclusion may be true through some other valid unit of reasoning with true premises. We only know that a valid syllogism with a false premise proves the conclusion neither true nor false.

Without assuming motivation for the reasoning used by this campaign speaker, we can gather from it that use of the enthymeme lends itself to possible trickery. The fact that the major premise in this case, the area for a large proportion of our possible doubt, was suppressed tends to divert our attention from it. A person who wants to disagree with an argument like this one has to go to the considerable bother of working out the syllogistic structure and developing the suppressed premise. We suspect that most people would not go to the bother of doing all that in casual reading of a column or listening to a speech, and possibly they might not have the background in logical reasoning necessary to accomplish that analysis. Hence, because an enthymematic form looks "logical," some people may be misled into accepting a conclusion without *examining* the steps leading to it. Persuaders can use enthymemes that suppress doubtful premises and conceal the suppressed element of their syllogistic reasoning in a cloud of colorful rhetoric.

A common syllogistic fallacy, one which has been intentionally and unintentionally used widely, is illustrated by this nonsense syllogism with true premises:

$$\begin{array}{l} \text{All tomatoes} < \text{vegetables} \\ \underline{\text{All potatoes} < \text{vegetables}} \\ \text{All tomatoes} < \text{potatoes} \end{array}$$

The Venn diagram for this example will reveal the theoretical weakness of its structure. But the more reasonable sounding enthymeme, "Both Socialists and Communists favor government ownership of industries, hence to all intents and purposes are the same," shares the same fallacy. Expand this enthymeme to a syllogism and draw its Venn diagram.

Before we take up syllogisms with particular premises and conclusions, we should consider popular variations of the enthymeme. Either of the premises or the conclusion, or more than one of these elements, can be suppressed. These possibilities can be demonstrated through presenting a syllogism in the several forms of enthymeme in which it might be found.

You can take our sample syllogism seriously or not, as you choose. A few people have believed it!

Major premise: All absent-minded people **are included in** brilliant people.

Minor premise: All professors **are included in** absent-minded people.

Conclusion: All professors **are included in** brilliant people.

To complete our standard procedure of treating a syllogism we will symbolize it and check validity with the Venn diagram:

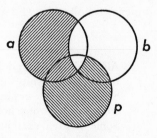

VALID

Now, what would be the result if we worded an enthymeme from this syllogism in which we suppress the major premise? Here is one form such an enthymeme might take: "All professors, being absent-minded, are brilliant." Let's suppress the minor premise. It could be worded then, "Absent-minded people are brilliant; hence, all professors are brilliant." If the conclusion is suppressed, we get an argument like this: "All absent-minded people are brilliant, and professors are known to be absent-minded!" In this last example the conclusion is implied, but, we believe you will agree, clearly so.

Examine these enthymemes carefully. You will see that even though they are condensed considerably when compared with the original syllogistic form, each contains or implies all the ingredients of the complete syllogism. If you expand any one of the three, you can reach only the one result, the same syllogism with which we started. Hence enthymemes, though their wording seems to be subject to considerable variation, represent as rigid structures of thinking as do formal and complete syllogisms. Sometimes it takes some experiment and careful thought to rearrange the material in the enthymeme into the proper syllogistic form, but if it is done carefully any good enthymeme can be expanded to one and only one syllogism. The arrangement of the class categories in the enthymeme is just as fixed as the arrangement of classes in the complete syllogism.

Particular premises and conclusions necessitate an adaptation of the Venn diagram as a validity check, and the use of "some" instead of "all" as quantifier. Otherwise, they can be handled as were universal propositions in the syllogisms we have studied. An example will illustrate the differences. We will begin with an enthymeme selected from a class discussion. "Some written examinations are not fair tests of a student's scholarship, and so it is wrong to base his grades upon them."

Major premise:	All fair bases of grades **are included in** fair tests of scholarship.
Minor premise:	Some written examinations **are excluded from** fair tests of scholarship.
Conclusion:	Some written examinations **are excluded from** fair bases of grades.

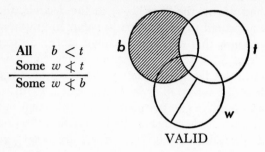

All $b < t$
Some $w \not< t$
—————
Some $w \not< b$

VALID

While "shading" a part of the diagram indicates *absence* of instances (emptiness), the "bar," as found in the w circle, indicates the *presence* of *some* (one or more) members of the class within the boundaries where it is drawn. How does the diagram show this syllogism to be valid? As with universal premises, we graphed these in turn, then inspected the diagram to see if it accurately represented the conclusion. The conclusion tells us that some w is to be found outside b, and surely enough it is, right there in the Venn diagram.

There is one rule to be remembered if you are to avoid trouble in using the Venn diagram to check syllogisms with particular propositions: *Always draw the "bar" through as many open compartments in the diagram as you can and still conform to the premises.* Let's look at another example to see how that works out.

"Not all doctors are wealthy, and wealthy folks are snobbish. Hence, some doctors are not snobbish."

Major premise:	**All** wealthy folks **are included in** snobbish people.
Major premise:	**Some** doctors **are excluded from** wealthy folks.
Conclusion:	**Some** doctors **are excluded from** snobbish people.

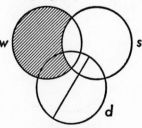

All $w < s$
Some $d \not< w$
—————
Some $d \not< s$

INVALID

Note that if we had drawn the "bar" *only* in the *d* circle, the syllogism would have appeared to pass its test as *valid*. In graphing the minor premise, we know that only *some* (one or more) doctors are to be found outside of the category of wealthy people. Since we have no authorization to put this *some* quantity (possibly only one instance) either inside of the *s* overlap or in *d* outside of *s,* we draw our "bar" through both possible compartments, indicating that our *some* may be found in one or the other or both. A little reflection will confirm that this procedure is necessary if we are not to go beyond information supplied in the premises.

Remember that every premise or conclusion must begin with a *quantifier,* and that it is either "all" or "some." "All" (universal) propositions seem to give no trouble, but the fact that all quantitative expressions indicating less than the whole of any class are translated as "some" causes difficulty. "Not all," "a few," "many," "a great number" are a few expressions which come out as "some" in the syllogism. Note this typical example.

"A few college athletes are demonstrably above the average in scholarship. For various reasons many students of above average scholarship deserve monetary help in getting their college educations. It follows that at least some proportion of college athletes deserve to be aided financially while going to college."

Major premise:	**Some** students above the average in scholarship **are included in** students deserving financial help.
Minor premise:	**Some** college athletes **are included in** students above the average in scholarship.
Conclusion:	**Some** college athletes **are included in** students deserving financial help.

Some $s < d$
Some $a < s$

Some $a < d$

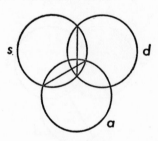

INVALID

Students who have studied logic will recall that you cannot evolve a valid syllogistic conclusion from two particular propositions. This rule makes drawing the diagram unnecessary, but, should you forget the rule, the diagram furnishes a positive judgment on validity. From study of the diagram try to develop an explanation of the theoretical impossibility of drawing a conclusion from two particular premises.

The "substantially all" universal premise should be studied in the syllogism. So let us use the Radio Moscow generalization mentioned earlier as a minor premise:

All people who are strongly motivated to hear what the USSR has to say on current issues **are included in** Radio Moscow listeners who pay close attention to the program content.

All people who listen regularly to the North American Service of Radio Moscow **are included in** people who are strongly motivated to hear what the USSR has to say on current issues.

All people who listen regularly to the North American Service of Radio Moscow **are included in** Radio Moscow listeners who pay close attention to program content.

Symbols and diagram:

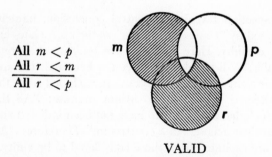

All $m < p$
All $r < m$
All $r < p$

m

p

r

VALID

Because we admit occasional rare exceptions to the second premise, we are bound to do the same for the conclusion. It might be a good idea to read the conclusion as a "substantially all" statement. Then it would sound like what it is, a description of a predominant central tendency that is as significant for purposes of the problem being considered as it would be if there were no possibility of individual exceptions. The important thing to remember is not to attempt an "each and every" conclusion from a syllogism that contains a "substantially all" premise. Be consistent!

Incidentally, this illustration demonstrates the saving of time and the minimizing of confusion by using symbols. Complex wording is common in syllogisms, and once the symbols are assigned, a lengthy structure can be examined quickly and accurately.

INTERCHANGEABILITY OF DEDUCTIVE FORMS

The three forms, condition, alternation, and syllogism, are to a considerable extent interchangeable. To illustrate concretely this interchangeability, we will rephrase a paragraph of argumentative writing in each of the three deductive patterns.

In widely publicized statements made in Congressional hearings by confessed traitors, many names of their associates have been mentioned. These persons may have participated in subversive activities, or they may have been completely loyal to this country and its government. We must remember that the named individuals have neither been indicted nor faced their accusers in court. The basic presumption of Anglo-Saxon justice, that a person is considered innocent until proven guilty, directly refutes any reasoning leading to a conclusion of guilt by association.

Preliminary inspection reveals the central conclusion, namely, that the people named by "confessed traitors" as their associates are not to be considered guilty. Here is a *syllogism* built on this argument. Major premise: "All people who have not been indicted and have not faced their accusers in a courtroom are excluded from the class of those considered to be guilty." Minor premise: "All the people named are included in those who have not been indicted and who have not faced their accusers in a courtroom." Therefore: "All the people named are excluded from those considered to be guilty." The reader can check the validity of the syllogism by symbolizing the premises and completing a Venn diagram.

Now, how could this same deductive progression be put in the form of a conditional argument? "If a person is to be considered guilty he must have been indicted and have faced his accuser in a courtroom. But the people named by 'confessed traitors' have not been indicted and have not faced their accusers in a courtroom, therefore the people named cannot be considered guilty." We reach the same conclusion that the syllogism yielded by a closely related process, the "if-then" sequence of antecedent and consequent. In this case the consequent was denied, which negated the antecedent. Now, let's word the argument in the form of an alternation: "Either the people named should be considered guilty or else it should be admitted that their guilt is an unknown quantity. But if their guilt were to be admitted, these people named would have faced their accusers in the courtroom and would have been indicted. Since this has not been the case there remains but one alternative—the admission that the guilt of these people is in doubt."

Opinions will differ as to which of the three forms represents the argument with the greatest accuracy. No arbitrary choice need be made, but it is the opinion of the authors that the syllogism represents the most faithful translation of the original argument.

There is no formula for determining which deductive approach is best for a given set of generalizations and a particular problem. When a limited number of definite possibilities are to be compared, alternation is usually appropriate. When the burden of the job to be done involves exploring the possible concomitants of a hypothetical assumption, implication seems indicated. And when related classes are fitted into or excluded from one another, try the syllogism first. Sometimes trying two or all three patterns clarifies a confusing relationship more than would staying with one approach.

Here are a few final bits of advice concerning use of the syllogism. Categories must be alike to be fitted into one another; horses can't go into a class of people. A common fallacy is the inclusion of four terms or classes in a syllogism instead of the legal maximum of three. This often comes about because two classes look a lot alike but are actually separate. When critically examining a syllogism, first symbolize it, then check its validity with a Venn diagram, and if it is valid, consider the truth of the premises. Why not consider *truth* before validity? Because judging truth is infinitely harder in most cases than checking validity. With respect to valid form, a syllogism either has it or it hasn't, but any test of the truth of its premises is often remote, and a judgment of truth often has to be speculative and is influenced by the critic's array of prejudices.

If you understand the Venn diagram, you know the basic theory of syllogistic reasoning and need no rules of the syllogism to identify fallacies. In fact, you don't need to be able to tell a major premise from a minor premise. Use the Venn circles freely, and soon the more often repeated variations of the syllogism will become so familiar you can judge their validity on sight. However, if you forget or encounter a rare syllogistic pattern, draw the three overlapping circles and you will not only get your answer concerning validity, but also a visual representation of the entire unit of reasoning that will enable you to diagnose its error or patch it up by revision to make it valid.

Syllogisms have great utility as summaries. Harry Hollingworth once said that a syllogism is a monument, erected to commemorate the thinking that has gone before. If you can so arrange your generalizations that a syllogism can consolidate them, it may impress your thinking upon the minds of other people better than any other device.

Discussion Procedures and Practices

PART THREE

Discussion Procedures and Practices

CHAPTER XI

Discussion Forms and Products

INTRODUCTION

The purpose of this chapter is to describe a number of forms within which discussion activity can take place, and to indicate some of the common products which are sought from discussion. In Chapter III we considered at some length the Round-table form, suggesting that the initial discussion experience of the student might well take this direction. However, the needs of various groups and the characteristics of various group situations in our society have given rise to a large number of discussion forms. Each of these has some distinctive advantages in particular situations, and by the same token, each form has certain limitations in terms of the results which it can achieve.

The student of discussion should participate in preparing and observing a large number of discussion forms. In this way he can best learn the uses and limitations of each.

BASIC FORMS FOR SMALL GROUP ACTIVITY

We distinguish two basic forms for discussion carried out by small groups. These are the *round-table* discussion and the *symposium*. We shall also identify the *case-study* discussion as a special form of the round table, and the *cooperative investigation* as a special form of the symposium.

The round-table discussion

Consideration of the nature, uses, and limitations of the round-table discussion has been given in Chapter III.

161

The case-study discussion   A special form of round-table discussion is that which proceeds from the consideration of a "case" rather than from the general statement of a problem. The selection of the case to be studied and the direction of discussion which will follow the reading or study of the case are determined by the general purpose of the discussion group. For example, the case conference has been used as a means of studying human behavior or human relations. Here discussion proceeds from the study of a particular instance involving a problem in human adjustment or human relations, the effort by the group being to gain insight into human-relations processes through discussion.[1] The case-conference method has also been used as a means of studying problems in business management, and has become, in fact, the principal method of instruction for the Harvard School of Business Administration. It has been used by the armed forces for training in military leadership, with cases involving military problems used as the basis for discussion; by parents of adult education groups for studying child care, with cases in child behavior as the basis for group deliberation.

Several advantages are claimed for the case-conference discussion. First, the concrete statement of a problem, as provided by the case, almost always assures a stimulating, animated discussion. Second, the case conference helps to free discussants from the preconceptions, slogans, or formulas which they may have invoked in problems of human relations, business management, and so forth.

For example, if we state a problem in human relations in abstract terms, many persons will have formula answers for the problem. Thus the problem, "Should people be honest in their dealings with one another?" seems no problem at all to a discussant equipped with the slogan, "Honesty is the best policy." On the other hand, a case study in which a medical doctor has a neurotic woman patient with a variety of psychosomatic ailments, an irascible husband, and a variety of other interested relatives who are convinced that the patient has cancer—such a case situation raises in concrete form the question of how honest the doctor ought to be in his conversa-

---

[1] See F. K. Berrien, *Comments and Cases on Human Relations*, New York, Harper & Brothers, 1951, for a collection of cases relating to problems in human relations and for a commentary on the use of discussion in relation to these cases.

Of particular interest to students of speech and discussion may be the cases on communication failure, included in the volume, Irving Lee, *Customs and Crises in Communication*, New York, Harper & Brothers, 1954.

tion with the patient and relatives. Discussants confronted with the complexities of a concrete situation may well find their old formulas for human behavior quite inadequate. Finally, the case conference tends to keep discussion focused, limited, and relatively concrete.

The form has certain limitations. Obviously, not all types of problems can be dealt with by the case conference. The problem, "How can the city of X reduce traffic congestion in the business district?" would not be readily approachable by a case conference on a traffic accident at Fifth and Main. Moreover, if the case conference is to result in more than a stimulating social experience, it requires skillful leadership and purposive participation, so that the discussion group moves toward the development of insights which will be useful in relationship to situations other than the specific case under consideration.

The symposium

The basic distinction to be made between the round table and the symposium is that the symposium replaces informal conversation among discussants with a series of short prepared speeches, presented in turn by members of the group. Usually the symposium topics represent a partitioning of a discussion problem into as many subtopics as there are to be speakers. Thus, a symposium might be set up as follows:

Problem: Can juvenile delinquency be reduced?

I.   Where do our delinquent children come from?
     Mrs. A. E. Overholse, School of Social Work
II. How extensive is our present juvenile delinquency problem?
     Professor John Useem
III. Our courts and the handling of juvenile offenders
     Judge H. A. Rockmeir
IV. The role of the church in combating juvenile delinquency
     The Reverend Billy Ulbert
V.   The role of the schools in combating juvenile delinquency
     Superintendent Robert Perham
VI. The Police Department and the juvenile offender
     Sergeant John Ferson

Notice that the rationale for this symposium came from the occupational "expertness" of the speakers. The partitioning of the discussion problem was a practical one based on the availability of certain speakers, each of whom had something to say relevant to the major problem. Could you suggest other kinds of rationale for partitioning a symposium on juvenile delinquency?

Sometimes the symposium is partitioned only in the sense that the speakers are invited to take opposing views on a controversial issue. Under such circumstances, the symposium becomes a sort of informal debate, with the speakers taking specific positions and generally holding to those positions.

Provision for interaction among speakers during a symposium The fact that symposium speakers present prepared speeches tends to reduce the amount of interaction or interchange among the speakers. However, some interaction can be achieved through careful planning. A brief period may be provided at the end of each speech during which other members of the symposium may address questions or comments to the speaker who has just finished. Another arrangement provides for a short period of questioning and "round-table" discussion at the conclusion of the entire set of prepared speeches.

Advantages of the symposium The symposium may be more suitable than the round table for public discussions before sizable audiences. The fact that the speakers make extended, prepared statements enables each speaker to deal with the problem of projecting coherent, organized speech to a sizable group—a problem not easily dealt with in the informal procedures followed in the round table. The symposium also simplifies the planning of a public discussion in that it minimizes the need for prior *group* preparation by the discussants. Symposiums can be successfully planned without any prior meeting of the discussants. In such cases, the chairman may partition the problem, suggest topics for the several speeches, and secure suitable persons to present these talks. The symposium is a good form for bringing together the ideas of several persons, each of whom is expert in some phase of a more general topic, but who may not, perhaps, be prepared for general discussion of the problem.

Limitations of the symposium Many of the values possible in round-table discussion are not readily achieved in the symposium.

The use of planned, prearranged speeches reduces the amount of criticism and clarification to which the ideas of any speaker may be subjected. Neither discussion as "conversation" nor discussion as "criticism" is very evident in the symposium.

The cooperative investigation   A special form of the symposium which has great utility is the cooperative investigation. Such a discussion form is suited to the needs of a group of persons who wish to become "expert" in a particular problem area, even though they may be starting with little information. It is a particularly useful form for gathering and sharing information, and is thus most commonly used in connection with problems of fact. Let us say that a group states as its problem, "What are the views of major religious groups in America on the question of birth control?" The group will meet to work out a reasonable partitioning of the research problem with which they are presented, perhaps deciding to divide the problem into four subareas:

(1)   The Catholic viewpoint.
(2)   The Jewish viewpoint.
(3)   The Protestant viewpoint (the larger denominations).
(4)   The Protestant viewpoint (the smaller denominations).

Following research, the members of the group will again meet for a "symposium" of reports on the findings of each member of the group.

The cooperative investigation has obvious merits for the situation in which a large group assigns a task of information-gathering and sharing to a smaller group. Thus, a college class raised the question, "How does our college get its money, and how does it spend it?" A discussion group from the class then partitioned this problem, carried out its investigation, and the members of the group reported their findings to the class.

On a more elaborate scale, community study groups may divide their membership into subcommittees, each with the task of gathering and interpreting information in a particular area. Thus, a community-wide "Committee on Public Education" set up study groups on such subtopics as personnel practices and needs; building needs; teacher recruitment and tenure; curriculum practices; finance; and so forth. The various subgroups had the task of gathering, evaluating, and reporting information for the larger group, thus providing the basis for a general understanding of the problem area being considered.

Advantages and limitations   The usefulness of the cooperative investigation form in gathering and sharing information is obvious. It should also be apparent that the cooperative investigation is often a valuable "ground clearing" basis for a round-table discussion. That is, persons with little informational background seeking to approach a problem-solving discussion of some important question of policy might well precede their round table or forum with a cooperative investigation on the informational aspects of their problem. By itself, the cooperative investigation, as a special sort of symposium, is only a starting point for the "conversation" and "criticism" which may follow.

Basic forms for large-group audience activity

A common form for public discussion involves the active participation of an audience in the consideration of a problem. This audience participation in discussion we refer to as a *forum*. While a forum may proceed just from the stating of a problem to an audience, it is more common to find the forum preceded by another form of speech activity—a "stimulus event"—designed to give the audience a specific basis for comments or questions. Thus, we might find a public meeting designated as a *lecture forum*, in which case the audience listens to a speech, and then members of the audience ask questions of the speaker or make comments supplementing or taking issue with statements of the speaker. The *round-table forum* would substitute a round-table discussion for the lecture as the stimulus event; and following the analogy of these titles, the general nature of a *debate forum, symposium forum, film forum*, becomes apparent. We shall consider in greater detail the form for the *debate forum* and the *film forum*, since both of these present special problems in organization.

The debate forum   The two-man debate on a controversial issue provides a stimulating basis for *forum* discussion. Two speakers can present, in a reasonably short period of time, basic pro and con positions on a problem which arouses controversy, following which members of the audience can be invited to contribute questions or comments or both on the problem under consideration.

The following agenda for a one-hour debate forum shows one of the possible time arrangements for such a discussion.

Problem: Do "crime" plays on radio and television increase juvenile delinquency?

I. Introduction of topic arrangements and speakers by the chairman.

II. A thirty-minute debate acording to the following time arrangements:

    A. The affirmative speaker, who answers "yes" to the stated question, presents his case in ten minutes.

    B. The negative speaker, who answers "no" to the stated question, answers the affirmative speaker, and presents his own case in ten minutes.

    C. The affirmative speaker has five minutes for rebuttal. During this period he seeks to re-establish the soundness of his initial speech and to answer arguments presented by the negative speaker.

    D. The negative speaker has five minutes for rebuttal —to answer the affirmative case and to re-establish his own previously stated position.

III. The chairman calls for questions or comments.

    Following the debate, members of the audience may address questions or comments to either or both of the speakers. Questions or comments should be brief, each stating one, and only one, point.

IV. The chairman summarizes briefly.

Varying time arrangements are possible for the debate forum. The radio program, "America's Town Meeting of the Air," is often presented as a debate forum. In such cases, the debate itself may be held to approximately fifteen minutes of the available time, with questions occupying the last fifteen minutes.

The film or film-strip forum A film or film strip dealing with a problem to be discussed provides an excellent stimulus to a forum. With small audiences, the film is shown after a brief introduction by the chairman, and general discussion follows. With larger audiences, or small audiences of persons not too familiar with the problem under discussion, it is often desirable to provide one or more "experts" to lead off the discussion of the film. These experts can then serve to answer questions from members of the audience. Such an arrangement is illustrated in the following form.

Problem : How have teaching methods changed in our elementary schools?

    I. The chairman introduces the topic and the principal discussants.

    II. The sound film, "Broader Concept of Method, Part I," is shown.

    III. A fifteen-minute symposium follows. Three "experts" who have previewed the film take five minutes to emphasize points in the film which they considered of most interest and importance.

    IV. The chairman asks for questions or comments from the audience.

    V. The chairman summarizes briefly.

An interesting variation possible in using a film strip is that of showing it in combination with discussion. The film strip is shown in a partly darkened room, with comments and questions invited after the showing of each picture, rather than reserving comment until the entire strip has been shown.

Leadership tasks in handling forums Since many members of an audience may be untrained in discussion, or unfamiliar with the procedures of a forum, or even unsympathetic to the purpose of a public forum, the forum leader faces heavy responsibilities. Some general principles concerning arrangements which will assist the leader are listed here:

1. With very large audiences it may be desirable to limit audience participation to the asking of questions, thus prohibiting the making of comments by members of the audience on the grounds that comments tend to develop into speeches and thus limit the chances for participation by a large number of persons. The chairman can announce this sort of limitation to an audience, but must enforce it with discretion. Members of the audience will often wish to precede a question with an explanatory remark, and unless such remarks are excessively long, the chairman might well decide to be permissive toward them.

2. If it seems desirable to reduce the possibility of disruptive or inflammatory statements in a forum on a very controversial issue, or if really strict control over the use of audience time is sought, the chairman may wish to limit audience participation to the stating of questions which have been written out and handed in in advance. This procedure gives the chairman maximum control over proceedings, but tends to limit sharply the sense of participation by members of the audience.

3. If comments and questions from the floor are permitted on a controversial topic, some ill-tempered or unpleasant remarks may be forthcoming. The chairman has an opportunity in such cases to seek to model, in his own behavior, more desirable attitudes toward discussion. He can restate inflammatory comments in milder language. He can attempt, with unfailing good humor, to restate the purpose of the meeting and to focus attention on the importance of hearing, and *evaluating calmly,* all points of view.

Buzz sessions The search for techniques of discussion which will achieve active participation by all members of large groups has found one answer in the "buzz session." In this form a discussion is opened with some stimulus event (a short talk, film, film strip, symposium, case study, and so on) or with the posing of a problem to the large group, followed by a short forum period. The large group is then broken into smaller groups, each of which continues discussion on a specific question arising out of the stimulus event. These small groups proceed as a conference-type round table for a designated period of time. At the end of this period a spokesman for each small group reports to the total group a summary of the thinking in his small group.

The "buzz session" form is sometimes known as the "Phillips 66 technique." Its use was developed by Professor J. D. Phillips, who customarily divided the larger groups into smaller groups of six persons, and alloted six minutes for the small group discussions; hence the "66" designation.

Some important considerations in using the buzz session form are as follows:

1. The posing of a very specific question—usually a single aspect of a larger problem—is necessary if the smaller groups are to make any headway in a brief (five-to-ten minute) period of discussion.

Of course, the small groups can be given a somewhat more extended period for discussion, in which case the issue being dealt with can be extended accordingly.

2. Preorientation of the leaders of small groups is a desirable step in planning buzz session meetings. If the leaders have had discussion training and are familiar with the handling of buzz session groups, the progress of the meeting will be facilitated.

3. Reports from the small groups should be kept brief. Unless leaders are carefully instructed in this point it often develops that the report from a six-minute buzz session will occupy as much time as the discussion itself.

Advantages and limitations   There is evidence that people who participate actively in a meeting are: (1) more interested in the products of the meeting, (2) more friendly with other members of the group, and therefore (3) more apt to effect changes in their own behavior when the meeting deals with a problem involving such changes. To the extent that these generalizations apply, the buzz session form may be a way of increasing the productivity of learning activity by large groups dealing with complex problems. The form has been used by teachers seeking active participation by the members of large classes; by home economists and social workers in adult education meetings; by large groups looking for "action plans" for their club or committee.

There are obvious limitations to the amount of critical analysis of a serious issue which can take place in five or ten minutes. Hence, we may conclude that the buzz session form has limited utility in promoting the use of dialectical skills in the rigorous analysis of a serious problem.

Miscellaneous forms using witnesses and cross-examination

There are public discussion situations in which it seems desirable to make use of the service of "expert" witnesses, or to mix discussion among experts and lay people. We shall suggest three forms which have been productive, while recognizing that endless variations are possible.

The "open hearing" with cross-examination OF experts   A student-gathering considering proposals for improving higher education organized one meeting in which three experts were invited to make brief presentations to the entire group of students concerning their views on higher education. Following each presentation by an expert, a panel of four students, selected by the larger group, cross-examined the expert as to the testimony which he had presented. The questioners sought clarification of certain ideas expressed, elaboration of argument at points at which the experts disagreed, and elaboration of argument at points at which the experts seemed to disagree with other points of view held by or known to the students.

The "open hearing" with cross-examination BY experts   An obvious variation of the cross-examination of expert testimony is the use of experts to criticize, through cross-examination procedures, the speeches of lay observers. At another meeting on higher education a group of four students made short speeches suggesting specific changes in instruction and curriculum at the college which they attended. Two experts—a teacher and an administrator—cross-examined each student as to his testimony, and provision was made for counter cross-examination by the students and for summaries by both students and experts. The somewhat complex form follows:

Problem: What specific changes in instruction and curriculum should be made at *X* University?

    I.   The chairman introduces the participants.

    II.   The first student speaks for five minutes, presenting his suggestion.

   III.   The experts cross-examine this student for three minutes.

   IV.   The three remaining students follow, and are cross-examined according to the same time schedule.

    V.   There is a ten-minute period during which students question the experts.

   VI.   One of the experts makes a ten-minute summary, stating his analysis of the various proposals which had been made.

  VII.   Each of the students takes three minutes to summarize the meeting as he sees it.

 VIII.   A short forum follows, with questions from the audience.

The mock trial   To some extent, open hearings using experts and cross-examination techniques are borrowed from the familiar use of such hearings by legislative committees. A form borrowed from the court of law provides a reasonably dramatic way of presenting what is substantially a debate over a specific *charge* or *proposition*. The mock trial makes use of the familiar courtroom figures—the judge, the prosecuting attorney, the defense attorney, and one or more witnesses for each side of the case. A sample of such a form follows:

The charge: Big-time intercollegiate athletics are subverting the purposes of higher education.

I.   The judge opens the meeting by introducing the charge (one minute).

II. The prosecuting attorney overviews the case of the prosecution (two minutes).

III. The defense attorney overviews the defense against the charge (two minutes).

IV. The prosecution witness is sworn in and is examined by the prosecuting attorney; he presents his evidence in response to questions (six minutes).

V.   The prosecution witness is cross-examined by the defense attorney (three minutes).

VI. The defense witness is sworn in and is examined by the defense attorney (six minutes).

VII. The defense witness is cross-examined by the prosecuting attorney (three minutes).

VIII. The defense attorney summarizes his case (five minutes).

IX. The prosecuting attorney summarizes his case (five minutes).

X.   The judge polls the audience for a decision, the audience serving as jury

The mock trial may serve as the stimulus event for a forum period, during which questions and comments are taken by the judge from the members of the audience.

Advantages and limitations   We have already referred to the desirability of arranging certain meetings in which expert and lay testimony are mixed. The careful study of the form for such meetings can regulate the use of expert testimony so that the experts do not dominate or inhibit the free expression of opinion and information by lay persons.

Students working with cross-examination as a technique for eliciting and criticizing testimony will soon learn that this method, while very slow in the production of information and opinion, also tends to lead toward a real clarification of a limited area of testimony and comprehensive interpretation of that testimony. In other words, cross-examination meetings tend not to get very far very fast, but they do tend to produce vigorous, critical examination of statements which are made.

The mock trial is frequently extremely interesting, with dramatic moments of conflict when a cross-examination question reveals an inconsistency, or the judge must rule on an objection of one of the attorneys. However, thorough preparation by the teams of attorney and witness is needed if the trial is to be a fast-moving stimulus event.

Discussion over an extended period of time

The forms we have considered thus far have all served the purposes of discussion groups with relatively short meeting periods. There are many situations in which discussion groups meet over an extended period of time in the consideration of a single problem. So-called "workshops" often take this form. We have workshops on foreign policy, higher education, juvenile problems, mental health, highway construction, safety and safety education, and so on as an ever-present aspect of American life.

Extended discussion may use any and all of the forms previously described, but they often follow an over-all structure for deliberation suggested by the steps in problem analysis given in Chapter III of this text. Thus a workshop on American relations with India might extend over a period of four meetings, with the focus of each meeting described as follows:

Meeting   I: Definition of the problem and consideration of its history.

Meeting II: Exploration of the problem: Causes and results; criteria for judging an adequate solution; attitudes of various interest groups.

Meeting III: Suggested courses of action and critical examination of each course.

Meeting IV: Further examination of courses of action, with an effort to define areas of agreement and disagreement as they now exist in the workshop group.

THE PRODUCTS OF DISCUSSION

Thoughtful readers examining the variety of discussion forms described in this chapter might well wonder what has happened to the rigorous definition given to discussion in Chapter I of this text. Where, for example, is the opportunity for critical conversation among thinking people if the discussion follows the rigid procedural controls of the mock trial? What happens to rigorous examination of ideas in buzz session groups limited to a six-minute discussion period? Is a public gathering in which questions must be written out and handed to the chairman really a discussion at all?

As we see it, the basic form for discussion activity is the round-table discussion, participated in by people who have had extensive opportunity to become reflective and informed concerning the problem at hand. However, the large variety of forms listed all represent adaptations to the great variety of situations in which people meet together for purposes of participating in the process of problem solving. All of the forms partake to some extent, in some particulars, of the form of discourse known as discussion. All forms are derived from the recognition and statement of a problem. All seek some sort of sharing of information and opinion, and all involve some sort of interaction among a group of participants.

After each discussion experience, participants and observers ought to raise the question as to the actual products of the discussion which has taken place.

Has the discussion served merely to stimulate interest in a problem? Short discussion, in which the opportunity for sharing information and opinion are limited, can often claim no greater product.

Has the discussion served merely to "warm up" the climate of opinion within which a group can continue to meet together in the consideration of mutual problems?

Has the discussion served to provide for efficient gathering and sharing of a large body of information relevant to some problem area? Cooperative investigations may result in this product, without leading a group into the examination of policy questions which derive from the information gathered.

If the discussion purports to be moving a group toward decisions as to solutions of real problems, what is the actual merit of the positions reached by the group members at the conclusion of their discussion period?

COMMITTEE REPORTS AS AN EVIDENCE OF THE PRODUCT OF DISCUSSION

Students of discussion sometimes become so interested in the discussion process, or so impressed by the joys of discussion for its own sake, that they stop short of asking about the intrinsic worth of the decision made or the conclusions reached by members of discussion groups. We have witnessed groups concluding a discussion period with a great show of harmony, with the feeling expressed that useful and worth-while decisions have been reached, even though these decisions would not stand the cold light of scrutiny by anyone remotely expert in the implications of the problem under consideration.

We would suggest that many discussion groups might profit from the effort to present the results of their deliberations in the form of a "committee report"—a brief written statement presenting the major conclusions reached by the group, and its major recommendations for action together with the key evidence, or lines of reasoning, upon which these proposals rest. The production of such reports tends to force discussion groups into more realistic consideration of the thesis that their deliberations, if worth-while, ought to result in statements worthy of serious consideration by persons outside their own group. Such reports also provide for a dimension for the criticism of discussion activity purely in terms of its intellectual products—a dimension often overlooked in the friendly social atmosphere developed by discussion groups.

CHAPTER XII

Interpersonal Relations in Discussion

A discussion brings people into a limited, specific relationship with one another. This relationship is ideally defined as a search for useful answers to a commonly experienced problem. But inevitably, the social interaction set up by discussion calls into action all of the personal needs and personality patterns of the several discussants. The thoughtful observer of any discussion group must necessarily be impressed by the extent to which the behavior of various discussants is related not simply to the task which the group may have set for itself, but more profoundly to the whole of the problem faced by each member of the group as he searches for ways of relating himself as a person to the various people with whom he is brought into interaction.

We observe, perhaps with irritation, the monumental assurance of a discussant who dismisses the remarks of an associate with the phrase, "You're entirely wrong," or, "No one looking at the evidence could make that statement." But behind this behavior we may sense an insecure ego, seeking to bolster itself through assertions of intellectual superiority. We observe how often a discussant's behavior seems to stem from a personal need for recognition or attention rather than from the problem identified by the entire group. We see appearing, however faintly, the jagged lines which separate persons with racial, religious, economic, and social differences; the lines which separate young from old, the man of experience from the theoretician, the practical man of affairs from the moralist, Cassandra from Pollyanna, and Mr. Peepers from Milton Berle. And in all of this play of personality against and with personality, we see the extent to which discussion is involved not simply in the search for understanding *about* a problem, but also in greater or lesser degree with the search for understanding *among* people.

THE STUDENT OF DISCUSSION AS A STUDENT OF HUMAN RELATIONS

Inescapably, the student of discussion becomes a student of human relations. And the activity of discussion involves an on-going quest by individual seeking to achieve a mutually acceptable or satisfying relationship to one another. In this chapter we shall explore some of the attitudes and actions on the part of discussants which help to generate a satisfactory climate of personal relations in the discussion group. The basic concept with which we shall work is that of *understanding.* It is our point of view that as people come to understand one another better, there is a tendency for them to build closer, warmer relationships with one another; a tendency for suspicions and antagonisms to be abated, and for feelings of mutual confidence and respect to grow. We are aware that this point of view has its limitations. It is entirely possible that under some circumstances, the more people come to understand one another, the less liking they will have for each other. But this is not, we think, a general tendency; moreover, the development of understanding as a basis for improved human relationships is a primary mechanism open to the discussion group, and is therefore the logical subject of study for the student of discussion.

UNDERSTANDING IS POSSIBLE ONLY IF DISCUSSANTS PRESENT REAL ATTITUDES AND BELIEFS

To some degree, adults practice concealment of their real attitudes, motives, and feelings in their conversations with other adults. These habits of concealment may rise out of real, often bitter, experiences. Most of us have undergone experiences in which the revelation of our real attitude or feeling resulted in some punishing consequence, perhaps because we revealed our lack of conformity to the supposed "normal" attitude of the group with which we were associated. Most of us can easily construct situations in which an individual might find it prudent or expedient to conceal his real purposes or feelings. Habits of concealment, therefore, are both widespread and inevitable among adults who converse with one another. Unfortunately, in many persons, these habits have become so extensive, so deep-seated, so generally practiced, that these persons lose the capacity to be open, or honest, or spontaneous in any communicative situation. We identify this generalized loss of spontaneity or openness as one of the real barriers to good interpersonal relations in discussion groups.

As an illustration let us suppose that in a discussion of the problem of population growth in the Orient, a suggestion is made that the government of this nation ought to promote an extensive program of education for birth control in so-called overpopulated regions of the world. Let us suppose further that John, one of the discussants, opposes this proposal on the basis of religious conviction, but that he has formed the habit of concealing his religious belief as the basis for his positions on certain questions of policy. John may now proceed to offer innumerable technical objections to the proposed policy of birth control, even though these objections do not represent the real source of his conviction, and even though in some cases he may use specious evidence or reasoning simply to gain time as he searches for some supposedly "safe" justification for his viewpoint. Other members of the group, confronted with John's adamant opposition and not understanding its basis, may work diligently, but with increasing frustration and irritation, toward a hoped-for integration or compromise. A real "meeting of the minds"—a real understanding which would permit the discussants to respect and appreciate each other's position, even though those positions might not be reconcilable—becomes impossible in the face of John's practice of concealment.

Concealment and conflicts in group loyalties

The illustration above presents a case of concealment based upon a discussant's habitual avoidance of any revelation of his religious beliefs, even though those beliefs are important to him. With slight variation it would also illustrate concealment which results from the conflicts of loyalties which occur among discussants who are simultaneously members of a variety of groups in our society. For example, a discussant might find himself simultaneously a member of an active, partisan political group and a member of a group organized for nonpartisan consideration of problems of political action. In discussions with members of the latter group, he might choose to represent himself as "nonpartisan" in attitude, even while secretly nourishing the ambition to operate as a partisan persuader—a real representative of his political affiliation. Thus, he might be ostensibly a member of a group discussing the problem, "What should be the policy of the United States toward the Nationalist Chinese Government on Formosa?" But in reality he would have set for himself the problem, "How can I justify a Republican [or Democratic] interpretation of American foreign policy toward the Nationalist Government of China?" The "hidden agenda" [1] of this discussant serves to subvert the intellectual processes of the group by introducing concealed purposes into the meeting. And in the absence of real openness of attitude and motive, it will contribute to the development of interpersonal conflicts.

The management of concealment

We have emphasized that habits of concealment are in part a personal problem, for each person participating in discussion. The discussant who consciously seeks more open communication of his own motives, attitudes, and feelings is likely to experience almost immediate reward for such action in terms of improved interpersonal relations. He may also find himself a contributor to a much more productive discussion.

Openness encourages a like response

One of the fortunate aspects of the problem of concealment is that any one member of a discussion group may initiate action toward more open, spontaneous communication without waiting for a commitment from his fellow discussants. Initiative in this area is almost certain to evoke response in kind. Persons most fearful of revealing themselves are stimulated by the warmth with which they will ordinarily respond to an open attitude on the part of a fellow discussant, and, thus encouraged, they may join in this new action pattern.

[1] For an extended discussion of "hidden agendas," see Braden and Brandenberg, *Oral Decision Making*, New York, Harper & Brothers, 1955, pp. 271–277.

Protecting unorthodox opinion

The importance of real opinions to productive discussion places a special responsibility on the discussion group to protect unorthodox opinion. Most persons are motivated strongly toward conformity, and in any discussion situation the greatest threat to open communication rests in the conscious or unconscious arrogance assumed by majority opinion toward the unorthodox or minority viewpoint. A real belief in the method of group discussion carries with it a particular responsibility on the part of each discussant to see to it that discussants who are open and honest are not punished for their contributions. We shall have more to say on this later in this chapter.

Reconstructing discussions in search of concealment

It is useful for discussants to analyze concealment in discussions in which they sense the existence of problems which were never fully brought into view. Recorded discussions offer special opportunity for such reconstruction. A group asking itself the question, "Did all of the attitudes and purposes which operated to shape this discussion come to light during the course of the discussion?" may find many useful insights appearing from members of the group. We have heard discussants identify the motivation for certain of their comments in terms of hostility aroused by a preceding remark, or in terms of a belief that "all good discussions end with everybody agreeing with everybody else," or "because I generally go along with the majority," and so on. Groups usually discover that the concealment practiced by members was needless and frequently destructive to both pleasure and productivity in the discussion.

UNDERSTANDING IS POSSIBLE ONLY IF DISCUSSANTS IDENTIFY THE OBJECT OF THEIR CRITICISM

Thoughtful students may sense a certain tension between two criteria for good discussion which have been considered in this text. We have insisted that good discussion involves *criticism*—that the uncritical acceptance of opinion, evidence, or reasoning destroys the intellectual purpose to be served by discussion. We have also insisted that discussants must be open in expressions of opinion or feeling, and that this openness is possible only in an atmosphere in which the unorthodox or minority view is protected rather than punished. Yet criticism in itself can be punishing, and the intellectual rigor of a good discussion may in itself be a deterrent to openness on the part of the less intellectually secure members of the group.

We do not think that this tension can be resolved in all instances. But we do think that certain habits or procedures concerning criticism may serve to lessen the shock of criticism upon some discussants and at the same time to increase the worth of the criticism. These habits we shall identify as: (1) the habit of seeking understanding prior to criticism and (2) the habit of dissociating ideas from the persons who state those ideas.

The habit of seeking understanding prior to criticism

Most of us have little sympathy for the deer hunter who fires his rifle prior to full identification of the object at which he is aiming. Too many cows, hunters, and game wardens have fallen victim to such "trigger-happy" marksmen to make them honored members of our society. Yet the "trigger-happy" arguer seems almost endemic to discussion groups. He is impatient in listening, reluctant to ask questions, skilled at restating a co-worker's idea to place it in the worst possible light, and adept at finding fault with the target which his own imagination has created. The solution to this problem is as obvious in theory as it is difficult in application. It requires simply this: that the discussant must, as a matter of habit, seek full understanding of the opinion and reasoning of another discussant prior to any effort at criticism. This understanding must encompass as a minimum a search for the meanings which the contributor *wishes* to be assigned to his language. It should go beyond this into a real search for an understanding of the implicit frame of reference, or point of view, from which the contributor offered his comment. There is only one way in which a discussant can get this full understanding, and that is through the conscious effort to get into the "other person's shoes"—to *feel with* the person who has made a statement, with enough sympathy to be able to sense fully the meaning of his statement.[2] Certain procedural routines may help in gain-

[2] For a longer discussion of the importance of this search for full understanding, see Carl R. Rogers, "Communication: Its Blocking and Its Facilitation," in *Language, Meaning and Maturity,* ed. by S. I. Hayakawa, New York, Harper & Brothers, 1954, pp. 53–60.

ing this understanding. One is the practice of asking for amplification or illustration of an argument which seems potentially to be an object of criticism. The limitations a contributor wishes to place on a general assertion may be better discovered, ofttimes, through his illustrations than through the implications of an assertion itself. A second practice is that of restating an argument and asking if the restatement is an accurate representation of that which the original contributor wished to imply. To be successful both questions and restatements must be animated by a genuine wish for understanding, a curiosity to know precisely what it is that has been said.

Two important consequences of this search for understanding prior to criticism may be noted. First, as discussants achieve real understanding of one another, they may find that many of the grounds for criticism or disagreement have disappeared. Contributors may often criticize the limitations of their own comments, thus relieving others of that task, and the merely verbal aspects of disagreement sometimes disappear altogether. Second, even though a real disagreement may be laid bare by the establishment of understanding, the search for understanding enables discussants to relate themselves to one another in a cooperative venture prior to the elaboration of their differences. Thus, a contributor experiences first the appreciation and sympathy of fellow discussants, and disagreements may then be considered among friends rather than in an atmosphere of hostility.

The habit of dissociating ideas and persons

We do not believe it possible for persons completely to dissociate their egos from the opinions which they hold. We believe, however, that many discussants carry ego involvement to the point that they regard any attack upon their opinions or reasoning as an attack upon their persons. The discussant with a lively sense of the limitations of human reasoning and of the limitations of proof as applied to matters of probability, will be able to accept and appreciate the fact that an attack on one of his opinions need not be construed as an attack on the integrity of his person. Discussants will find it helpful to observe the great variety of responses manifested by persons whose opinions have been challenged. They will find it helpful to compare their own responses with those of other members of their group, and to become alert to any evidence indicating that they have become habitually resentful of any challenge to their opinions.

The responsibility for achieving a reasonable dissociation of idea and persons rests equally with the criticized and the critic. There is a small but important difference implied in the statements, "I disagree with you" and "I disagree with the opinion you have presented." The latter statement does not readily extend itself into an imputation of bad faith or unworthy motivation on the part of the author of the statement which is under consideration.

UNDERSTANDING IS FACILITATED BY PERSONS WHO USE SPEECH WITH DISCRIMINATION

We define speech broadly as including the systems of audible symbols (language and voice) and visible symbols (expression, posture, gesture) by which men communicate. In discussion, as in the bulk of human relations, our speech is our way of behaving toward one another. Thus, in a very real sense, all misunderstanding in discussion is either intentionally or accidentally the product of an act of speech. If we assume that the avoidance of misunderstanding is a requirement of good discussion, then the presence of such misunderstanding in discussion represents a failure in speech.

Incongruities of voice, action, and language

One of the common sources of misunderstanding among discussants is the habitual use of incongruous or conflicting systems of symbols by members of the discussion group. This would be illustrated by the discussant who thanks a co-worker for his contribution in accents which suggest extreme disapproval of that contribution; or the questioner who asks, "Is that what you mean?" with a show of verbal objectivity which is accompanied by the vocal suggestion that "if it is, you are certainly foolish"; or the discussant whose verbal responses indicate close attention, but who assumes postures and attitudes suggesting preoccupation or repose; or the discussant who relates an "exciting incident" in sleep-provoking tones and attitudes. Of course, discussants may on occasion use incongruity as a source of satirical or humorous effect. But the student of discussion needs to identify and study habitual limitations in his vocal or physical behavior which affect the clarity of his communication. We refer here particularly to (1) items of behavior such as querulous or aggressive intonation which do not promote the sought-for warmth of good discussion; (2) the important summary presented with insufficient force or articulatory clarity; (3) the habitual avoidance of physical directness in talking with fellow discussants; and (4) the monotonous voice. The student of discussion needs to work toward modification of these poor speech habits if he is to make maximum contributions to understanding.

Misinterpretation of the meanings of words

Lack of care in the use and interpretation of language seems almost the rule among discussants we have observed. We think that much of this lack of care or accuracy proceeds from a fundamental misunderstanding among many discussants of the nature and limitations of language, and for this reason we devote a chapter of this text to an examination of language in discussion. We call attention here to two common sources of linguistic confusion, noting, however, that these examples could be extended.

Discussants frequently confuse statements of fact with statements which are inferential in character Such confusions rise from the tendency of discussants to place into discourse not the data on which their conclusions or interpretations rest, but the interpretations themselves. This process is often accompanied by the implicit feeling that the interpretations have now become "facts" and are to be treated as such. Thus a discussant says, "As we all know, it is an established fact that dictatorships are more efficient than democracies," and proceeds to develop a line of thought based upon this so-called fact. Examination of the asserted "fact" shows it not to be a fact at all. At best, it is an interpretation of some possible facts about the performance of governments which have been identified as dictatorships, and governments called democracies. At worst, the discussant may be merely repeating an assertion which he has heard, and for which he accepted the misleading label of fact. He is thus passing along a very loose inference, without any substantial *fact* from which to infer. Discussants who accept this inference as fact become contributors to the linguistic crime which is under way. In this particular instance the gravity of the crime is magnified by the probability that any real examination of the evidence of how democracies and dictatorships have performed would show that the so-called "fact" is an exceedingly poor inference.

The tendency to confuse fact and inference is magnified by our tendency to take into the language certain value terms—i.e., terms in which we assert that certain facts are good or bad, on the assumption that these value judgments are facts. As an example, take the term "underprivileged." Would you assert that it is a "fact that certain people in America are underprivileged"? This statement would not be a surprising one, since it is a commonly accepted assertion. But closer examination reveals that the term "underprivileged" is a value judgment. It asserts that certain groups have less income, eat different sorts of food, live in different sorts of dwellings, and so on—*and* that this situation is regrettable. As we see it, there is no reason that a discussion group should not accept the inference that certain groups are "underprivileged" as a basis for further discussion, but we would insist that only discussants who understand that this statement is an inference, and not a fact, can hope to escape misunderstanding.

Discussants assume that a value "assigned" to a word with many possible values is understood alike by speaker and listener This tendency may be productive of both "verbal" disputes—quarrels in which the discussants are in agreement about everything except the value each is assigning to a particular term—and pseudo-agreement or agreement in which discussants are assigning a different value to a term, but are able to agree because they assume the assignments to be of the same value. As an illustration of a "verbal" dispute, let us take a situation in which a discussant asserts that "a society cannot be both capitalist and Christian at the same time." Anyone making an assertion so sweeping in nature, and involving two concepts so multivalued as Christianity and capitalism, probably deserves to be involved in a dispute of some sort. But the dispute can become prolonged and unproductive if it is undertaken by a listener who assumes that both he and the originator of the assertion have a common understanding of the particular values being assigned to these terms. Thus, the discussant might have meant by "capitalism" the phenomena peculiar to the working of the factory system in England and America in the early part of the nineteenth century, while assuming that the present system of economic organization in America cannot be called "capitalism." His adversary may assign to "capitalism" the value of the present system of economic organization in America, and assume that this is the system that is being criticized as "un-Christian." Pseudo-agreement, while less immediately unpleasant than "verbal" controversy, may be equally destructive of interpersonal feelings in the long run. Post-World War II discussions between Russia and the United States were livened, but not aided, by the fact that representatives of these two powers were able to agree at certain conferences that the governments of Eastern European nations should be "democratic." The agreement was a "pseudo" one, based on different values assigned to the word "democratic" by these two nations. One may question the good faith of the Communist nation in assigning its own meaning to the term "democratic," but certainly the pseudo-agreement thus fostered did not serve the cause of international understanding, at least from the viewpoint of the United States.

It is apparent that discussants who practice the procedures designed to seek understanding before criticism would relieve themselves, for the most part, of the burdens of verbal dispute and pseudo-agreement.

UNDERSTANDING IS FACILITATED AMONG DISCUSSANTS COMMITTED TO A PLURALISTIC SOCIETY

By a pluralistic society we mean one in which persons of different races, religions, political persuasions, and social and cultural backgrounds undertake to work together. Many societies have achieved stability because of homogeneity in the racial, religious, and cultural backgrounds of their members. But such societies have always warred with one another and have often made life uncomfortable or impossible for minority groups within their area.

In a real sense the United States has been, and continues to be, an experiment in the possibility that a stable and productive society can be organized by persons who differ in important ways, but who share fundamental respect for one another and therefore a willingness to work together. We sometimes refer to this fundamental respect among persons who differ as "tolerance." But "tolerance" seems a sort of negative virtue, and beyond tolerance lies the possibility of a positive belief that variety is not merely a necessary, though unfortunate, condition of society. Rather, it is a desirable and valuable condition. It is this positive belief in the worth of variety which we identify as an essential to good interpersonal relations and hence to good discussion.

A commitment to the values of variety permits the discussant not merely to acknowledge opinions different from his own, but to welcome these differences of opinion as potentially creative in the task of problem solving. It permits the discussant to regard the search for understanding of differences as not merely a necessary burden in discussion groups, but as a stimulating and rewarding enterprise.

There are many ways in which students may examine the contributions of variety to a creative and productive society, and thereby seek increased appreciation of its positive value. The study of history, sociology, anthropology, and political science, for example, may produce insights which relate to the development of appreciation of the contributions of racial, religious, cultural, and political variety to the development of civilization. There is, however, one way of studying the contributions of variety to the discussion group which is particularly important to the student of discussion, since this study best proceeds by an examination of the workings of discussion groups themselves. This is the study of "role-organized" behavior within the discussion group.

Role variations contribute to the productivity of discussions

In one sense good discussants share a common role. That is to say, if they study the function of discussion, they seek, while discussing, to adapt their behavior to the behavior patterns which we associate with good discussion. In this sense the whole significance of a course in discussion may be viewed as that of seeking to help persons learn the requirements of the role of the discussant. It goes without saying that the thoughtful discussant fills a role somewhat different from that of the debater or the public speaker and, of course, a role much more specific and definable than that of a job-holder, or parent, or citizen. But within the general role of discussant, there are a number of more specific roles which may be perceived as contributing to the tasks of a discussion group. Thus, we may find one discussant—perhaps the group leader—who serves the group as an "expediter." He is the person who reminds the group of the extent of the task before it and of the possible time limitations faced. He searches for and discovers ways of increasing the speed with which the group moves, helping other members to avoid irrelevant excursions, to identify and eliminate time-consuming disagreements over the values to be assigned to particular terms, and so on. This discussant may well share many other tasks in the discussion, but, as contrasted with his fellow discussants, he may be observed to make a more significant contribution in this one direction. Other roles, important to the over-all task of the group, may be similarly identified and named. We may observe one person especially adept at the task of conciliation; another at the task of criticizing the relationship between evidence and inference; another at organizing the over-all pattern of an agenda, and so forth. Students of discussion will find it profitable to examine discussion groups to see how variout discussants fill one or more of the following roles needed by the productive discussion group:

The expediter	The conciliator
The information-seeker	The information-giver
The critic	The organizer
The clarifier	

This list is suggested as a useful starting point for observation, but it may be amplified or reconstructed by any thorough student of discussion. We would emphasize the value of such examination of role behavior within the discussion group as twofold. First, it is productive of some insight into the differences between creative and disintegrative roles in discussion, and second, it permits observation of the contributions of variety to the discussion group. That is, it reveals how different persons, with different personality potentialities, different backgrounds, and different skills, may each make a significant contribution to the group productivity. In this sense it reveals the way in which group problem-solving activity may be more rewarding than the effort of even the most talented individual, precisely because of the variety present in the behavior of discussants.

Nonproductive roles

This is not to say that certain discussants may not play parts which are destructive to the purposes of discussion groups. Such persons, we believe, exhibit a sort of generalized alienation from the over-all role of discussant. Having failed to make a commitment to the purposes and needs of the discussion group, they may use the discussion situation to play social roles expressive of their own personality needs. Thus we observe the *recognition-seeker,* for whom all social situations are simply an avenue to fulfill his own need for attention. We observe the *dominator,* who is less interested in the product of a discussion than in the matter of seeing to it that he determines this product; the *pessimist,* who seeks to use each social situation to demonstrate the futility of any sort of action, and who has a real, if subconscious, desire to see the group fail. And so on.[3] Students may find it productive to observe persons who seem to be primarily exhibiting such individual social roles in the discussion group. They may, in this way, gain insight into conflicts between the role of discussant and some of the personality needs which they carry into the discussion situation.

In general, however, we are more impressed with the contributions of variety to the discussion group than with the frequency with which destructive roles obstruct its progress. We would caution against the tendency to label any role as destructive without careful consideration of the possibility that it brings a form of creative variety into the discussion group.

Role-playing in discussion training

Our preceding discussion has suggested that the behavior of persons who are "being themselves" can often be profitably studied by considering the behavior of the individual as organized in terms of the role he sees himself as taking in a given social situation. Another possibility for studying interpersonal behavior consists of the creation of situations in which discussants are asked deliberately to "play" or assume a given role in a discussion. Such "role-playing" may serve a number of purposes. It may be a way of providing discussants with the opportunity to practice roles which they would like to fill, but in which they feel inadequate in real discussion situations. It permits objectification of types of individual roles which may be destructive

[3] An interesting set of titles for a variety of personal roles is to be found in McBurney and Hance, *Discussion in Human Affairs,* New York, Harper & Brothers, 1950, pp. 260–265. They label these roles as Mr. Pontifical, Mr. Parlor Pink, Mr. Sweetness and Light, Mr. Doom, Mr. Smug, Mr. Milquetoast, Mr. Blue Nose, Mr. Smart Aleck, Mr. Prima Donna, Mr. Lunatic Fringe, Mr. Tycoon, Mr. Politico, and Mr. Suspicious.

to group discussions, and may be productive of insight on the part of observers concerning their own behavior. It permits the creation of difficult leadership problems, and opportunity for the practice of leadership skills. And it may serve as the starting point for a discussion based upon a problem illustrated in a "role-playing" scene. We list here examples of three types of situations which have been used as the basis for role-playing activities.

A problem in the handling of behavior   Teachers studying the handling of classroom discipline problems prepare two "role-playing" conferences between a teacher and a problem student. In each case the teacher is asked to represent an attitude toward the handling of discipline problems. Thus, in one case the teacher plays the role of stern disciplinarian, determined to apply as much force as his position permits in an effort to control the behavior of the student. In the second case the teacher is to epitomize sweetness and light consistent with an absolute belief that "there are no problem children." Facts of the case are given both the person playing the part of the problem student and the person playing the part of the teacher, but instructions as to the role to be played by each individual are given to that person alone. Thus, the conference as enacted is essentially spontaneous. The scenes are "cut" as soon as they seem to have lost spontaneity or development.

A problem-reduction exercise   Two students are asked to participate in an informal "argument" on some controversial issue, with a third student serving as moderator. The disputants are instructed to engage in a variety of "destructive" behavior, such as name-calling, misinterpreting the other person's statement as a basis for attacking it, confusing fact and inference, and the like. They are instructed, however, to be responsive to efforts by the moderator which show that the moderator sees, and is attempting to reduce, the sources of their conflict. The moderator is not informed as to the instructions given the disputants. He knows only that they will start with a disagreement which he should try to help them to "reduce" to its smallest possible proportions.

Regular discussion with "roles" superimposed   A group plans a round-table discussion and prepares its agenda. Each member is then asked to assume and maintain a consistent role expressive of some personality need or pattern. Members are not informed as to the roles to be played by fellow discussants. Observers follow the discussion, seeking to identify the roles being played as preparation for discussing the impact of such individual roles on discussion.

A SUMMARY

We have in this chapter explored some of the attitudes and actions which are particularly relevant to achievement of satisfactory personal relationships in discussion groups. We have considered a variety of ways in which individuals and groups can seek to develop the insights and types of behavior which will improve the climate within which people carry on discussion. In closing we wish to affirm our belief, already stated in Part I of this text, that discussion is best viewed as a specific, purposive enterprise in problem solving; that the skills most basic to this enterprise are dialectical; and that persons who believe in the possibility of critical thinking and have some skills in its exercise have secured the most stable possible foundation for building good interpersonal relations in discussion groups.

CHAPTER XIII

Language in Discussion

We cannot avoid a penalty for using verbal symbols as a means of communication in discussion. If mental telepathy were possible, group problem solving would be much more efficient. Spoken language must be classed as a "low fidelity" mechanism for transmitting intelligence, due to obstacles that are analogous to the bad atmospheric conditions and defective receivers that reduce the precision of radio communication. Many language difficulties can be understood and partially overcome. This chapter is to acquaint you with key concepts in language theory which not only are important to the kind of communicating we do in discussion, but are problems which we as individual leaders and participants can do something about. Study of language cannot but increase discussion skills.

WHAT IS COMMUNICATION?

Communication includes both purposive and accidental transmission of meanings from one mind to another. The "accidental" part suggests that the communicator is not always in control, that his intent does not necessarily circumscribe the impressions perceived by the person to whom he sends his message. Herein lies the distortion that costs time and reduces achievement in discussion. Let us begin our search for the sources of "accidental" meanings by an example of a simple experiment to determine the nature of responses to a single verbal stimulus.

A hundred people are seated in a small auditorium and supplied with pencils and paper. They have no knowledge of what is to come.

Without warning, as soon as the room has become completely quiet, a single word comes over a loudspeaker. It is clearly enunciated by a male voice, the loudness is such that all hear clearly, and the word is in isolation, preceded and followed by silence. The single spoken word is "huge." After a moment the same voice requests the listeners to write down whatever came into their minds when they heard the single spoken word. Will all these people reproduce the dictionary definition of "huge" on their papers? Most assuredly not.

Many will write down names of objects which in a particular context have the characteristic of "hugeness." These range from "Empire State Building" to "twenty-seven inch screen" and "magnification of the electron microscope." Some will note ideas or problems in which "hugeness" plays a minor part, such as the dilemma of getting married or going to college that may come to one person's mind because to him it is a "huge" problem. Some will write synonyms, "large," "great," "extensive," "enormous." To some the voice may be a stimulus that overshadows the word, and responses might be "tall person," "handsome man," "radio announcer," and so on, or "pleasant voice," "loud sound," "conversational quality." The means of communication might most impress the technically minded, who might write "loudspeaker" or "P. A. system." The reader can add to the list of probable or possible responses. In addition there is certain to be a small number of listeners whose minds, as far as they can tell, respond not at all to the stimulus. They have no conscious response to write and will either think up something that seems to be appropriate, which is not a reaction to the stimulus but to the request, or they will write "nothing" or leave the paper blank.

At the moment the word "huge" was reproduced in the little auditorium, *what did it mean?* You can see that, at least in terms of recorded responses, there is no simple or uniform answer.

WHAT IS MEANING?

We expect our reader at this point to be conscious of two kinds of meaning, (1) that which is assumed to be "in" the symbol (e.g., the dictionary definition) and (2) the interpretation supplied by the particular mind upon which the symbol is impressed. To label and refine these concepts:

Logical denotative meaning: to the logician the denotation of a term (a unit of communication) is the sum total of things to which that term can be applied.

Pragmatic denotative meaning: to the pragmatic-minded student of communication the denotation of a term (a unit of communication) is the sum total of the things it calls to mind (considered responses) *for a particular person perceiving it*.

To the logician a term "stands for" or denotes a finite number of things, whether any individual receptor knows it or not. To the pragmatist a term has meaning only when it hits somebody, and for that person the nature of the meaning is determined by his perception. The pragmatist says that while dictionary-makers and logicians may arbitrarily allocate meanings to words, the vitally important view for the practical communicator is the recognition that individuals respond differently to the same term.

Suppose an American with no knowledge of Japanese is walking down a street in Tokyo and comes to a sign which bears the Japanese word for "danger." The sign *means* danger, says the logician. But another view is that the sign actually *means* something else to the American who walks into the open manhole.

Let us say, then, that the context of "meaning" is the process of communication. Because communication is a stimulus-response phenomenon, the purpose of any communication study is to enable the student better to understand responses of individuals to units of communication. Focusing attention upon meanings intrinsic to symbols but which may or may not be perceived is at best a roundabout means of studying stimulus-response patterns. Hence, let us accept this assumption: For purposes of communication study, *meaning is perception*. If someone alleges a certain meaning to be present in a unit of oral communication and, for example, an auditor A behaves as though it were not there, for him it is not there. Further, if a communicator sends the word "square" to auditor B and auditor B represents what he has received as "circle," then for auditor B the meaning of "square" is "circle." "Meaning is perception" is a pragmatic assumption based upon the belief that the meaning which counts is the one which gets through to the nervous system of the person to whom it is communicated.

This chapter will treat language concepts with this assumption, that the meanings talked about are perceptual phenomena. If reference is made to meanings intrinsic to a symbol, attention will be called to the exception. We thus hope to avoid one of the pitfalls of language communication, the popular assumption that because a unit of language has within it a particular content it is certain to produce uniform or identical responses from the different people who receive it.

Carl R. Rogers summarizes neatly the significance of this approach to the meaning of language in the process of communication by saying:

"Often, of course, the perception has a high degree of correspondence with reality, but it is important to recognize that it is the perception, not the reality, which is crucial in determining behavior." [1]

THE NOTION OF ABSTRACTING

Accepting the proposition that "meaning is perception" explains the observation that certain words produce more uniform responses from different people than do others. We say that "specific" terms are more easily understood, that "general" terms are unclear and possess multiple meanings. "The fine for speeding is high" and "the fine for exceeding a speed of thirty miles per hour on lower Hennepin Avenue is $25" illustrate abstract and specific statements. Quite naturally the first sentence produces a great variety of response because "speeding" and "high" are relative terms with no absolutes supplied to help us interpret them. The second sentence has concrete elements that mean almost the same thing *to individuals with driving experience in Minneapolis.* Hence, we can expect among such an audience less varied responses but still some variation in details supplied in its interpretation. Thus, within a particular set of circumstances and for people with homogeneous language background, we can generalize about word meaning as though the meaning were in the word. That it is really *not* in the word, however, becomes obvious when we remember that a generalization about meaning does not apply to all groups of people everywhere.

We can classify units of language on a scale of uniformity of response to them within a population. A continuum that reaches from a category of language symbols that produce no uniformity of response (e.g., unfamiliar foreign words) to symbols which produce

[1] D. C. McClelland, ed., *Studies in Motivation,* New York, copyright 1955 by Appleton-Century-Crofts, Inc., p. 86.

a predominantly uniform response (e.g., writing on a blackboard before the local PTA "$2 + 2 = \underline{}$") is useful in comparing the "communicative specificity" of verbal stimuli. It is frequently desirable to narrow the range of probable responses to a symbol communicated, thus reducing probable error in its interpretation. Where there is a choice of alternative symbolic patterns, we should be able to select for our particular audience the one least likely to precipitate contradictory or conflicting meanings. The reward of "specificity control" is higher fidelity of communication.

A much used visual device for dramatizing differences in range of probable responses to verbal symbols is the "ladder of abstraction." This is a vertical continuum with "high level" terms being those which bring about many varying responses, i.e., mean all things to all people. These are "abstract" in the sense that the central core of details transmitted to all receivers of the message is small, and many details are "abstracted" or left out. At lower levels on the ladder more details of meaning are capable of being faithfully reproduced in the minds of listeners and readers and the language is said to be less abstract. At the bottom of the ladder of abstraction are symbols which for the group concerned trigger the most uniform responses, in other words, communicate the most details and produce the fewest accessory differing ideas.

We can illustrate the abstraction continuum by using names of things familiar to English-speaking people on the North American continent, thus creating a large group with the required language homogeneity. Suppose we want to communicate to a listener or reader the characteristics of a certain object and are limited to a language unit, a noun, and a few modifiers. We might use any of the levels of this continuum:

Levels of Abstraction

(1) Personal possession
(2) Household article
(3) Piece of furniture
(4) Chair
(5) Upholstered chair
(6) Plastic-covered, upholstered chair
(7) Plastic-covered, upholstered rocking chair
(8) Red plastic-covered, upholstered rocking chair

As was the case with the word "huge" in isolation, "personal possession" by itself is very nearly meaningless (produces no uniformity of response or very little). But as we proceed down the ladder it is quite obvious that similarities in responses of different English-speaking people will increase. By the time you get to levels (7) and (8) it is likely that a group of a dozen random-selected people would be able to reproduce images called to mind by the symbolic unit that have many elements of identity. Communication of the concept from one mind to another becomes measurably more accurate than it is at higher levels.

The moral of this example is clear. If you are interested in increasing the accuracy of your communication via language, you will attempt to use the lowest practical level of abstraction for the purpose to be served.

One important function served by the application of this principle is definition. When someone says, "What do you mean by a 'private utility'?" and you answer, "I mean a corporation," you have moved *up* the ladder by supplying as a substitute for the original term, which produced too many different responses, another which is even more abstract. Then, if you define "corporation" as a "business enterprise" you will have left your listener in the clouds that always surround the top of the abstraction ladder. Moving *down* the ladder is a better way to help him get his feet on the ground. If you reply to his question, "By 'private utility' in this instance I mean a business organization, independent of government, that supplies electric power to large groups of people," you will have increased the common ground of understanding.

Many definition difficulties in discussion—and elsewhere—come from lack of knowledge that definitions are most "meaningful" when they proceed to lower levels of abstraction. Dictionary definitions are usually too abstract for the very good reason that they must embrace the major possible interpretations. Communication is usually best served by a definition which is deliberately specialized in the context of the topic being discussed. "Stipulated" arbitrarily narrow definitions which apply only to one discussion are often helpful in avoiding possible misunderstandings. Early in Chapter V there is an example of an agreement to so limit a term. We suggest that the student reread the section of Chapter V that deals with definition in light of the theory of the ladder of abstraction.

AMBIGUITY AND VAGUENESS

The future of democratic government and personal freedom is dependent upon accurate verbal communication. If citizens are to sift the wheat from the chaff, and through their votes choose the wiser of available alternatives, then they must understand not only the issues but the evidence and reasoning that support them. They can gain requisite knowledge and understanding only by listening to and reading words. It is in the interest of good government to labor for increasing precision of verbal communication. We regret that powerful forces are systematically and perceptibly reducing the power of words to communicate by forcing familiar symbols up the ladder of abstraction, thus increasing the amounts of ambiguity and vagueness abroad in the land.

Reproduced by permission © 1954 The New Yorker Magazine, Inc.

"Our problem, as I see it, is to get across to the American public, that fattening foods are non-fattening."

The accompanying *New Yorker* cartoon calls to mind the efforts of advertisers to blunt the meanings of familiar terms. In tremendously extensive efforts through mass media of communication, the nation is blanketed with language opposites put together as though they were compatible. The purpose is to appeal to as many people as possible, even those who are seeking totally different product characteristics. A mattress manufacturer claims "yielding firmness," an automobile provides "economical luxury," a headline in a soap powder ad shouts, "Cleans dishes without washing," and in the small print below supplies the reservation, "If stubborn dirt clings, a flick of the dishcloth will remove it."

Advertisers train us in the habit of forgetting that relative terms must refer to some fixed standard to have any meaning. "This cigarette has *fewer* irritants," "*X* car has *more* power," "*Low*-priced *high* fidelity," "*Best* TV picture," "Termed *outstanding* by *those who know*," "*Medical authorities* agree that *Y* cigarette is *easy* on the throat," and so on. What do these *underlined* terms mean? Precious little without the suppressed context. These are further examples of a purposeful interest in dulling critical faculties of the general public to the point that vagueness and ambiguity will go unquestioned. A nationally known coffee company radio campaign requests people to send "key strips and jar labels" and in return the company offers to buy Christmas gifts for orphans. *The ratio of strips and labels to gifts is not specified.* Yet each year thousands of strips and labels are sent in by trusting, unquestioning listeners. Vagueness in the promotional material would make it possible for the company to set any ratio it chooses, e.g., ten thousand labels per ten-cent gift.

How serious are the effects of advertising on other purposeful communication? We don't know because we can't measure the extent to which the American public understands the abuses of language that occur in advertising. The present writers believe that damage has been done and that our national language is shifting toward the "group-think" ultimate in which those who control the mass media are able to make any word mean anything to the general citizenry. "Yielding firmness"; "vigorous, yet mild"; "progressive conservatism"; "smaller on the outside, bigger on the inside"—these are phrases not far removed from "war is peace" and "freedom is slavery."

Certainly words that once served high purposes have been prostituted to common ends. Whether the values they represented have eroded with the blunting of their symbols is a topic for speculation. Childs and Cater think language and ideals are so interwoven that in all probability we have lost important cultural and moral ground:

"The advertiser must accept some responsibility for the confusion of values that is a symptom of our time of troubles. Words such as character, faith, belief, integrity are used to commend the quality of beer and pills. If you buy a certain car you are exalted, exultant, magnificently at ease." [2]

A second major area of contribution to increasing vagueness and ambiguity of language is political rhetoric. What is Radio Moscow after when it uses the terms "democracy," "socialism," and "communism" interchangeably? It is intentionally creating an ambiguity, a series of definite meanings for the same term. A word is ambiguous when it is difficult to decide among alternative and appropriate meanings in a particular context. Certainly the Radio Moscow ambiguity would make it unlikely that a regular listener could preserve his original distinctive concepts of democracy, socialism, and communism.

The Secretary of Agriculture says: "Controls are bad. The American farmer deserves freedom to produce what he thinks he should. But production must be tailored to consumption. We must rely on voluntary cooperation with the suggestions made by government to produce a balanced supply of needed farm commodities."

The crusading Senator summarizes his accusation of a prominent official: "He is either a member of the Communist party, or a fellow traveler, or sympathetic to socialistic ideas." The serious charge in the first alternative somehow carries over to the largely meaningless third and most likely possibility. Similarly, a related example of *vagueness* is the label, "Fifth Amendment Communist." Vagueness is word confusion resulting from inability to "pin down" a term to a particular definite meaning. A vague word is so "fuzzy around the edges" that it produces primarily an acceptance-rejection type of response but no clear image, and it selects no definite referent. The idea that exercise of the constitutional privilege of refusing to testify

---

[2] M. W. Childs and D. Cater, *Ethics in a Business Society*, New York, Harper & Brothers, copyright 1954 by the National Council of the Churches of Christ in the U.S.A., pp. 168–169.

under prescribed circumstances is linked to communism is sufficiently confusing to guarantee that most people will accept the idea that something bad has occurred without attempting to analyze it. Thus, vagueness serves its purpose.

Language resembling the above samples is certain to find its way into discussion. Part of the answer to the problem it presents is found in persistent insistence upon resorting to lower levels of abstraction. After all, vagueness and ambiguity increase the range of probable responses to the point where too many are likely, so by definition the level of abstraction is too high for the purpose to be served. Other tools for dealing with vague and ambiguous language are the abilities to distinguish between emotive and report functions of verbal symbols and to translate "loaded" (emotive) language patterns into equivalent neutral report language.

EMOTIVE AND REPORT LANGUAGE

Occasionally, an appealing idea invades even academic disciplines. Often it turns out to be unusually helpful because it fires the imagination. It catches the fancy of students and teachers alike, and because they enjoy the idea they remember and apply it. The process of "loading" or "slanting" language is such a concept. Few people who learn about "loaded" words cease to be conscious of the differences between emotive and report language, and as a result their responses to language become more discriminating.

The communicator has a choice in many instances, the option to slant or not to slant a message. He can transmit information with little influence on its interpretation, or he can, by choice of words and even by inflections, transmit the same conceptual content and with it *a predisposition to accept or reject it.* That characteristic of a communication which adds to the ideational content something which prejudices response pro or con is termed *slanting.* It is accomplished by using "loaded" or "emotive" language, words or combinations of words which because of their associations tend to produce favorable or unfavorable attitudes not intrinsic to the message transmitted.

Slanting of terms representing institutions or objects is prevalent and easy. A governmental money-lending agency may be called a "Federal Land Bank" or a "New Deal Mortgage Bureau." One's business associates may be termed "colleagues" or "henchmen." Campaigning via mass media is described in headlines as "Politicos educate the American voter" or "Money buys American elections." Youth entering military service are "guardians of our democratic heritage" or "cannon-fodder to be." In the political campaign of 1954 the period of Democratic administration that ended in 1952 was characterized as either "twenty years of progress" or "twenty years of treason."

These are obvious and heavy-handed, though common, examples of slanting. But it is not safe to assume that the person who speaks or writes even heavily "loaded" language is *intentionally* slanting his message. Frequently a firm personal conviction makes use of impartial words difficult. Hence, many a person has felt unjustly accused when the biased nature of his word choice has been pointed out. The personal involvement causing us to think in loaded language makes it very unlikely that we will speak in report language about matters that are vital to us.

Calculated or accidental use of emotive language occurs with all degrees of subtlety. Some of the most effective attempts to prejudice listeners and readers have been almost imperceptible. Consistent, conservative slanting has a cumulative effect. Here are bits of language selected from an editorial that reviewed, with apparent impartiality, recent campaign efforts of a state governor and a rival candidate. Singly, any item is not particularly derogatory or flattering. In the aggregate the slanting effort may well have some effect.

Describing pretender's campaign:	Describing incumbent's campaign:
(1) Hired staff of speech writers.	(1) The Governor's aides.
(2) Barnstorming activities.	(2) Series of personal appearances.
(3) Applied the vote-getting pressures.	(3) Sponsored by leading citizens.
(4) Charged that the state highway department paid too much for manhole covers.	(4) Quiet appreciation, modest but sincere applause.
(5) Centered attention upon the need for protecting wildlife.	(5) Spoke of the accomplishments of his administration.
	(6) Promised better school support and lowering of income taxes.

We are tempted to generalize that slanting is a universal characteristic of communication from a prejudiced source, and that most of us are prejudiced with respect to issues concerning us. At any rate, dealing with emotive language is an ever-present problem. People carrying on discussion must systematically discount these protective colorations of advocacy. One of the best means of surmounting the obstacle of slanting is the deliberate and conscious conversion of the suspect unit of communication into "report language," words which are accurate but neutral. This will be facilitated by understanding of connotation and denotation and of signal and symbol response.

SIGNAL AND SYMBOL RESPONSE

Further understanding of the "meaning is perception" assumption comes from an examination of the nature of responses people make to language. Perception involves awareness, and awareness takes time. Any mental interpretation of a stimulus, necessary to perception (the formation of meaning), is therefore delayed and contrasts with another sort of response, that which is *immediate* or as nearly so as the communication of nervous impulses permits. This immediate response of which we are unaware but which influences later meaning is termed *signal* response. The delayed reaction that adds meaning to the stimulus already received is called *symbol* response.

Signal response resembles the simple conditioned reflex. A soldier trained to respond to the shouted command, "Duck!" may act as quickly and unthinkingly as his dog responds to "Down, Shep!" But not only actions may be triggered by verbal stimuli. Word associations may result in one word causing the hearer to think of another, as "Communist-traitor" or "Communist-friend." Or the repeated association of a word or phrase with a certain type of context may result in its having a built-in, generalized, acceptance-rejection response for certain people. The word "propaganda" is a good example of a term that, because of dominant use in the context of something that is against our interests, has come to have a negative signal response effect upon many people. For contemporary Americans a term with a similar but positive built-in signal bias is the word "democracy." The signal responses to "democracy" and "propaganda" amount to predispositions to accept or reject what is conveyed by or associated with them. These predispositions are called *attitudes*.

So signal responses can be actions, verbal symbols, or attitudes, or any two, or all three. Important to remember is that signal response is immediate and unthinking, hence dependent upon previous learning or conditioning that makes automatic reaction possible. In communication of information and ideas, as in discussion, signal responses are usually attitudes. These predispositions of favor or disfavor color the perception (meaning) that develops as the individual interprets (thinks about) the verbal stimulus.

Individual differences in signal response to the same unit of language are great. What to one person is a stimulus to set off a strong rejection response to another individual may produce a weak negative reaction and to a third a strong predisposition to favor or accept the associated content. During a political campaign among voters in the Upper Midwest such a term was "New Deal." Weak signal-response attitudes may interfere little with reasoned development of a concept, but strong attitudes may influence perception and associated thinking to a point that these become stereotyped and ritualistic. The conservative Republican may find it difficult to think critically about or even comprehend a proposal that is labeled "socialistic," and a liberal Democrat may experience the same sort of inhibiting stricture with respect to suggested labor legislation that is characterized as "Old Guard Republican." A third person who has learned no reflexive patterns to these stimuli may attend only to the informative content of the labels and experience a signal response to either so weak that it can be ignored.

One type of signal response is both immediate and delayed. It resembles posthypnotic suggestion. Language slanting may arouse an attitude which becomes latent or hibernates until the event with which it is associated comes along. Then the attitude again becomes active. For example, an emotional denunciation of an individual may arouse an antagonism that subsides, but which becomes active and intense upon meeting that person a week later.

While signal response cannot be said to be perception or meaning, it contributes significantly to that meaning, as the above examples demonstrate. Certainly the communicator needs to be conscious of the signal responses he may accidentally or purposefully precipitate and of the resultant distortions of the ideas and information he is attempting to transmit.

Symbol response is, in part, the meaning we are talking about when we say, "Meaning is perception." The person receiving the stimulus fits it into a context, whereupon it acquires significance. The nature of the pattern supplied by the receiver is completely dependent upon his experiences and the elements these have in common with the stimulus. So we listen with the sounds we have heard and see with the sights we have seen. We recognize in the stimulus only that which is familiar. It is little wonder that a group of people from different places find it difficult to communicate for long without some misunderstanding.

Symbol response continues beyond the first awareness of a unit of communication. It includes testing and modification of the first conscious reactions, and sometimes elaborate processes of comparison and critical evaluation follow in chain sequence. All delayed, thoughtful mental manipulations that result from reception of a unit of language are included in its symbol response.

One important part of responding symbolically to language is becoming conscious of one's own signal-response tendencies and compensating for them. The mature discussant knows his areas of pronounced bias, and when operating within them is on guard. He looks for language that might predetermine his thinking through its slanting, and takes the precaution of translating slanted items into report language. He tries to accomplish a similar objective for the group by converting heated or otherwise colored contributions into neutral terms more likely to produce thoughtful response. He always finds that lower levels of abstraction are less productive of signal reactions. When terms are vague and abstract, we tend to substitute acceptance-rejection response for understanding.

For discussion, indeed for all thoughtful communication, we want as much symbol response and as little signal response as possible. The desirable characteristics of discussion are those which facilitate critical thinking on the problem confronting the group. Signal responses limit thinking and predispose its outcome. The objective of limiting the incidence and severity of signal responses may be approached through understanding of the associated element in language, connotative content.

CONNOTATION AND DENOTATION

Early in this chapter we used the terms "logical denotative meaning" and "pragmatic denotative meaning" to designate what a word might represent conventionally (e.g., its dictionary meaning) and what might occur in the mind of one person hearing it in a specific context. We decided that our discussion of language would be in terms of pragmatic denotation of communication units. The communicator is interested in *responses*, which are momentary and in the minds of particular people. This behavorial approach to the interactions of people communicating, forces us to select one of the several interpretations of the denotation-connotation duality, one not based upon the logician's assumption that meaning is in the word.

For our purposes let us consider denotation to be whatever there is in a message that *directly* influences the choice of a context to give it meaning in the mind of the communicatee. This excludes the slanting factors of loaded language which arouse latent attitudes and thus indirectly influence meaningful interpretation. The denotation of a message produces symbol response. We can speak of "denotative content" of a communication including any of its characteristic features which for a particular audience at a certain time seem likely to evoke delayed and thoughtful responses.

Whatever we can find in a message (and the message includes its delivery and surroundings) that will precipitate immediate and unthoughtful rejection or acceptance tendencies in a certain audience at a particular time we can label *connotation* or *connotative content*. Or, more simply, connotation refers to those characteristics of a message which will produce signal responses in an audience under specified circumstances.

Any description of message content as connotation or denotation is a guess, because to some degree people are unpredictable. Where meaning is considered to be perceptual, we must recognize, in fact emphasize, that its estimation is subject to error. We say typically, "These elements in our communication are connotative, for, under specified circumstances, they will probably trigger signal responses."

Why do we need the terms "connotation" and "denotation" when they bear such close relationships to signal and symbol responses? Because they are useful in thinking and talking about language. We can analyze discussion of a controversial issue most directly if we refer to connotative and denotative elements in the discourse itself rather than make explicit the signal and symbol response patterns that are implied. As long as these terms are understood to be related to particular responses of specific people, it is convenient and helpful to be able to talk about connotation and denotation in a communication.

PRACTICAL APPLICATION OF LANGUAGE CONCEPTS TO DISCUSSION

The language habits of our times are incredibly imprecise. Discussion, because of its resemblance to conversation, suffers more from a transfer of sloppy language practices than does any other mode of purposeful communication. The prevalent idea that fluent discussion is good discussion places emphasis upon flow and volume rather than upon clarity. Finally, the personal aspects of utterance are an ever-present threat to accuracy. Individual interests may sometimes be served by concealment through ambiguity, high level abstractions, oversimplifications, and deliberate or accidental arousal of intense signal response.

Two-valued orientation is a frequent result of the forces of imprecision. This is a bipolar generalization, usually in the form of an "either-or" proposition. "So it amounts to this: Either Anderson is re-elected or we have a depression." "Well, can we agree that the counseling system should either be drastically changed or thrown out entirely?" "It seems that Jones did some cheating on that examination. Let's take a vote to clear him or expel him." "Coach Lilligren has to play Smith in the fullback position or we'll lose the next game." "He's either a friend of the USSR or a friend of the U. S. A. There are no degrees of loyalty."

The incisiveness of the method makes a two-valued approach attractive. What was confused in a multitude of pros and cons seems suddenly, for the first time, to stand out clearly. No longer does it seem that there is much to say on both or several sides. Decision is facilitated. Our only criticism of the method is that it may not lead to the best decision.

We suggest that the discussant resist the connotative elements in a bipolar approach and substitute for it the more realistic *multi-valued orientation*. After you think about it for a while you may decide that there are more ways of improving the team than just by playing Smith, that one person might well be "more loyal" than another, that some possibility other than expulsion or exoneration might better help Jones to benefit from his ethical lapse of cheating on one exam, and so on. Two-valued orientations can be neutralized only by stubborn people who insist that we scrutinize other possibilities as well as the pair suggested.

The discussant who uses language conservatively often makes a signal response to another admittedly deplorable habit of our times; that of overstating everything for effect, evidence and opinions alike. The speaker resorts to hyperbole to jolt his listeners into an appreciation of the importance of his contribution. We generally accord each other the privilege of exaggeration. As one college debater complained, "We don't mind exaggeration, but on this point our opponents have overexaggerated"! What the maker of striking statements overlooks is the fact that his listener is habituated to excessive claims. The twentieth century American has reached at least the point of apathy when confronted with a sweeping generalization.

A study of motion picture advertising will increase your appreciation of verbal extravagances. In the fall of 1954 a new "production" was publicized with these phrases:

". . . the most eagerly awaited motion picture of our time."

". . . the best picture ever made."

". . . furnishes a standard for measuring the greatness of all motion pictures from this time onward."

The concensus of the reviewers who commented upon the above-described motion picture was: "Mediocre."

Possibly understatement is more thought-provoking than overstatement. In discussion exaggerated claims blur the picture and it takes time and effort to turn attention back to the details. The remedy for overgeneralization as well as its preventative is reverse motion down the ladder of abstraction. The attempt to substantiate an overstated conclusion with specifics will cut it down to size.

Unnecessary complexities deserve mention in our collection of language habits that handicap discussion. Part of our surplus complexity is accidental, a product of talking around a point while we try to think through it. Some may be purposeful in an effort to confuse the issue. But most unneeded language complications probably stem from a deep-laid conviction that worth-while ideas must be difficult to grasp. All of us share this to varying degrees. Hence we all tend sometimes to use technical terms, long words, and elaborate sentence constructions when a simpler approach would be adequate and much clearer. Recent "plain talk" crusades have opposed these tendencies to be elaborate in language, and many business organizations have attempted to eliminate unnecessary and stereotyped "businessese" from their communications.

Scholars are noted for habitual, unnecessary complexity in their writings. Here are three sentences that illustrate the introduction of extraneous language elements which, at least to the present writers, seem to cloud the central point made by each statement.

"The rhetoric of catastrophe weakens with the general semantic palsy of our time." [3]

"The United States has gained nothing by the Greek intervention, but has merely avoided an important loss." [4]

"Part, at least, of the communists' strength is a reflex of the fact that non-communists think them to be so strong." [5]

The above sentences are quite typical of language complexities in discussion. How does one penetrate the fog to locate the core of meaning? Probably by rewording statements like these in simple report language, although gems like the first may defy all rewording attempts. Fortunately, discussion is frequently aided by the participant who says with appropriate tact, "Let me see if I get what you mean . . . ," and who then interprets the elaborate contribution in simpler report language.

Often, however, the contributor of elaborate confusion must be called upon to help in clarification. This is facilitated by the asking of skillful questions. One question in particular is almost magical in its wide usefulness and therapeutic effect: "Will you give an example to show what you mean?" An answer is almost certain to lower the abstraction level and simplify the difficult language. Remember this question and experiment with it. Almost everyone who does is pleased to find how it helps people to understand each other.

---

[3] James Burnham, *The Coming Defeat of Communism,* New York, The John Day Co., Inc., copyright 1950 by James Burnham, p. 1.

[4] *Ibid.,* pp. 30, 31.

[5] *Ibid.,* p. 107.

Figurative language, a special sort of complexity, may add color to discussion, but often the color is paid for in loss of precision. Verbal figures are always at least once removed from "life facts." They produce the illusion of understanding, but when you ask the question, "What, exactly, has become clear?" you will see how little figures of speech contribute to problem solving. Figurative terms are slanted more often than not. Report language translations may be necessary for figurative contributions if their ideational content is to be used by a group.

The reader will find many other applications of the few language concepts we have discussed in this chapter. We trust that he will be always conscious of the difficulties inherent in the process of converting thoughts into words, sending the words into another's nervous system, and decoding the words there. Discussion will increase in efficiency if participants and leader understand and systematically attempt to surmount these obstacles.

PART FOUR

The Criteria of Discussion

CHAPTER XIV

Listening to Discussion:
Description and Evaluation

The student of discussion will make progress only if his practice of discussion is accompanied by a deepening insight into the nature of discussion activity. Hence, thoughtful listening and observing are essential to the development of discussion skills.

But listening to a complex discussion can often turn into an exercise in frustration or futility. Two or more students observe the same discussion, and are asked to make a generalized judgment of its worth. One says, "It was a good discussion." His neighbor asserts, "It was a poor discussion." Are we to conclude that one of the two observers was inattentive, or lacking in perceptiveness, or obstinate? Probably not. The greater likelihood is that we have had a demonstration of the influence of selective attention upon the reactions of two observers to the same complex act. The one observer, for example, may have been pleased with the harmony, good temper, and energy of the conversation. The other observer may have been displeased with what seemed to him a lack of productivity in the problem at hand. Or any one of a half-hundred legitimate standards for judging the discussion may have been operating to direct the attention of various observers, causing them to *see* and *react to* certain events, and to *fail to notice* or *ignore* other events.

We conclude that thoughtful students of discussion ought to spend time in discovering and experimenting with a *variety* of ways of looking at discussion. By systematically changing his *frame of reference*, the student may develop insight into the nature of this

213

complex interpersonal relationship. This chapter will explore systematically a number of different ways of describing and appraising discussions. Combined with the check lists in Chapters XV and XVI, the materials in this chapter will provide enough different ways of looking at discussion to serve most evaluation needs in the discussion course.[1]

BASIC CATEGORIES OF EVALUATIVE ACTIVITY

In Chapter III we recommended that students listening to an initial discussion react to this experience by describing aspects of the discussion to which they reacted favorably and aspects to which they reacted unfavorably. Such "basic" reactions by listeners serve to give discussants a sense of the range of factors which enter into the rating of a discussion.

As discussion experience continues, it is desirable that listeners sharpen the focus of their observations. An initial step emphasizes the distinction between the "description" of a discussion and its appraisal. It is our view that maximum insight into the nature of discussion will be attained by listeners who become skilled in *description* of a discussion, and who consider *description* as an essential prerequisite to useful appraisals. The student who exercises freely his capacity to "like" or "dislike" discussions may well fall short of ever realizing exactly what it was that he "liked" or "disliked"— and thus lack insight into the significance or insignificance of the particular aspects of a discussion to which he is reacting. Productive listening in the discussion class, therefore, should stress accurate descriptions of the events which take place.

DISCUSSION PROCESSES AND DISCUSSION PRODUCTS

A second discrimination which will be useful in listening to discussion is that of distinguishing the discussion *process* from the discussion *product*. Observations of discussion *process* encompass the extent and flow of participation, the balance and precision of reporting, criticism, and climate-making contributions of members of the

---

[1] An excellent compilation of evaluative procedures may be found in Chapter 16 of *Oral Decision Making* by Waldo W. Braden and Ernest Brandenberg, New York, Harper & Brothers, 1954. We suggest this chapter for students seeking additional materials on evaluation.

group, and the nature and efficiency of leadership exercised during the discussion. However, the final test of the adequacy of discussion comes from an examination of the productivity of the discussion. The *products* of a discussion may be observed in terms of the understandings arrived at by the members of the discussion group. These understandings may be considered the primary product, but a second category of discussion product is to be found by examining the effect of the discussion upon the members of the group. Do the group members report having gained information and insight as a result of discussion? Do they feel discussion to be productive, and feel inclined, therefore, to further discussion? Yet a third aspect of discussion product is the effect of a public discussion on its audience.

Ways of describing discussions

The simplest observation to be made of a discussion involves recording the frequency of contributions by members of the group.

PARTICIPATION RECORD			
Discussant	0–10 min.	10–20 min.	20–30 min.
1. John	///	THH ///	THH /
2. Helen	THH /	THH //	/
3. Henry	//	THH ///	THH ////
4. Jim	/	////	/
5. Betty	//	//	/

Remarks:

‾‾‾‾‾‾‾‾‾‾‾
Observer

Fig. 1

Information gathered in a participation record is of some use to the discussants themselves, and may form the basis for certain interpretations of the nature of good discussion. It is obvious that there is no one-to-one relationship between the worth of a discussion and the extent to which participation is widely shared by various members of the group. On the other hand, students studying discussion are often surprised to find out how little or how much they are participating overtly in discussion groups, and may find this information useful in regulating their subsequent behavior. Moreover, observers may find that certain subjective judgments made of a discussion will be confirmed or modified by a record of participation. Thus, a judgment that the discussion was *dominated* by one or two persons, either throughout or at certain stages, may be supported, modified, or interpreted through reference to a participation record.

Charting participation flow

It is often significant to find out not merely who contributes to a discussion, but also to chart the directions along which contributions flow, i.e., to observe who talks to whom during the discussion. A simple flow chart will serve to record not only frequency of contributions, but also direction of flow.

This chart seems a little complicated at first glance, but once understood it is easy enough to use it in recording data. Beneath the name of each participant is a box in which may be tabulated the comments which are addressed to the entire group. Then there are lines connecting each participant with each of the other participants. Comments which are primarily directed to a single person, such as answers to questions, specifically directed questions, or comments on the statements of a preceding speaker, will be recorded as a mark on the "line of direction" at a point near the speaker.

Such a chart may reveal a number of interesting types of data. For example, it may show that in a particular discussion, most of the contributions were responses to questions posed by the leader, with very little interaction among the members of the group. It may show that little or no effort was made to draw a reticent member of the group into the discussion, or, if effort was made, it will show by whom. It may show that the discussion was dominated by frequent interchanges between two members of the group. It will show whether the leader tended to present his questions to members of the group as a whole or directed them to particular individuals.

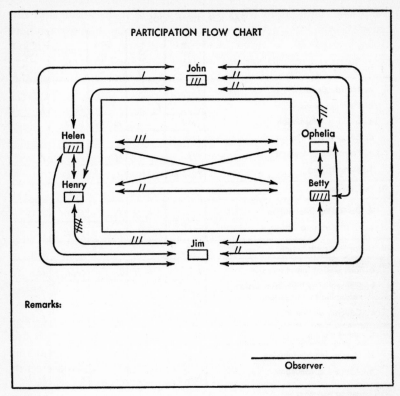

Fig. 2

Classifying the function of contributions: coded observations

Observers of discussions will not be long content merely to record the fact that a discussant made a contribution. A more informative level of observation can be reached when the observer employs a code to describe the nature or primary function of each contribution. Thus, in place of a mark (1), the observer records a letter (*a* or *b* or *c* and so on) which stands for a statement classifying the functioning of the contribution.

A simple code for classifying contributions could take the following form:

(a) Reporting: gives information, or clarifies information.
(b) Dialectical: interprets information; generalizes from infor-

	John	Helen	Betty	Henry	Ophelia
I. Discussion regulation					
a. Introductions	/				
b. Defining terms		/		/	/
c. Seeking information	卌		//		
d. Seeking clarification	//				
e. Proposing procedure	///		//		/
f. Summarizing	卌 /				
II. Reporting					
a. Presenting information		卌 //	/	///	/
b. Clarifying information		//	//	卌	
III. Dialectical contribution					
a. Interpreting information	/	卌 //	/	卌	//
b. Generalizing from information; reasoning to conclusions		////	卌	/	/
c. Criticism of reasoning	//	卌	卌 /	/	/
IV. Climate-building					
a. Humor; tension-relaxing	卌				
b. Approving comment	卌 /		//	/	////
V. Disrupting comment					
a. Irrelevancy					卌
b. Recognition-seeking		/		/	
c. Personal hostility		///			
VI. Unclassified	//				

Remarks:

_____
Observer

Fig. 3

218

mation; criticizes argument or interpretation; presents solutions.

(c) Discussion regulation: introduces members, asks questions, summarizes, rephrases.

(d) Climate-building: humor, expressions of approval.

(e) Irrelevancy.

(f) Unclassified.

Note that this code contains only six classifications. Since one comment may serve more than one function, more than one code letter may be recorded for a single contribution. Observers should be encouraged to make liberal use of the "catch-all" classification (f), so that the contributions receiving other numbers will have been definitely identified. It is also well to have several observers check their records against one another after using the code. If observers cannot apply the code with some degree of reliability, it indicates that the study group needs further study of examples of the application of these classifications to particular types of comments.

Coding contributions on a participation chart may reveal the progress of a discussion in terms of the major functions which are stressed at various stages. It may reveal that the early part of a discussion is dominated by discussion regulation (c), climate-building (d), and reporting of information (a); while the latter part of the discussion is dominated by dialectical activity (b). Such coding will also indicate which members of the group contribute most in terms of information and which members make other sorts of contributions.

Using more elaborate codes   If the code for classifying contributions contains more than five or six categories, the observer will find it easier to use a chart on which both the code and the names of the participants are listed:

Analysis of the data from a participation code chart will tend to indicate the different parts played by different discussants in the development of the discussion. If it is desired to use both an elaborate code, as in Fig. 3, and to show the time distribution of the various coded contributions, this can be done by assigning code letters to the participants and recording these "name letters" in the appropriate time division, thus:

Students may be interested in developing classification systems

PARTICIPATION CODE			
I. Discussion Regulation	**0–15 min.**	**15–30 min.**	**30–45 min.**
a. Introductions	j		
b. Defining terms	h, o, a	h, o	
c. Seeking information	$j, j, j, j, h\, h$	r, r, r, a, a	j, j, j, a
d. Seeking clarification	j, j	j, j, j, j	j, j, o, o, o, h
etc.			
John—(j) Helen—(h) James—(a) Henry—(r) Ophelia—(o)			

Fig. 4

of their own after a few experiences in observation. We would emphasize that there is no inevitable "rightness" about any system of classification, and developing a system which will be productive of useful data is an excellent way of gaining insight into the nature of discussion activity. Please keep in mind that good discussion involves investigative activity (reporting), dialectical activity (reasoning, criticism), and human-relations activity (climate-building), plus those activities we have classified as "discussion regulation." Within this general framework, a variety of systems for coding contributions can be developed.

Another approach to the observation of discussion seeks to classify the behavior of the various discussants according to the role or roles being played by each. As we have already indicated, the participation codes give helpful data on roles being played. At a slightly more impressionistic level of observation, however, one can seek to perceive the total behavior of a discussant as it fulfills the requirements of one or more roles. The observer does not attempt to classify each comment of each discussant, but rather classifies the over-all function of each discussant. Students attempting this sort of observation will find it helpful to make up their own list of roles to be identified, giving each an appropriate title. The list used in the following chart is an example.

ROLE IDENTIFICATION CHART			
Discussant	0-20 min.	20-40 min.	40-60 min.
Helen	O	E	E
Jim	I T	I T	T
Henry	F	F	F

Role code:

   O-Organizer (introduces, summarizes, keeps agenda in mind, etc.)
   I-Information source
   E-Expediter (looks for ways to keep discussion moving)
   C-Climate-maker (harmonizes, approves, builds rapport)
   T-Thinker (seeks valid generalizations, proposes solutions, criticisms, argument)
   F-Follower (takes attitudes, opinions from others)
   D-Disturber (seeks recognition, blocks reasonable progress, is disaffected)
   L-Listener
   U-Unclassified

Remarks:

_____
                                                Observer

Fig. 5

The reader is reminded at this point that the evaluative methods illustrated thus far are all ways of recording "descriptive" observations of discussions. To be sure, the observer "describing" a discussion will seldom wish to content himself with description. He will ordinarily have made, or want to make, certain judgments about how good or poor a discussion is, or about the value or lack of value in the work of certain discussants. For this reason we have indicated that a space for remarks is a desirable part of any observation chart. It gives the observer a chance to interpret some of the data he has gathered, and to make value judgments on the discussion as a whole. A second order of evaluative activity, however, is that which invites the observer to concentrate his attention on appraising the worth of the activity he observes rather than on analysis of the nature of the activity.

Semistructured appraisals of discussions

By semistructured appraisals, we mean appraisals in which the observer comments freely on the worth of a discussion as he sees it, using only a few "division lines" to increase the focus of his ap-

---

APPRAISAL FORM: DISCUSSION PROCESS

I	Planning:	Had the discussants arrived at a useful agenda for considering their problem? Did they follow the plan?
II	Information:	Was sufficient relevant information presented to provide an intelligent basis for discussion?
III	Reasoning:	Was information carefully interpreted? Did the group arrive at generalizations justified by their information? Were generalizations subjected to critical examination and analysis? Were points of agreement and disagreement clearly identified?
IV	Climate:	Were attitudes of cooperativeness and permissiveness generally evident? Were minority views given an adequate consideration? Was widespread participation encouraged?

Observer

Fig. 6

I	Clarity of conclusions:	Were the points of agreement and disagreement clearly defined by the end of the discussion?
II	Value of conclusions:	Were the solutions or other interpretative statements on which consensus was achieved practical and desirable? Were they adequate in terms of the problem proposed?
III	Value of "shared information":	Were participants and observers "better informed on the problem at hand" as a result of the discussion?
IV	Effect on the group:	Was the discussion personally satisfying to the discussants? Would they be likely to seek further discussion with the members of this group?

Observer

Fig. 7

praisals. We have already indicated that one useful "division line" is that which separates the appraisal of the discussion *process* from its *product*. Following this major division we can indicate certain simple forms for appraising the worth of a discussion.

Measuring the impact of public discussions: the shift-of-opinion ballot

One obvious product of a public discussion is the effect of that discussion upon listeners. The discussion may affect the attitudes of an audience toward the value of the discussion process; it may stimulate members of an audience to continuing interest in or study of the problem at hand; it may result in members of the audience being better informed; and it may produce changes of attitude or opinion toward the problem.

Some of the effects of a public discussion upon audience opinion can be measured through the use of a simple device known as the shift-of-opinion ballot. In using this ballot, it is necessary for the evaluator to phrase one or more *propositions* which relate to the problem to be discussed. Thus, if the problem for discussion is, "Should the United States adopt a program of universal military training?" a related proposition might be easily formulated as, "The United States should adopt a program of U.M.T." Prior to the discussion the members of the audience could be asked to record their opinions on this proposition on a simple three-point scale:

(1) I approve of the proposition _____.
(2) I am undecided about this proposition _____.
(3) I oppose the proposition _____.

After the discussion, the members of the audience may be asked to record their opinion concerning the proposition on a five-point scale, as follows:

(1) I approve of the proposition more strongly than before _____.
(2) I approve of the proposition _____.
(3) I am undecided about this proposition _____.
(4) I oppose the proposition _____.
(5) I oppose the proposition more strongly than before _____.

This ballot permits the person using it to record either that his opinion has remained unchanged or that he has shifted his opinion. Analysis of the pre- and postdiscussion ballots will produce certain data, such as the number and percentage of the audience reporting shifts of opinion and the tendency in terms of direction of shift, i.e., a tendency for audience opinion to become more "pro" or more "con" on the proposition. Or was there a tendency for initial opinions to be modified toward the "undecided" position?

A "product-centered" discussion appraisal: the committee report

The "Appraisal Form: Discussion Product," presented in Fig. 7, asks an observer to evaluate the worth of the conclusions arrived at by the discussion group. We regard this appraisal as a particularly significant one if we are to keep in mind that the primary function of discussion as we have defined it is not that of social conversation but is rather that of problem solving. Discussions, however harmonious, interesting, literate, or seemingly informed, invite serious reservations if they result in consensus on statements or solutions too vapid to have any real meaning, or too ill-considered to withstand the scrutiny of a thoughtful student of the problem discussed.

An excellent procedure for focusing attention on the product of the discussion is that of asking a discussion group, meeting as a committee, to prepare a written committee report which will summarize the essence of its deliberations, particularly the recommendations which the committee wishes to advance. A suggested procedure for handling such "product-centered" discussions is as follows:

1. The discussion group is asked to reduce the products of its deliberations to a two- to four-page committee report. This report should indicate:

(a) The definition of the problem under discussion.

(b) A statement of the major criteria which were used in judging the recommendations to be made by the group.

(c) A statement of courses of action rejected by the group, if any.

(d) A statement of the recommendations of the group, together with an indication of the evidence considered most important in supporting these recommendations.

2. The committee report may represent the consensus of the entire committee, or if the committee is unable to reach consensus, it may prepare majority and minority reports.

3. Reports are duplicated and distributed to members of the audience (discussion class or study group) at a date prior to a "committee hearing" (open forum).

4. At a "committee hearing" members of the committee explain, defend, or reconsider their report in the light of questions and comments made by members of the audience.

5. As a further optional procedure, it may be possible to get an acknowledged expert in the problem area to analyze and present a critique of the committee report.

It is apparent that a discussion activity of this sort serves to direct the attention of the discussion group to the development of an intellectually competent product. It also permits a more searching and deliberate examination of the product of the discussion group, to the extent that that product can be summarized in report form.

Contingent criteria for the evaluation of discussion

Since discussions are carried on under a wide variety of circumstances, it is clear that certain criteria for evaluating a discussion will be derived from the particular requirements of each situation. We will suggest a few of these "contingent criteria," while recognizing the impossibility of anticipating all of the criteria which might be reasonably applied to particular discussions. For example:

1. It is clear that a public discussion should be interesting to the audience. Discussants in such circumstances need to be mindful of the various ways in which good speakers secure and hold the interest and attention of listeners: by talking in terms of concrete situations; by talking with animation; by using colorful figures of speech; by using humor; and so forth.

2. In some circumstances a public discussion may seek as its major product the effect of stimulating the study of a problem by members of an audience. In such cases the discussants may be held less responsible for making apparent progress toward the solution of the problem as stated, than for dramatizing the issues which are raised by the problem so as to make these issues seem important and interesting.

3. A radio discussion faces special problems in helping the audience to keep the members of the group clearly identified. It would be expected that a group broadcasting would pay particular attention to the frequent use of identifying names as a part of its discussion. It is also probable that extended periods of silence, which may be desirable in some conference-type situations and which may be at least interesting in public discussions with the audience present, are almost inevitably confusing to the audience of a radio discussion.

A comprehensive check sheet for discussion leadership and participation

In this chapter we have presented a variety of ways of describing and appraising discussions. Good evaluation demands that the observer make an intelligent synthesis of accurate observation and interpretation; that is to say, the observer must "see things as they are" and be able to fit these things as they are into interpretations which are made meaningful by his knowledge of the nature of discussion—of what discussion might ideally be.

A final form for observing and evaluating discussion, which asks for simultaneous acts of description and appraisal, is presented at the outset of Chapter XV, and is explained in some detail in Chapters XV and XVI. These two chapters continue our consideration of the evaluation of discussion.

Criteria of Discussion: Participation

For three years students in the basic discussion course at the University of Minnesota were asked to identify items of behavior in discussion participants and leaders which they thought contributed positively to productive discussion—or which they thought were deterrents to productive discussion. From their observations a list of questions was developed as a means of focusing the attention of observers upon the symptoms of good or poor discussion.

We do not assert, of course, that the list of criteria suggested by these questions is in any sense an ultimate or comprehensive list. As noted in the preceding chapter, many discussions take place under circumstances which call for the application of special criteria. We have found the following list a useful one in that it encourages the observation of specific items of behavior and discourages excessively impressionistic observation.

THE PLAN FOR CHAPTERS XV AND XVI

We propose to present first the criteria of participation in discussion. Then we shall examine the rationale of each question on the list. And finally, we shall give examples of *verbal indicators* that the discussant is or is not observing a particular criterion. By *verbal indicators* we mean phrases or sentences which we have frequently found associated with positive or negative behavior by a discussant in relation to a particular criterion. It should be clear that such indicators are not in themselves a sufficient basis for saying that student *A* is a good or poor discussant. It is possible, for example, that *positive* indicators might be used in a purely superficial or inappropriate manner. Nevertheless, we invite the attention of students to the indicators which we describe in these chapters, and we suggest that students of discussion will find it useful to add other indicators to this listing. This activity will direct the attention of the student to a closer examination of the specific verbal behavior of discussants and to the significance of this behavior for the ideal functioning of discussion. For most of the criteria we have listed both positive and negative verbal indicators. In other instances only one or the other is easily observed, and only positive or negative examples are provided. Chapter XV will consider the criteria which apply to the discussion participant; Chapter XVI will be concerned with a similar analysis of the criteria of discussion leadership.

CRITERIA OF DISCUSSION PARTICIPATION

REPORTING INFORMATION

(1) Is the participant's evidence pertinent, plentiful, and documented?

(2) Does the participant recognize the limitation of his own evidence?

(3) Does he supply information to supplement or test information contributed by other members of the group?

CRITICAL THINKING

(1) Does the participant contribute one point at a time?

(2) Does he answer questions directly, specifically, briefly?

(3) Does he test all thinking by critical analysis?

(4) Does he distinguish fact from opinion?

(5) Does he distinguish disagreements in language from more fundamental disagreements?

(6) Does he seek a useful "plan of attack" on the problem at hand?

COOPERATION

(1) Does the participant listen attentively?

(2) Does he stay on the subject?

(3) Does he make every reasonable effort to bring out all points of view?

(4) Does he exhibit willingness to change his opinion when change is justified?

(5) Does he support needed leadership?

(6) Does he define areas of agreement and possible agreement?

(7) Does his manner of disagreeing or criticizing promote group harmony?

(8) Does he recognize and approve useful contributions?

(9) Does he contribute to the enjoyment of the discussion?

ANALYSIS OF THE CRITERIA: REPORTING INFORMATION

(1) Is the participant's evidence pertinent, plentiful, and documented?

The importance of pertinent, plentiful information to a discussion scarcely needs further emphasis here. The importance of documentation may need clarification. By documentation we mean the clear indication of the source of the evidence which is being furnished, including the time or date at which this evidence was reported. In general, such documentation should be furnished if the evidence bears upon a matter concerning which there is any controversy; concerning which there is any dispute as to the question of "What are the facts?"; or concerning which the nature of the facts may be changing. In such cases it becomes important to the discussion group to know if the evidence cited is personal experience, or the "remembered" résumé of some conversation with an expert; if it comes from a reputable source, or from a source known to be unreliable; if it is recent evidence, or out of date. The discussant who furnishes such documentation as a matter of habit gives evidence of his own recognition of the importance of the source and the time of evidence, and helps call these matters to the attention of the group. Why would it be important to have documentation of evidence bearing upon the following matters?

(1) The relative size of the Russian and American air forces.

(2) Statistics on "trends" in juvenile delinquency.

(3) Evidence concerning the size, preparedness, morale, and leadership of the Nationalist Chinese army on Formosa.

Positive indicators

"Concerning the first question we have raised, the following facts are pertinent."

"This evidence is taken from _____."

"The trend as reported in these statistics is confirmed by three other reports I examined, which can be found in _____."

Negative indicators

"I read some place that some insecticides are dangerous to human beings."

"Now if you are interested in knowing who Mr. _____ is, the man from whom these figures are taken, I can report that he not only is an expert, he is quite reliable."

"These figures on the cost of home construction are quite recent. They might even be figures gathered last year."

"I thought these facts are interesting, although they probably aren't relevant."

"I'm not sure about the date of this survey, but _____."

"No, I can't support that with evidence, but common sense will tell you it's true."

"The exact figures are unimportant. The main idea was _____."

(2) Does the participant recognize the limitation of his own evidence?

One of the surest indications that a discussant has a real respect for evidence is provided by his willingness to clarify the limitations of his own evidence. To be sure, it is the responsibility of all members of a discussion group to examine the limitations of all evidence presented, but this operation is greatly facilitated in the group in which participants are motivated, not so much by the desire to use evidence to make a point, as by the desire to present evidence for what it is worth—no more, no less. Indeed the evidence-giver may well be in the best position of any member of his group to indicate the limitations of the evidence he is giving.

Positive indicators

"These facts may be significant if they are supported by evidence from other parts of the country. Have we been able to find further evidence on this point?"

"I want to emphasize that these are only two or three examples, and we ought to be cautious about generalizing from them."

"General _____ has always been a strong advocate of the policy which would be supported by these facts. This doesn't mean that the facts he presents are wrong, but it means that he might be more apt to collect evidence of the sort I have just presented than he would be to collect evidence of a contradictory sort."

"These trend statistics are now three years old. We ought to have more recent figures before we conclude positively that this is the trend today."

Negative indicators

"This is only one example, but I think we can conclude that it's typical."

"There's no question about the meaning of these statistics, because an enormous amount of time and energy went into their preparation.",

"I've a good deal of experience working with alcoholics, and I can state it as an undeniable fact that _____."

"I don't think we ought to quibble about this evidence. After all, the man from whom I got it has studied this problem more than any of us."

"These facts [a small sample] indicate a trend which we can conclude will continue indefinitely."

"What I gave you was a summary of the evidence which shows that the income tax is unfair. You can't present all the evidence on this because then we would have no time to discuss the issue."

(3) Does the participant supply information to supplement or test information contributed by other members of the group?

Orderly thinking is generally promoted by the effort to establish the extent of information available *prior* to the effort to generalize from this information. This process, in turn, is expedited by discussants who introduce all of the evidence available on a specific problem at the time that such evidence is first considered. Advocates (persuaders) will sometimes withhold key bits of evidence for strategic purposes. For example, the evidence may be withheld for purposes of attacking a conclusion or generalization which the persuader wants to oppose. This strategic use of evidence, important to persuasion, is destructive to discussion, since it invites certain discussants to extend their thinking in the absence of relevant information rather than with full realization of the evidence available.

Positive indicators

"Your evidence agrees with some information I have _____."

"Here is some information which seems to contradict the evidence just presented."

"How can we reconcile these conflicting bits of information?"

"Can we agree upon any criterion for judging the relative worth of the conflicting evidence we have on this point?"

CRITICAL THINKING

(1) Does the participant contribute one point at a time?

This important criterion needs to be sensibly interpreted. Its importance rises from the impossibility of a group's giving adequate critical attention to more than one significant item of evidence, or one generalization, or one segment of reasoning at one time. The discussant who is so eager to unburden his mind of all available thoughts that he presents several thoughts as a single contribution will scatter the intellectual energies of the other discussants and promote less-than-thorough examination of one or more of his ideas. While the principle of "one contribution, one point" will tend to keep each contribution relatively short, it cannot be concluded that the length of a contribution is a sure indication of its singleness. The unity of a contribution may best be tested by asking whether or not it will tend to focus the attention of listeners upon a single statement, or tend to disperse attention in two or more directions. There are no important positive verbal indicators for this criterion, but there are negative indicators associated with contributions which violate it.

Negative indicators

"Before I answer your question, I want to develop another point I was making a few minutes ago."

"Now I have three points I want to make. First _____."

"Before you answer my question, Jim, I have another point I'd like to put before the group."

"So much for that point. Now I'd like to return to a matter which came up earlier."

"I'll take up Jim's objection first, and then I'll go on and deal with the idea brought up by Alice."

(2) Does he answer questions directly, specifically, briefly?

Asking and answering questions is the major avenue by which discussants achieve verbal understanding. The more divided people find themselves, the more important it becomes that they halt the piling of "reason upon reason," the making of charges and counter-charges, and turn to the "search for understanding" implicit in the activity of questioning.[1] The potential for understanding in a good question is, of course, lost if the answer is not responsive.

Positive indicators

"Yes."

"No."

"Is this what you meant by your question _____?"

"I haven't any information on that point."

Negative indicators

"Your question is very interesting. However, _____."

"In general, your question leads us into this related subject which I was discussing a few minutes ago."

"Before answering your question, I would like to preface my remarks with a few observations which may help us to clarify the situation in which we now find ourselves."

"Rather than answer your question, I'd like to pose one of my own for the entire group to consider."

"That's a good question, but it evades the real point of what I was saying. To get back to the basic issue: _____."

(3) Does the participant test all thinking by critical analysis?

This question asks us to attend to the quantity and quality of the critical thinking carried out by the various members of the discussion group. Our assumption is that one of the greatest foes of rigorous, intellectual, productive discussion is the failure on the part of discussants to "dig into" the worth or worthlessness of generalizations and other interpretations of information or opinion. This failure may result from the confusion of discussion and social conversation; in social "chit-chat," all assertions are credited as a matter of convention, and most thought is viewed as equally worth-while. Or the lack of criticism may result from the use of generalized objections to arguments and to the meaning of evidence, without any real

[1] Questions can be used as a weapon to discredit a person. Legal cross-examination, when it seeks to discredit a witness by forcing him into contradictions, takes this form. Such aggressive questioning is usually one-sided in nature —i.e., one person acting as questioner, and another as respondent, under procedural controls. This specialized use of questioning does not contradict the general function of questioning in the problem-solving discussion or in conversation.

analysis of the basis for objection. Yet a third reason for lack of testing is the use (and acceptance of the use) of sanctions for certain arguments which are so powerful as to silence analysis. Thus, to call an opinion *American* may suggest strongly that it not be analyzed or tested. We call such statements "discussion stoppers." We are aware that discussion groups which apply seriously this criterion will find their deliberations slowed. Members may be frustrated by what they regard as picayunish restrictions upon their fluency and expressiveness. But the issue at stake is a fundamental one. Do we want discussion to be merely pleasant, or do we want it to be productive? Assuming the latter to be our goal, the best resource available to discussants is the rigorous testing of all thinking; the relentless pursuit of generalizations which are justified by available evidence; and the development of reasoning which will stand close inspection.

Positive indicators

"Joe, your conclusion takes in only a part of our evidence. How do you account for the facts which seem to contradict the evidence which you cite?"

"I don't think we'll have any difficulty in agreeing with Jim. But I don't think this sort of agreement gets us very far. His statement was so general, so open to a variety of interpretations, that even though we agree with him, we may all be attaching different meanings to what he has said."

"We ought to remember the circumstances at the time that Mr. Churchill expressed this opinion. We can't simply conclude that his opinion, in view of present circumstances, would be the same."

"Is there any evidence available to support that conclusion?"

"What was the basis upon which these statistics were gathered? That is, what was the nature of the sample used, and over what period of time was the study made?"

"Isn't there another way of interpreting those same statistics?"

"I have gathered opinions from a number of teachers—five to be exact—on this point."

"The evidence indicates a possibility, I should say, but not a probability that this type of campaign will backfire."

Negative indicators

"Certainly no fair-minded person would disagree with you, Jim."

"You seem to have been doing some poor thinking. Here's my idea."

"Of course some people will agree with you, but the majority of careful thinkers will feel otherwise."

"I feel that you are wrong, but the whole thing is too complicated for people with our preparation to analyze."

"We won't get anywhere if we quibble over the meaning of a word like democracy. Let's just assume that we all understand pretty well what is meant, and then go on to make our proposals for improvement."

"Your evidence doesn't support your reasoning. Why not? Well, let's ask others in the group if they don't feel the same way."

"The only way we can get any place is by cooperating, so I suggest that we stop raising objections to the meaning of various pieces of evidence which we bring in."

"I don't think it's a good idea to criticize Joe's evidence. After all, he spent a lot more time gathering those facts than any of the rest of us did."

"Some things are just naturally right [wrong] and we don't need to try to analyze them."

"There's absolutely no doubt whatsoever about this, so here's one point we won't have to discuss."

"Since we know that this is the sort of argument used by Communists, we don't need to analyze the argument further. It is obviously bad."

"I think we ought to know that this is the position which would be taken by all loyal Americans."

"Human nature doesn't change."

(4) Does the discussant distinguish fact from opinion?

There is no more common or distressing symptom of poor discussion than the tendency to label as "facts" assertions which are at best interpretations of facts, and at worst mere opinion. To be sure, some discussants use the label of "fact" for statements which they would readily acknowledge to be opinion. But the use of the label may confuse not only the person hearing the assertion; it may equally confuse the user. Having called an opinion "fact," the discussant may be less ready to examine rationally the limitations on his opinion; less willing to admit possible merit to conflicting opinion.

Positive indicators

"Those are the facts. My interpretation of them is _____."

"But that is opinion. Are there facts which support it?"

"It is true that your authority made that assertion. But how did he arrive at his conclusion? We can't really judge the worth of his opinion until we know the facts upon which he based it."

"Before we debate our differences of opinion, let's see if we can agree as to the facts which are relevant to this issue."

Negative indicators

"Since it is a fact that our candidate is more moral and has higher ideals than yours, we ought to place more reliance in what he says."

"Now it's a fact that taxes are too high. We don't need any figures on the present level of taxes, therefore. All we need to do is talk about what we ought to do about this problem."

"_____ has presented some interesting data, but his motives are wrong. This fact about his motive ought to outweigh any consideration we give to the other facts."

"Now we know for a fact that the administration intends to liquidate the small farmer."

"It's a fact that the leaders of Asia are anti-American."

(5) Does the discussant distinguish disagreements in language from more fundamental disagreements?

The real differences which divide people are serious enough without complication through verbal disagreements. By a verbal disagreement we mean a dispute which arises because two persons are using the same word or phrase in two different ways. Unaware of this ambiguity in their conversation or unwilling to resolve the ambiguity, they continue their disagreement without the possibility of discovering the nature of the reality, if any, which divides them. Thus, two discussants might feel themselves seriously at odds as to the way in which juvenile delinquents ought to be handled. Speaker A says, "I don't believe in coddling junior-grade Dillingers." Speaker B says, "That's a foolish attitude. I don't believe in taking a punitive, revengeful attitude toward law violators simply because they disturb our peace of mind. We know that the goal of our

system for handling delinquents is rehabilitation, not revenge."
A answers, "I can't go along with your milquetoast attitude."

One can visualize the potential explosiveness of the argument thus joined. But notice that so far neither disputant has given any indication of the exact way in which he would handle a specific juvenile offender. It is possible that the dispute undertaken rests in different reactions to the meanings of such words as "coddling," "punitive attitude," or "rehabilitation." Careful exploration might reveal that *B* doesn't believe in the sort of action which *A* calls "coddling." Indeed, it is possible that *A* and *B* agree substantially as to the handling of juvenile offenders. If they disagree, it would be better for them to discover the real nature of their disagreement so that they could focus their discussion. That is, exactly what is it that *A* would do in relation to specific juvenile offenders which *B* would not do?

Positive indicators

"Let's both leave out the colorful labels, and see if we really interpret our available evidence differently."

"Let's not argue about whether this proposal is American or un-American. Let's find out specifically what it is that you object to in the proposal."

"You say the schools are doing a bad job, and I say they're doing a good job. Yet I'm pretty sure that you don't disapprove of everything the schools are doing, and I don't approve of everything they are doing. Let's see if there are any specific parts of the program of our local high school that we disagree about."

"Instead of calling the Senator a demagogue, as you do, or a statesman, as I do, let's find out what specific actions of the Senator you wish to disapprove."

"I'm not sure I know what you mean when you say that government interference in the life of the private person is bad. Do you oppose all governmental regulations? If not, can you specify just which function now being performed by our government you think the government ought to abandon?"

Negative indicators

"As opposed to the high-minded campaign conducted by this party, we have the unprincipled politics of the opposing party."

"You have asked for my real objection to present-day education.

I can pin down my objection in a single word. Present-day education doesn't give attention to fundamentals."

"The real reason we aren't making headway here is that some of the group don't know the true meaning of the word 'law.' "

(6) Does the participant seek a useful "plan of attack" on the problem at hand?

We have already discussed at some length the importance of an agenda to the orderly conduct of discussion. But unless a discussion is completely "dramatized," the search for and selection of an order of procedure and method of analysis is an on-going task. As problems arise, the group needs to ask constantly the simple procedural questions: "What are we now doing?" "How can we proceed with maximum productivity?" While these questions may be a particular concern for the chairman of a discussion group, they are also properly the concern of each member, since clarity of discussion is seldom achieved save among discussants who have sought and found an agreeable and useful procedure.

Positive indicators

"Before we propose ways of improving the counseling procedures in our college, shouldn't we try to agree as to the criteria by which we might judge an effective counseling set-up?

"Can't we divide our consideration of the effects of a change in American policy in the Far East into three parts? We could first consider the possible effects of this proposed change on our Allies. Then we could ask about its possible effects on the Communist bloc of nations. And perhaps we ought to consider the possible effect on the Nationalist Chinese Government as a separate item."

"As I see it, we're now trying to find out if we can agree as to the nature of the problems, if any, which are raised by the present security system in our national government. I suggest that we throw a rough list, including everyone's ideas, on the blackboard, and then see if we can classify the possible types of problem with which we may want to concern ourselves. We might be able to talk about two or three types of problems rather than the ten or twelve examples of problems which have already been suggested."

"It seems to me we're trying to cover too much in this group if we talk about the problem of censorship in general. Why don't we limit ourselves to that aspect of censorship which is currently getting the most attention in this community—namely, censorship of comic books?"

COOPERATION

(1) Does the participant listen attentively?

It is perhaps sufficient to say of listening that without effective listening no worth-while discussion is possible. The discussant whose attention is always on the formulation of his own next comment is not participating in a discussion in any real sense. If the essence of good listening is a part of discussion by definition, let us also observe that the appearance of good listening is a stimulus to good discussion. Members of a discussion group are stimulated if their listeners make instantly apparent the fact that they are following each comment closely. It costs a discussant who *is* listening but little additional effort to look as though he were listening.

Positive indicators

"Let me see if I understood what you were saying."
"Is this a fair restatement of your idea?"
"I didn't follow you. Would you explain your point once more?"
"Here is an example which relates to the point just made."

Negative indicators

"I'm sorry. I didn't get your question."
"Did you just say that?"
"To continue the comment I was making before Jim got the floor, _____."

(2) Does the participant stay on the subject?

"Staying on the subject" means not merely staying within the bounds of the total problem under consideration, but rather talking to the point which the group accepts as the immediate focus of its conversation. This criterion is closely associated with the criterion of attentive listening. But even good listeners may choose irrelevance as a mode of procedure if they are inclined to place their own needs for expression ahead of cooperation with the agenda being followed by the group.

Negative indicators

"What we really ought to be discussing is the solution to this problem, so I'll start out on this point."

"Let me jump back to a point we left a few minutes ago."

"This isn't our subject at the moment, but it's really important that we do not forget the attitude of the city council toward this problem."

(3) Does the participant make every reasonable effort to bring out all points of view?

One of the persistent problems faced by discussion groups is that of giving adequate recognition to points of view not presented on the panel, or to points of view represented by ill-prepared or ineffective participants. Ignoring such points of view may promote seeming progress among the members of a group, but the group which does not see itself as a segment of a broader society will achieve only an illusory harmony. The effort on the part of a discussant not only to give a fair hearing to all points of view, but actually to aid in the adequate airing of views other than those which he himself holds, is an effort in support of the theory of discussion as free, open inquiry—in which no advantage is sought for certain ideas through accidents of circumstance.

Positive indicators

"Jim, I'm not a Republican, but I've heard the Republican administration's position on farm price supports defended in this way—and I'd like you to check me to see if you think my statement of the case is fair."

"We have pretty good harmony among the people here, but we ought to keep in mind that there is a considerable body of opinion contrary to that which we have been expressing."

"I want to point out that Dr. _____ disagrees sharply with the interpretation I have just given to these facts. His idea is _____."

"Henry, I don't know that you concur with all the talk that has been going on for the last few minutes. Would you like to give your interpretation to the facts we have presented on the traffic problem?"

Negative indicators

"There are only Democrats here today, so we won't expect any presentation of Republican points of view."

"Since we have no Catholics on our panel, we are going to eliminate discussion of Catholic attitudes toward the problem of divorce."

"Henry, everyone seems to disagree with the point of view you
expressed. Can we get you to go along with the group?"

(4) Does the participant exhibit willingness to change his point of view when change is justified?

From the viewpoint of the student of discussion, one of the most
attractive facts about people is that they do change their minds. To
be sure, some people find this business of change more difficult than
do others, but we generally find little to praise either in the person
who is so rigid and defensive that he will resist all evidence rather
than have his propositions jeopardized, or in the person to whom all
opinions are as one, and who is therefore willing to go along with
whatever opinion seems most comfortable, convenient, or popular.
Our ideal discussant needs to avoid the personality extremes characterized by Professor Allport as the "chameleons" and the "beavers."
The chameleon, lacking faith in reason or evidence, changes his
opinions to suit whatever environment of opinion in which he finds
himself. The beaver, equally lacking faith in evidence or reasoning,
pursues his settled goals and convictions regardless of the impact of
new information or thinking.

Positive indicators

"This new evidence certainly alters the position I expressed a few
minutes ago."

"I'd like to modify the position I originally stated. I'm still in favor
of flexible price supports, but I can see better than I did before that
such a program is no cure-all for our farm problems."

"I'm attracted to the force of the argument you just presented. I
think I want some more time to think about this question, and I'd like
to hear several of you comment on Jim's argument."

Negative indicators

"Your evidence sounds convincing, but I'm sure that if we look at
it long enough, we'll find something wrong with it."

"I'm willing to admit that my evidence won't hold up, but I'm still
certain of my conclusion. I do need more time to find new evidence."

"Certainly my evidence isn't conclusive, but then we all know that there is no such thing as conclusive evidence. What we need is less effort to pick apart the argument I presented and more effort to see that this is the position which any moral person would inevitably take."

"Alice has given a lot of specific suggestions for improving our anti-gambling laws, but she has overlooked the one real basic fact about gambling. And that is that you can't change human nature."

(5) Does the participant support needed leadership?

We assume that every group profits from orderly procedures. This in turn implies that the group must either share or delegate the responsibility for promoting order—and in the group characterized by cooperative behavior the promotion of order is best when widely shared. Discussants who have difficulty adjusting to the activities of a group will often resist suggestions made by the nominal leader, seemingly for no other purpose than to express a sort of generalized and immature resistance to constituted authority. We have observed persons enter a group *after* that group had spent some time in preparing an agenda to guide its deliberations, and proceed to assert the need for a complete revision of the order of deliberation already selected. To be sure, not all leaders deserve support simply from the fact of their position. But the decision to resist a leader's suggestions, or to work to alter deliberative procedures generally agreed to, is not a decision to be undertaken lightly.

Positive indicators

"We've had two or three orders of procedures suggested here. Since there seems little to choose among them, why not follow the procedure suggested by our chairman?"

"I'll be glad to defer discussion of the possible solution until _____."

"I think either procedure suggested would work if we all agreed to give it a try. Why not let the chairman select the next order of business?"

(6) Does the participant define areas of agreement and possible agreement?

We have emphasized that good discussions need not attain consensus on all points under dispute. Nevertheless, the reduction of differences is one of the constant goals of discussion, and the securing of areas of agreement is one of the significant achievements toward which discussants properly work. All discussants, therefore, need to be oriented not merely to the testing of all thinking proposed to their group, but also to the locating of all potential or real areas of agreement. Such identification is not only intellectually sound; it has important implications in terms of promoting good human relations.

Positive indicators

"I sense that we are in agreement as to the general ends of American foreign policy. Let me see if I can state this area of agreement in a way which will be generally acceptable to this group."

"Before we continue to examine this proposal for a new tax, can we state that we all agree as to the desirability of avoiding any regressive tax?"

"I do not object to Bill's emphasis on the need for integrity in our elected officials. In fact, I think we can agree that we all desire representatives who will not take a cynical view toward campaign speaking."

(7) Does the participant's manner of disagreeing or criticizing promote group harmony?

If the intention of a discussant is to voice dissent, there are two extremes of verbal gesture which need to be avoided. The first is the extreme which clothes the dissent in such thick layers of euphemism, or surrounds it with so many qualifications, that the essential fact that disagreement occurred is lost to view. Dissent which is not recognized as dissent can serve no useful purpose in clarifying a problem. The other extreme is the use of dissent as a form of aggressive assault upon the personality of another discussant. Disagreement stated in such a way as to imply that another discussant is lacking in intelligence, insight, or good will can create more problems than it solves. Disagreement so stated is incongruous in a situation which asks for cooperative thinking.

Positive indicators

"I'm sure there's a great deal to be said for your argument. But don't you think it possible that _____."

"I don't believe I'd see that evidence in quite the same light. Let's try this approach _____."

"You can probably guess from what I've said before that I don't go along with Richard. May I try to clarify what I believe is the essence of our disagreement?"

Negative indicators

"A man would have to be an idiot to believe that those facts lead to that conclusion."

"It's pretty clear to me that this form of argument is a form of narrow, political partisanship, no matter what language is used in its statement."

"You're wrong there. And you're wrong because you haven't taken the time or trouble to get at the real facts."

"I suppose people who have never had any practical experience in these affairs might get off such woolly-minded arguments. But let's take a hard-headed look at the facts."

"Undoubtedly your grandfather would have thought the same."

(8) Does the participant recognize and approve of useful contributions?

The importance of recognition to nearly all persons suggests that the time spent by discussants in acknowledging approval of worthwhile contributions is time well spent on promoting a favorable climate for discussion. There are many physical signs of approval which ought to be used by the discussant wishing to give assurance to fellow participants, but these are immeasurably strengthened by brief spoken acknowledgments.

Positive indicators

"I liked the way you put that idea."

"That evidence will help us a lot. It bears directly on our problem."

"I'm interested in what you say."

"I don't agree, but I hope I can put my point of view half as clearly as you expressed yourself."

(9) Does the participant contribute to the enjoyment of the discussion?

We see some tendency for discussions to move toward two extremes. One is represented by the discussion which is lively, entertaining, and spontaneous, but so lacking in intellectual control that it is all but useless in producing understanding of a problem. The other extreme is represented by the discussion which is profound, informed, and intellectually vigorous, but which proceeds with the use of speech designed to chill the attention of all but the hardiest and most highly motivated participant. We see no real reason why a discussion cannot be at once intellectually respectable and colorful. And we believe that the effort by discussants to add humor, personal experience, and intrinsically interesting anecdotes to a discussion is an important contribution to the development of rapport among the members of the group.

Positive indicators

"Here's an experience I had yesterday which bears on this point."
"A close friend of mine tells this story: _____."
"Helen, I was interested in the story you were telling yesterday about the discipline problems in the school you attended. I wonder if you'd repeat it?"

CHAPTER XVI

Criteria of Discussion: Leadership

GROUPS NEED LEADERS

One of our common experiences with living in groups is the selection or emergence of leaders. But it is an equally common experience to note the tremendous differences in the activities of these individuals. The leader of the neighborhood gang, the leader of an army regiment, the leader of a parent-teachers' association, the leader of a parliamentary body, the leader of a homecoming day planning committee—all these are perceived as doing vastly different sorts of things. These differences are not merely between successful and unsuccessful leaders; more important, they are differences in the functions of leaders whose roles resemble one another only in the superficial sense that all are in a position of special responsibility.

In this chapter, therefore, we seek to define only the criteria for leadership appropriate to discussion. These criteria do not define the "good" leader for every special circumstance. Rather, they are criteria we developed by watching groups in action; by seeing what sorts of leadership contribute to successful discussion, and what activities of the leader keep discussion groups from realizing their potential.

LEADERSHIP STYLES INAPPROPRIATE TO DISCUSSION

Two extreme interpretations of discussion leadership result in ineffective discussion. The first we shall call the concept of authoritarian leadership; the second, the notion of the leaderless group.

The authoritarian leader conceives of himself not as the servant but as the master of the discussion. Procedures are to be those he suggests, or to which he gives assent. The decisions of the group are the decisions which the leader initiates or approves. His only interest in the group may lie in the challenge it offers to his ability to influence and control members of the group, or in the prestige which may be added to his views when he can say that these views were approved in a discussion. Authoritarian leadership contradicts the notion that discussion groups exist to carry out inquiry through reflective, cooperative thinking. Successful authoritarian leadership marks the destruction of critical thought.

The concept of leaderless discussion is based on an idealized view of "the group" as being able to achieve a type of identity among members so that the normal functions of leadership are so widely shared that no single person is identifiable as the group leader. We do not say that it is impossible that groups of this sort can come into being and operate productively. We do say that we have yet to observe a productive discussion group in which one or two persons did not emerge as leaders. So diverse and difficult are the language functions of the discussion group that certain duties are best performed when they are made the particular concern of a leader. We see the pursuit of so-called leaderless discussion as the pursuit of an illusion. Groups which by design or lack of organizational foresight stumble into such a situation can only look forward to reduced productivity.[1]

LEADERSHIP STYLES APPROPRIATE TO DISCUSSION

Between authoritarianism and anarchy lies the arena of democratic leadership. The democratic leader determines his activities from the needs of the discussion. That is to say, his role is not merely to aid a group toward a speedy and useful completion of the task at hand, but to operate in such a way as to promote the full development of group thinking. His concern is not simply a concern for

---

[1] A study by Maier and Solem comparing leaderless groups and groups with democratic leaders supports the view that the leader makes important contributions to group productivity.

Norman R. F. Maier and Allen R. Solem, "The Contributions of a Discussion Leader to the Quality of Group Thinking: The Effective Use of Minority Opinions," *Human Relations,* 5 (1952), pp. 277–288.

stating solutions to the problem at hand, but also a concern for the growth of the discussion process as a way of getting at social problems.

A considerable range of leadership styles may be observed to fall generally within the category of democratic leadership. Many leaders working in unique situations will tend to assume a somewhat *directive* role in relation to the activity of the group. Their leadership will be quite apparent. They may assume leadership in posing the agenda agreed to by the group; in supervising the problem of keeping discussion relevant to the question at hand; in keeping the problem of time limitations before the group; in moderating or clarifying points of dispute; and so on. Groups working under severe time pressure, groups which have been newly organized and whose members have had little experience in working together, and groups in which discussion skills and understandings are not widely shared may well profit from leadership of a relatively *directive* style.

The work of other leaders may be quite unobtrusive. Such leaders may be said to follow a relatively *nondirective* style. Procedural suggestions emerge from the group, and rather free exploration of different ways of attacking a problem may take place. Common leadership functions, such as clarifying points of agreement and disagreement, summarizing, and proposing new lines of investigation, may be undertaken by any and all members of the group. It is our view that the leadership style most appropriate to discussion will be as nondirective as the circumstances and the group permit. Groups in which knowledge of discussion procedures are widely shared have less need for directive guidance and achieve their fullest development through widespread, general participation in leadership functions. Groups which have been together over a long period of time and those which are not confronted by any time pressure may frequently achieve their greatest productivity with a minimum of supervision or direction from a designated leader.

A SUMMARY OF LEADERSHIP STYLES

We may summarize this point by observing that the styles of leadership appropriate to discussion tend at their extremes to become the styles which we consider inappropriate. This relationship may be visualized as follows:

Discussion Leadership

Inappropriate	*Appropriate*	*Inappropriate*
	Democratic leadership	
Authoritarian Leadership	Directive ⟷ Nondirective	Leaderless group
Results in	Results in	Results in
Destruction of critical thinking	Facilitation of productive group deliberation	A loss of productivity

DETAILED ANALYSIS OF LEADERSHIP

Our procedure for the remainder of this chapter will be the same as that in Chapter XV. We shall first state the full list of leadership criteria as a set of questions which direct attention to items of leadership behavior. Then we shall consider the rationale of each criterion separately, and list positive and negative verbal indicators which we have found associated with behavior relevant to that criterion. We emphasize that leadership is not necessarily always performed by the designated leader of a group. Indeed, one of the marks of a superior discussion may well be the widespread sharing of these duties among the members even while the responsibility for seeing that the functions get performed continue to rest with a designated leader.

CRITERIA OF DISCUSSION LEADERSHIP

(1) Does the leader build a permissive climate?
(2) Does the leader follow a plan?
(3) Does the leader give or get accurate summaries?
(4) Does he give or get clarification of vague statements?
(5) Does he promote evaluation of all generalizations?
(6) Does he protect minority opinion?
(7) Does he minimize extrinsic conflict?
(8) Does he perform only necessary functions?

(1) Does the leader build a permissive climate?

The leader can do much through his own reactions to suggest the attitude appropriate to the members of a discussion. If he reveals enthusiasm for the possibility of a productive meeting; if he is warm and personal in his attitude toward all members of the group; if he makes manifest a real interest in *everything* that is said and avoids either the manner or language of impatience or contempt, he can do much to set the "tone" which is desirable for the entire group. We have commended the attitude of impartiality toward all proposals as suitable to the dialectical activity of all discussants. But we have also observed that the best discussions embrace strong differences of opinion among the discussants, and the vigorous critical examination of all assertions. A designated leader has a particular mission to preserve his neutrality among opinions. He must show concern for and interest in all opinions, and by so doing keep ever before the discussion group the idea that their commitment to the process of discussion itself must not be overshadowed by their passion for particular opinions.

Positive indicators

"There's no opinion, honestly given, which can't help us all in our work with this problem."

"Just a minute—I don't think Al has finished his comment yet."

"Three of you want to comment, and we'll all have a chance. Let's start out with Betty, since we haven't heard from her for awhile."

"We're moving a bit more slowly than we can afford to in view of the hour. I suggest that we limit ourselves to one point at a time, and in this way everyone will get a hearing, and at the same time we can make better headway."

Negative indicators

"Try to keep your next comment shorter, will you, Bill?"

"I can't see where that argument will take us, so let's get back on the track."

(2) Does the leader follow a plan?

Unstructured conversation may be entertaining; it may even be stimulating to the persons who participate. But it can scarcely contribute to solid progress toward the solution of a problem. We have stressed the importance of an agenda, cooperatively achieved, to the success of a discussion. Once the agenda has been secured, the leader becomes its particular guardian. His responsibility includes reminding the group of the agenda, calling attention of participants to digressions when they occur, and consolidating the sense of the group that the discussion is ready to move from one item of the agenda to the next. As "guardian" an inflexible leader can perform a real disservice if he forgets that the agenda is to serve the group and is always subject to revision and alteration by productive lines of thinking which evolve during the discussion. The effective leader stresses need for order, but is ready to assist the group in the discovery and development of new plans at any stage of the discussion.

The main responsibility of the leader in relation to the agenda is discharged by reminding participants of answers to these questions: "Where are we going?" and "Where have we been?" He also has certain "housekeeping" responsibilities if the group is to achieve maximum efficiency. The good leader will have planned how to get the discussion under way; how to secure proper introduction of members; how to keep accurate records of the group's activity if such records will be useful; how to keep the group fully aware of its time limitations.

Positive indicators

"The first major question we have to consider is _____."

"Before we move ahead to the discussion of possible solutions to our problem, is there any more to be said about the nature of the problem?"

"Ron, would you act as recorder for the group? We need someone to keep track of the points on which we seem to reach agreement, and to report back to us occasionally as to our progress."

"We have fifteen minutes before a number of our group will have to leave. Can we try to pull together our major points of agreement and disagreement at this time? This will give us the point from which we can start our next meeting."

"We'll want to get into your proposal before the end of the meeting, Barbara. But would you mind holding discussion of that point until we've finished with our consideration of the possible causes of this problem?"

(3) Does the leader give or get accurate summaries?

A discussion should "take account" of its progress at regular intervals during the discussion. This task is usually carried out in one of three ways. Either the chairman assumes personal responsibility for keeping track of the discussion and for furnishing the discussants with a report on their progress at the completion of each major issue; or the chairman or group selects a member of the group to serve as a recorder who is instructed to furnish summaries of progress on request; or the chairman asks the members of the group to summarize the progress of the discussion as they see it. Use of a combination of these methods is common. It should be observed that the need for accurate summaries is one of the reasons that a group may wish to provide itself with an active, observant leader. It is not easy for all participants in a discussion to keep perspective on the movement of group thinking. A designated leader, who sets himself apart from participation in particular controversy, may be in a

Reproduced by permission © 1953 The New Yorker Magazine, Inc.

"Then it's agreed that we adopt Running Elk's proposal to plow the first quarter's profits back into exploratory drilling."

much better position to pull together the sense of a meeting than will any other person in the group.

Summaries are always offered to a discussion group, and never imposed on the group. The good summary is the one which gains full assent from all members of the group through their recognition that it is an accurate account of their deliberations.

Positive indicators

"Let me see if I can state our points of agreement up to this time."

"Would this be a fair summary of the position at which we have now arrived?"

"Would anyone be able at this time to state a definition of totalitarianism which will summarize the sense of our discussion?"

"Let's see if we can sharpen the issue over which we seem to be disputing. What would be the clearest way of stating the issue at which we have arrived?"

(4) Does the leader give or get clarification of vague statements?

The discussion leader can provide a substantial service to the group by serving as a semantic supervisor. In this role he asks himself constantly, "Do I understand what was just said?" or "Was the statement just made sufficiently clear to be interpreted in approximately the same way by different members of our group?" Participants in a discussion have the same responsibility as does the leader for being sure that they understand all that is said. But participants confront a dual task—that of understanding what has been said, and at the same time wording their own contributions.

Hence, the leader can perform a particular service to the group by virtue of his freedom from some of the pressures which bear upon participants.

To be sure, the leader with an obsessive commitment to the semantic purification of all statements can bring any discussion to an abrupt stop. As in all his activities, the leader's motivation should be to serve the group, not to demonstrate his superiority. He must, therefore, seek to engage the cooperation of the group in the search for clarity of statement.

Positive indicators

"Could you give us an illustration of the point you are making?"

"Let me see if I can restate what you have said. Check me to see if I have your meaning straight."

"Would you elaborate a bit as to what you mean by 'freedom' in this instance?"

"I don't think we're all giving the same meaning to the term 'censorship.' Can we illustrate different types of censorship, and then agree as to what operations we have in mind when we talk of censorship in this discussion?"

Negative indicators

"Let's don't use any general words like 'peace,' 'freedom,' or 'democracy.' Who knows what these mean, anyway?"

"There are four words in that last sentence of yours which need defining. Are you prepared to give definitions which we can all understand and accept?"

"Let's don't argue about the meaning of the American tradition. After all, we're all Americans, and we know what it means even if we can't make a statement."

(5) Does the leader promote evaluation of all generalizations?

This criterion suggests that the leader may serve as a sort of "critical conscience" for the group. Once again, his freedom from some of the pressures of participation permits him to keep in view the important consideration of the quality of the critical thinking which is being carried on. If the group stops its deliberations short of critical examination of an important issue, the chairman may ask for more examination "in depth" of the problem at hand. If generalizations are generally proposed and accepted without examination or criticism, he may recall for the group the fact that a good discussion needs to be more than an exercise in good will.

Positive indicators

"We seem to accept John's view that 'all religions believe pretty much the same things.' I wonder if we really all agree to this? Are we prepared to underwrite this generalization without any more examination?"

"We have listed a number of possible causes for the rate of auto accidents, but not all of these seem to be supported by the evidence which was introduced earlier. Shouldn't we try to see which of the causes seem to be most important according to our evidence?"

"We seem to view all of the proposed solutions as equally desirable. Have we asked yet about the practicality of these solutions?"

(6) Does the leader protect minority opinion?

This criterion of leadership might seem to be a subdivision of the criterion which asks that the leader promote a permissive climate. To be sure, a permissive group will tend to be one in which all views are welcomed, and in which, therefore, representatives of minority views should feel free to contribute. But the dynamics of "permissiveness" are not always conducive to the fullest development of minority opinion. The condition of permissiveness may encourage the confident spokesmen of majority opinion to "run away" with a discussion. Protected as they are by the powerful sanction of majority approval—whether this sanction is stated or unstated—these discussants may give both inadequate opportunity and inadequate consideration to the views of a member who has little backing in the group. They may treat this minority representative politely, even with manifest good will, while at the same time using the leader's permissiveness as the basis for brushing by any genuine consideration of minority opinion.

The leader, understanding both the importance of minority opinion and the tendency for it to be buried, may well wish to protect minority opinion at the expense of reducing his permissiveness toward the flow of majority opinion.

Positive indicators

"I think we ought to give more time to Jim's suggestion. It seems contrary to the opinion most of you have expressed, but let's not dismiss his idea. It might contain some valuable insights."

"Willis, you've been out of action for quite a time. I think we'd all profit from hearing a fuller development of your attitude."

"We simply tossed out that idea on the grounds that most of us disagreed with it. Certainly, that's no indication of any real effort at analysis on our part. I suggest we pause here and try to get some understanding of this point of view."

Negative indicators

"I think we can dismiss this idea, because very few people in our country support it."

"Keep in mind that we want to reach some agreements, and we'll never get together if we aren't all willing to go along with the group."

"We'll always have some hard-headed objectors, I suspect. But if we leave out a few of the left-field ideas, we will reach consensus sooner."

(7) Does the leader minimize extrinsic conflict?

Good discussion is born in conflict and thrives on conflict. But the conflict must be one of ideas rather than one of personalities. By "extrinsic conflict" we mean that which is not strictly relevant to the problem before the group. Two discussants who have become irritated with one another may exchange insults, with each discussant calling into question the motives, good sense, or character of his "enemy." We must recognize that there are occasions in which questions of motive, good sense, and character are relevant to a discussion problem, but for the most part such personality clashes are irrelevant to the intellectual tasks of the discussion group. Sometimes the extrinsic conflict occurs over the personality of an individual not present at the discussion. We recall a discussion concerned with the problem, "Can the system used by our national government for the elimination of security risks be improved?" One discussant was presenting information on the way in which present security measures are administered. He included in his evidence a parenthetical comment on the character of a well-known United States Senator, offering a few gratuitous insults to the Senator. Another discussant, burning with zeal to defend the Senator, joined the battle, and soon an argument was raging over the irrelevant issue, "Is Senator _____ a scoundrel or a hero?" In another discussion the problem was, "Is released time for religious education a desirable arrangement for public education?" An argument developed as to which of two high schools, the alma maters of two discussants, had provided the best administration for its released time program. One of the important and continuing functions of leadership is that of seeking to separate relevant conflicts from those which are extrinsic, and the consequent effort to minimize or eliminate the extrinsic conflicts. Two faulty attitudes toward conflict are: (1) the attitude that all conflict is good, because it adds color and excitement to a discussion, and (2) the attitude that since discussion is cooperation, any expression of conflict, whether intrinsic or extrinsic, is to be minimized.

Positive indicators

"Instead of calling this idea pernicious, can we simply state the particular reason for offering objection?"

"Let me rephrase that criticism if I may. Is this the essence of your objection?"

"I don't know that we have any real evidence on the motives for which this bill was offered. Why don't we talk about our evidence that the bill will have good or bad results and try to judge it on these grounds?"

"We've begun to use a lot of colorful adjectives in our argument. Before we go on, let's try to clarify the real issue at stake here, regardless of our feelings toward the persons involved."

Negative indicators

"Let's liven things up. No real spirit in this argument."

"This is going to turn into a bad discussion if we keep disagreeing with one another."

"Now I think that when we really understand one another, we won't have any disagreements at all."

(8) Does the leader perform only necessary functions?

An ultimate test of a leader's understanding of the nature of discussion is his willingness to subordinate his own personal drive for recognition, status, or approval. The leader has responsibility for helping leadership functions get performed. He has equal responsibility for keeping out of the way of discussants who are making progress. He should take pride in the work of a group in which leadership functions are widely shared, for it is a crowning achievement of good discussion leaders that they help groups to become progressively less dependent upon the leader, and progressively more resourceful in working out their own solutions to problems. We do not provide examples of verbal indicators for this criterion. Its application is altogether contingent. That is to say, by this criterion any action of a leader, however valuable it may seem in and of itself, becomes undesirable if it is unnecessary.

ROLE SPECIALIZATION AND LEADERSHIP FUNCTIONS

We have emphasized three complementary ideas in this chapter: First, a designated group leader may have special opportunity to serve the group by reason of his dissociation from some of the responsibilities of participation. He may, accordingly, give special attention to the *process* of the discussion as opposed to the *content* of particular stages. He can serve as a climate-maker, guardian of the agenda, clarifier, harmonizer, issue-sharpener, and summarizer. Second, able discussants share in the responsibility for accomplishing leadership functions. Third, appropriate behavior of a designated leader varies a great deal with different topics, circumstances, and groups.

Indeed, so varied and complex are the leadership activities which we have been describing that it is common to find individuals in a group emerging as "leaders" with respect to a particular function. Thus, we may find the designated leader serving as guardian of the agenda. But one of the discussants, with a particular capacity for stimulating warm interpersonal relations, may serve as the leader in developing a permissive climate. And yet another discussant, with an eye for vagueness or ambiguity, may serve the group as a leader in the task of clarification. The best discussion leaders will recognize and welcome the contributions of discussants with these capacities.

PART FIVE

Discussion and Society

CHAPTER XVII

Inquiry, Persuasion, and Social Action

THE CULT OF DISCUSSION

The speech form "discussion," as we have defined it in this text, embraces many of the positive values in contemporary democratic society. We speak of the necessity of impartiality to the discussant, and we invoke the powerful sanction of the scientist whose power for creativity comes from his willingness to confront and follow evidence, his vision undimmed by stubborn adherence to preconceptions. We speak of the need for openness among discussants—for the elimination of hidden motives, assumptions, and purposes as a prerequisite to the search for common understanding among men. And surely, openness so conceived idealizes the possibility that men, however separated and divided they may find themselves, can discover some of their original oneness to the extent that they relinquish deviousness and the seeking after self-advantage.

We speak of discussion as cooperative thinking, linking it to the aspirations of democratic citizens to be freed from the rancor of unresolved conflict with their fellow men. We emphasize that discussion provides a situation in which men can exercise all of the powers of rationality which they may possess. We express thereby the hope of most people that man's rational capacity freely exercised is sufficient to the building of a better, more decent society. Because of its intimate relationship to democracy, discussion carries a not inconsiderable value status for most educated persons, at least those in Western cultures.

The association of discussion with many positive values accounts in some part for the considerable attention which has been paid to this form of discourse by scholars and community and business leaders in the last three decades. The idealization of discussion has gone so far that the word is now often offered as a "formula answer" to problems. "We have a problem? Very well, the answer is discussion. We will organize discussions, and through the magic of the process our problems will melt away!"

There are two dangers to this idealization of discussion. The first is that since the word is a good word, it will serve as a label for a wide assortment of verbal activities which bear only a superficial resemblance to the discussion envisaged in this book. The reader will recall in Chapter I our description of the group of speech situations we termed "pseudo-discussion." The second danger is that persons who find discussion "good" may be inclined to suspect that forms of discourse other than discussion are at least "less good," if not altogether degraded. It is not difficult to find evidence that some persons in our society have concluded that discussion, ideally practiced, is not only a useful part of the method by which men set about solving their social problems, it is indeed a sufficient way; therefore, the continued popularity of such forms of discourse as persuasive speaking or debate represents not a desirable condition in society, but rather the continuation of practices developed when mankind was less enlightened.

We are not opposed to the tendency to idealize the values of good discussion; we are, however, opposed to any tendency to extend this approval of discussion to imply animadversions on persuasion, whether that persuasion be undertaken by the public speaker, the political propagandist, the debater, the advertiser, or the clergyman. We would invite the thoughtful reader to seek to place the activity of discussion, rigorously defined, into perspective, to see it as a valued part of the communication methods by which men seek solutions to their problems, but as a *part* insufficient to attain most necessary social action and quite unsuited to the service of many "action-producing" demands.

THE LANGUAGE FUNCTIONS OF INQUIRY AND PERSUASION

We shall not engage here in an analysis of the several functions of language in the affairs of men. Rather, we shall limit ourselves to two separable functions which are closely joined in their relationship

oups, discussing, for example, a matter of national
ot be likely to achieve precisely the same sets of con-
ver rational the processes followed by each group.
attitudes so important to effective inquiry in them-
against action. Impartiality, the admission of doubt,
lore all possible assumptions, all possible significance
is dialectical attitude is the characteristic "imprac-
academic world which interacts with, but cannot by
e needs of society for decision, confidence, action.[1]
contrast, proceeds from a position of decision. It
e support, to dispel doubt, to instill confidence, to
It is communication by which political movements
being and political beliefs are translated into social
ds and supports the activity of the market place;
ion religious beliefs came to influence the decisions
racteristic pattern which connects verbal communi-
action is not *inquiry-action*; it is rather *persuasion-*

ACTION OF INQUIRY AND PERSUASION

ht into the relationship of inquiry and persuasion
by an examination of several characteristic uses of
society. In these the products of discussion are
the social need for decision and action.

CONFERENCE"

lication may be found in the "staff conference."
nay be called by an official who is responsible for
advancing action proposals. This person may en-
ticipate in inquiry, seeking to achieve maximum

that discussion at one level of excellence may be quite
for action is emphasized by Mortimer Adler in his analysis
itude appropriate to philosophizing. "The aim of philos-
"might almost be described as the attempt to achieve an
free from any intellectual prepossessions, and unhampered
her. So conceived, philosophy is the process of entertaining
ssible, and of examining its significance impartially. It has
oetry is usually the product of sincere feelings. It might
onversation that it is bad philosophically when it is moti-
victions."—*Dialectic*, New York, Harcourt, Brace & Com-

to the securing of social action—the functions of inquiry and persuasion. We shall seek adequate definition of these two functions, observe their application to discussion and to related speech forms, and finally observe their interaction in certain speech situations.

INQUIRY CONSIDERED

The functions of inquiry and persuasion arise from two separate positions men may take toward a problem. The first of these is the position of the learner, the inquirer, the person who suspends or withholds to some extent decision as to what position ought to be taken with regard to a particular problem. Persons taking this position of suspended judgment are prepared to enter into the linguistic exercise known as "inquiry." This position is the one we have described as appropriate to discussion.

It should be observed that the position of the inquirer can, but need not, proceed from actual uncertainty, doubt, or the absence of partisan feelings. A person may have rather strong convictions with regard to the answers which might be made to a particular problem, but he may be willing to submit his partisanship to a process of inquiry for one of several reasons. First, if the problem is a complex one, he may recognize the real possibility that however strong his partisan feelings, there is yet a possibility that through impartial inquiry he may reach an improved position. Or the partisan may enter honestly into inquiry to test the practicality of his position in terms of the opposing positions taken by fellow discussants. Actually, his inquiry is in search of a more satisfactory basis for social action than the positions which he presently prefers. Discussion among the representatives of interest groups may take this form. For example, representatives of labor and management might enter into a process of inquiry not through any lack of partisanship on an issue at hand, but through recognition that such inquiry may be productive of a more practical action proposal than could be forthcoming without such inquiry. Similarly, representatives of different religions may be able to enter into the process of inquiry concerning problems involving matters of dogma in their respective religious commitments. They can do this while acknowledging their unwillingness to abandon a particular position. Their willingness to submit to examination from the point of view of persons holding to different dogma makes it possible that the conflict thus raised for rational examination may be, if not reduced, at least better understood.

We wish to emphasize the seeming paradox that discussion can embrace at one and the same time the activity of men who are partisans, who are divided in opinion, and who are yet impartial in the sense that they are willing to submit their preconceptions, their assumptions, their evidence, and their reasoning to critical examination. Indeed, we would go further to assert that good discussion of important problems cannot take place among people whose only commitment is to be agreeable, and who feel no conflict simply because they have no strong or considered opinions. Rather, it proceeds among men who have thought, who have convictions, but who, recognizing the elusiveness of truth in the affairs of men, are willing to impose upon their convictions, their thought, and their evidence the discipline of deliberate impartiality, openness, and critical examination.

PERSUASION CONSIDERED

The second position men take toward a problem, that of the persuader, is assumed by the person who has committed himself to the support of a particular answer to a given problem, either through conviction that this solution is unalterably "right"; or that it is the expedient or practical position to be taken at a given time, and therefore deserves to be advocated; or that it is required of him by the social system which he serves. Thus, a political leader may seek to persuade the public that an increased appropriation for the air force is needed, and he may be reflecting a profound conviction that this course of action is the only prudent one for his nation to follow. On the other hand, considerations of expediency may rest behind the persuasion of another person. During the Presidential campaign of 1940, both candidates for President for the two major parties, President Franklin Roosevelt and Mr. Wendell Willkie, are reported to have believed that America's involvement in the European war, then in progress, was inevitable and should be planned. Yet neither candidate felt that public opinion in America would support such a position. Both candidates campaigned by advocating preservation of peace for America, a proposition which seems to have been somewhat short of the real conviction each might have expressed.

A third type of persuas position because it is asked ticipating, is less well unde the persuasion of an attorn in a court of law, using s disposal. The lawyer may cence of his client. Yet h existing systems for obta argues that in cases of alle a vigorous competition in an able defense attorney before an impartial judg "system" in our society convictions may or may practice of advertising. siderable evidence, that tisers are essential const America. Certainly it ha essential to a mass prod may well view his work regardless of his person persuasion may be sellin

THE RELATIONSH

Even a cursory exa is secured in America insufficient to attain su as primarily the "prea extent that reason is a lems, "discussion-inqu men discover, organiz action which they wi groups may reach d willing directly to a activity of *inquiry—*

But "discussion-i promoting the forms conditions of discuss sons can achieve co

numbers of gr policy, would r clusions, howe Moreover, the selves militate the wish to exp of evidence—th ticality" of the itself sustain, th Persuasion, by seeks to organiz produce action. are brought into action; it exten through persuas of men. The cha cation to social *action.*

THE INTERA

Further insig may be obtained discussion in our closely related to

THE "STAFF

One such ap The conference formulating and courage and par

[1] The possibility remote from the need of the dialectical at ophy," writes Adler, empty mind, a mind by one belief or anot any idea as merely p been said that bad similarly be said of vated by sincere con pany, 1927, p. 246.

understanding of the implications of any of the possible courses of action available. The position of the official in the discussion is ambivalent, and becomes increasingly so as the time at which decisions must be made approaches. He asks from his staff the reporting of thorough investigative activity and the efficient conduct of dialectical examination of evidence thus made available. But the burden of ultimate decision rests upon him, with the necessity of implementing that decision, and perhaps securing its acceptance, through persuasion, by groups not involved in the conference.

THE "STRATEGY CONFERENCE"

A specialized form of staff conference, and one even more obviously dependent upon a subsequent program of persuasion, is the "strategy conference." Here the problem faced by the staff group is not "What policy are we going to adopt?" but "How are we going to sell a given policy?" Consideration of the problem presupposes that the decisions reached are to be put into action through persuasion.

THE "POLICY-MAKING COMMITTEE"

Let us say that the mayor of a city appoints a citizens' committee to study and make recommendations concerning this civic problem: "What program of hospital support, improvement, and construction should be followed by this municipality?" When he appoints the committee, the mayor will envisage inquiry done by the group in its discussion as an integral part of a larger plan of action involving persuasion. He may want from the group not only decisions which are as soundly based as possible—decisions which he, as mayor, can support—but he may also see the practical advantages of presenting to the community proposals which have the support of a study group involving certain community leaders. And he may well plan to use the services of members of the discussion group to work for widespread public support for their recommendations, i.e., to work as persuaders.

COMPETITIVE PERSUASION IN SUPPORT OF INQUIRY

Another aspect of the interrelationship of inquiry and persuasion may be observed in contrasting attitudes which persuaders and listeners may bring to certain speech situations. We observe that the competing attorneys in a trial are engaging in persuasion. Their principal audience, however, is engaged in a process of inquiry. With some wisdom, society holds that the accused in an alleged law violation cannot be expected to supply damaging evidence in an impartial inquiry concerning his own guilt or innocence. The person or persons upon whom the burden of inquiry rests, therefore, may find the competition of persuaders the best possible way of conducting their investigation. Similarly, society does not expect candidates for political office to discuss openly with one another the important question of which is better fitted to hold office. But the citizen who may wish to make such inquiry may be aided in his efforts by listening to a debate between two candidates—either face-to-face, competitive persuasion reminiscent of the Lincoln-Douglas debates, or the more remote mass-media argument of modern political campaigns. Congressional investigations provide another interesting example of an intermingling of persuasion and inquiry. Here, committee members are supposed to bring attitudes of inquiry to the hearing situation—and it may be supposed that they sometimes do, even though many such hearings appear to be carefully planned as acts of persuasion. However, assuming the function of the committee to be inquiry, the committee may well invite a variety of persuaders to testify before it, hearing conflicting advocacy, and reserving to itself the task of interpreting such testimony through discussion.

SUMMARY

We observe in our society situations in which discussion, embracing the linguistic function of inquiry, operates as a relatively pure combination of form and function. We observe other situations—probably more numerous—in which discussions (acts of inquiry) are undertaken as part of a larger program of social action, with discussion serving to establish the grounds for action, and persuasion to precipitate the action. We observe yet other situations in which men, performing the function of inquiry, observe the acts of competing persuaders as the most practical way of furthering their own deliberations. We would conclude that democratic society should encourage the practice of inquiry for purposes of bringing intelligence to bear upon the problems of men, securing the best possible bases for human understanding and the best possible proposals for social action. It also has need to encourage the practice of persuasion, the means by which products of inquiry may be made effective.

CHAPTER XVIII

Ethics of Discussion

In medicine, ethical conduct is behavior which benefits patient, community, and the medical profession. Both long-range and immediate effects enter in. The doctor who would be ethical interprets the "principles of medical ethics of the American Medical Association" in a way that seems to him to serve best the ultimate ends of the practice of medicine as well as to meet a present emergency.

In discussion, ethical practices are those which promote thoughtful deliberation. To the extent that leader or participant knowingly or carelessly subverts this end, he not only harms the individuals in a group through restricting their access to the best solutions of their problems, but also reduces the usefulness of discussion as a method by which people may better themselves. This damage is analogous to that done to patient, community, and profession by an unethical physician.

Unethical discussion always prevents or reduces reflective thinking, but not all obstacles to critical thinking can be properly labeled "unethical." Motivation plays a part. Ignorant but sincere insistence upon the truth of misinformation often obstructs group thinking, but is not subject to ethical criticism. Rather, this would seem to be a failure in competence. A similar insistence when the discussant *knows* about the false nature of his evidence is certainly not ethical. When the participant or leader is interested in and works toward the interruption of thoughtful deliberation of the group for selfish or other reasons extraneous to problem solving, the stage is set for the practice of unethical tactics.

Can *unintentional* hamstringing of the problem-solving process

269

in discussion ever be unethical? To be classified as unethical, an item of behavior must be avoidable. Certainly, flagrant "careless neglect" of interests and rights of others in a group seems unjustified. A failure to cooperate on the part of an individual who understands the urgent need for group decision, even the careless wasting of other people's time through personal exhibitionism, seems to be to some degree unnecessary. Many of the unintentional "thought-stoppers" in discussion would never occur if the people perpetrating them had envisaged their harmful effects. Hence we may say that behavior illustrated by these examples is directly avoidable and unethical for reasons of carelessness.

Ethical shortcomings in discussion due to carelessness are about as serious as a head cold when compared to the cancerous growth of intentional unethical manipulations. For one thing, careless deficiencies can be attacked directly. A tactful group member or leader can open the eyes of an offending person to the results of his behavior. Or a persistent misfit can be excluded from discussion. But the discussant with an axe to grind, who has a vested interest in preventing true group deliberation, because of the permissive climate of discussion, has great opportunity to influence its direction subtly and almost imperceptibly. The glib, unprincipled, hidden advocate is a menace to discussion who has too long gone unrecognized. He can best be revealed on ethical grounds, and that is what we propose to do in this chapter.

The student of discussion will be interested in ethical implications of language usage in other types of communication and in various approaches to the development of ethical criteria. These matters are sufficiently complex to prevent our including them in this brief book. They are treated in some detail in the textbook, *Persuasion: A Means of Social Control*,[1] Chapter XXIV, "The Ethics of Persuasion."

TECHNIQUES FOR MANIPULATING DISCUSSION

For many years the present authors have been collecting examples of the ways individuals or groups of individuals "control" discussion. How does the "hidden agenda" of a participant show itself

---

[1] Winston L. Brembeck and William S. Howell, *Persuasion,* New York, Prentice-Hall, Inc., 1952, pp. 444–466.

and change the course of the deliberations of a group? We have been interested primarily in the advocate who used *apparently* impartial procedures of inquiry to advance his cause. Frequently his persuasive goal has been enhancement of his personal prestige. At any rate, we think we have unearthed some of the methods used in purposeful skulduggery, and that these manipulations should be called to the attention of students interested in promoting the discussion of inquiry.

At first we were inclined to label the collected phenomena "subversive techniques in discussion." But it soon appeared that each had, under unique circumstances, a positive dimension. With proper intent every manipulation could at some time or other be used to help the group attain its objectives. "Techniques for manipulating discussion" are most often used to thwart critical thinking and serve the purposes of an individual. But not always! We encourage the reader to imagine situations in which each manipulation might serve socially desirable ends.

To criticize is to point out the need for revision. We are critical of the following practices because, most of the time, their revision would improve discussion.

The five categories of manipulation methods proceed from the least offensive to the most unethical. "Positive" applications of type (5) techniques will not be numerous!

(1) Aggressive exploitation of interpersonal relationship

The extremely congenial, out-going, cordial good fellow usually dominates his discussion group, particularly if his natural talents are of a back-slapping, toothy-smile variety. He implements this approach by making a seating chart which immediately enables him to call all participants and the chairman by their first names. He leans forward eagerly, grins and nods constantly, seems to be fascinated by every contribution. He helps the chairman get the discussion under way, often subtly appropriating the chairman's duties.

He builds a friendly climate by liberally dispensing praise in all directions. He repeats the contributions of others, credits original contributors, and notes the exceptional wisdom of each. At intervals he comments that this is the finest discussion in which he has ever had the good fortune to participate. At the end of the meeting

he can be relied upon for a final statement glowing with appreciation of the utterly splendid contributions of all who participated.
Only a misanthrope can suspect the beguiling warmth of this ex-
ploiter of interpersonal relations.

(2) Pseudo-critical thinking behavior

Regrettably, the symptoms of critical thinking can be simulated,
and some discussants show that they have learned this lesson well.
The successful pseudo-deliberator manages to impress others as a
"brain" without necessarily having one, and here are some of his
procedures.

He appropriates and interprets other people's ideas and information. Somehow these sound like his own.

He speaks often of "integration" and "advancing the thinking
of the group." He selects items of information from widely spaced
contributions and "integrates" them, thus demonstrating his facility.

He asks many "penetrating" questions, most of them unanswer-
able. He demands evidence in support of every speculation. He rejects all opinions lacking conclusive proof. He insists upon specific
examples, particularly where they are difficult to provide and
inappropriate.

The pseudo-deliberator is aided by an impressive vocabulary. He
uses the language of the laboratory: "reliable," "valid," "low probability," "high correlation," "coefficient of correlation," "But what
is the standard deviation of that distribution?" "normal curve,"
"probable error," "skewed distribution."

From confusing complexities he often turns to attractive oversimplifications. "But can't we state our difficulty in common-sense
terms?" he asks, and reduces an intrinsically involved predicament
to elementary Main Street logic. International trade problems are
resolved by analogy to activities of retail and wholesale merchants
in the home town. Problems of peace and war he reduces to hus-
band-wife relations, asserting that people are basically alike every-
where. Damage done by an attractive oversimplification is difficult
to repair.

The most able pseudo-critical thinker shows finesse in a device
which, skillfully executed, almost inevitably places the manipulator
in a position of intellectual ascendancy. He labels all fallacies, using
Latin names, *without explanation.*

(3) Sabotage of rivals

The practitioner of sabotage techniques consciously appreciates the fact that reputations are relative. He knows that if others appear to be incompetent, he may seem to be the shining light. So he systematically sets about dimming the bulbs of those who might legitimately outshine him.

For example, let us suppose that an excellent contribution, succinct and well spoken, has been made. Our saboteur, alert to the threat posed by a rival, assumes a puzzled expression and says, "That is very interesting, but let's get back to the subject." Whereupon he asserts a different topic with confidence and energy. By the time the original contributor grasps the situation (if he ever does), the time for effective correction has passed.

He spots the person whose attention has wandered momentarily and asks him a pointed question based upon the conversation he has obviously missed.

He ignores the argument and centers attention upon possible motivation of the person who advances it, a vigorous adaptation of the classical *ad hominem* fallacy: "It is interesting that you, a native American, should take the side of Red China in this discussion. Why are you pro-Communist?"

The chairman can be made to seem incompetent by judicious usurpation of his functions. When the chairman is about to summarize, the sabotage artist summarizes first. When it is almost time to change the subject, he beats the chairman to the draw and makes the transition. He may then twist the knife by requesting plaintively that the chairman be more active and alert.

Because people in discussion are encouraged to be frank and open (i.e., have their guards down) they are vulnerable to personal attacks like those above. Fighting back in discussion is difficult. A participant who claims that he has been wronged in this context sounds like a bad loser. A glib and clever saboteur can often lower the prestige and effectiveness of all members of a group without any person in that group realizing what has been going on.

(4) Personal advancement devices

The converse of sabotage of one's rivals is artificial enhancement of one's own status. Rather than contribute to the lowering of prestige of others, this approach accomplishes the same effect by drawing favorable attention to the manipulator, making him pleasantly conspicuous.

The simplest technique for personal advancement is for the ambitious one to talk more than anyone else. He recognizes that in all probability the participant who contributes the most words in a smooth and effortless flow will get credit for greatest accomplishment. Long speeches spoil this effect because they irritate the rest of the group. Hence, successful application of the technique implies that its practitioner have as his goal the making of a terrific number of very short contributions.

Collaboration has been used for personal advancement in discussion. "Ganging up" with another person multiplies effectiveness. Two glib people in secret collusion can guide a group into almost any related ramification of a topic. Also, by reciprocal flattery they can do much to enhance each other's contributions.

A tried and proven technique for personal advancement is that of waiting until the other participants in a discussion on a controversial issue have revealed their positions, then taking the odd one. The single representative of a radical, minority point of view becomes a center of interest and has more opportunity to talk than do the others. A chart showing participation flow (Chapter XIV) would show a great number of contributions directed toward the minority member. As the discussion develops, he may allow himself gradually to become "converted," and this apparent change of conviction guarantees him a continued spotlight at center stage. Typically, the "reluctant" change of the radical to a more favored middle course is disarming. All participants feel a missionary glow of pleasure in helping one of their number to discover the truth. Truly, there is more joy in heaven over the return of the lost sheep than concern over the fate of the ninety and nine that did not stray.

(5) Extreme stratagems to obstruct discussion

The title of this division does not imply that the other types of manipulation activity do not obstruct discussion. All do this to greater or lesser degree when used for selfish purposes. But these "extreme stratagems" are so named because they have as their objective the harassment of reflective thinking until it grinds to a halt.

They are resorted to by persons committed to positions threatened by the developing discussion. These are "rear guard actions" employed in the interest of escaping the consequences of a foreseen and logical conclusion. They are diversionary tactics designed to preoccupy men's minds with side issues, thereby preventing concentration upon the central problem.

The simplest type of obstructionist engages in his activity by introducing, as frequently as necessary, diversionary items made as attractive and urgent as possible.

More complicated and usually more successful obstructionism may take the forms of inaccurate restatement and pseudo-summary. The obstacle builder may seem to be recapitulating some portion of the preceding discussion, but his version resembles the original only coincidentally. Trying to straighten things out after a half-hour of distorted summary and twisted restatement will stop the forward progress of very nearly any discussion.

A desperate obstructionist will combine all possible means of confusing the thinking of individuals in the discussion, including many mentioned in other categories of manipulations. Insisting upon meticulous definitions of everything, frequent reversion to previous points, arguing about the motives of various members, reducing arguments to inappropriate analogies—these are a few of the tools available to the person who has for his own reasons resolved to prevent deliberative consideration of a problem.

The ultimate goal of all extreme stratagems to obstruct discussion is to persuade a group that their problem is too big for them, that further discussion cannot be productive, hence should be abandoned. The obstructionist hastens this eventuality by repeating loudly and frequently that the problem is beyond the abilities of the group, that it demands unavailable information, and that it should be left to the experts.

We have listed a sampling of ways to manipulate discussion, but more were omitted than were reported. Why do people so frequently lend themselves to purposes as antisocial as manipulating discussion to selfish ends? Because belief is influenced by desire. If we want a thing badly enough, many of us tend to resort to unusual means (if necessary) to get it. Most people feel free to use some persuasion in discussion. "Techniques of manipulation" are devices of concealed persuasion which are, in the context of discussion, largely unethical. Reread the first section of the present chapter and see if you agree with this opinion.

People may manipulate discussion with conscious purpose or with little understanding of their own activities. All of us who have studied techniques of manipulation will at least recognize some symptoms of improper manipulation in ourselves and in others. Recognition of a difficulty is prerequisite to doing something about it. We believe that an understanding of ways in which individuals or groups may take unfair advantage of the deliberative nature of discussion is sufficient to enable intelligent leaders and participants to protect themselves. Unethical controls over discussion can achieve their selfish ends only when they go unrecognized.

LARGE-SCALE, CONCEALED PERSUASION IN DISCUSSION

Chapter XVII suggests that the relationships among inquiry, persuasion, and social action are in delicate balance in a democracy. This implies a possibility that an advocate might manipulate inquiry on a large scale so as to serve purposes other than the solving of obvious problems. Joseph Alsop presents an analysis of what he considers to be such an attempt, explaining in this way the growth of the Southern Vietminh. Apparently carrying out the highly publicized slogan, "Serve the people!" (First Principle of Ho Chi Minh) the Communist representatives (cadres) labored in small communities in this fashion:

The cadres in the villages gave no orders, except in emergencies, and submitted no reports, except in secret. They lived like the peasants and tilled the fields with the peasants. They were specifically instructed to fade into the peasant background in every way possible. During the resistance period, they did their main political work indirectly, through a bewildering variety of "people's organizations"—Peasants' Patriotic Associations (which provided the real village governments), Patriotic Youth, Patriotic Women, Resistance Artisans, Mothers of Combatants, and many more. When the peasants had to be persuaded to pay the rice tax, or when supply coolies were needed for one of the army's raids on the French, or even when the villages were "laying out the next month's work program and setting the norms" (which is Vietminh language for a meeting to discuss planting schedules), the village branches of all these innumerable organizations were called together for endless talkfests. This was the "democratic deliberation" Pham Thieu had referred to. Its simple object was to convince the villagers that they ought to do what the Vietminh wanted them to do. The discussion at the talkfests was discreetly guided, of course, by the village cadres. Equally, of course, if the first round of democratic deliberation produced an unsatisfactory result, there had to be more discussion, and some self-criticism, too. Yet the deliberation was genuinely democratic in the sense that everyone was allowed his say, and prodigious efforts were made to secure general agreement.[2]

. . . In this manner the Vietminh met the most vital requirements of their struggle, which was to mobilize the people and keep them mobilized. And in this manner they provided a resistance-period substitute for the bureaucracy they lacked. Finally, in this manner, with really devilish ingenuity, they solved a problem one would not have supposed they could safely solve in mid-resistance: They prepared for the time when the resistance period would end, when Vietminh power would be unchallenged, and when the Vietminh government would have bureaucrats in plenty. For the cadres are in the villages now—under the shells of the turtles, as it were. They are there to stay. They know the affairs and thoughts of every man and every woman in the villages. And what could be more helpful than this in the probably inevitable future when the Communist masters of the state will depend on the police and the Army for their support, when they will not care very much about the support of the people, and when they will care very greatly about controlling the people with a close and iron hand?[3]

Mr. Alsop's theory suggests a method of gaining social control well adapted to the mass media of modern times, yet suited to widely varying cultural conditions in a population of diverse origins. Undoubtedly, sponsoring discussion for the purpose of ultimately creating circumstances that will prohibit discussion is unethical. Perhaps this is an impossibility in a democracy. At any rate, we should be alert to attempts, at home or abroad, to use discussion as a tool of social control.

LANGUAGE, LOGIC, AND ETHICS IN DISCUSSION

The concepts of language and logic in this book have ethical implications when they are applied to discussion. When linguistic

[2] Joseph Alsop, "A Reporter At Large," *The New Yorker*, Vol. XXXI, No. 19, June 25, 1955, p. 51.
[3] *Ibid.*, pp. 52, 53.

devices or logical procedures are used carelessly or purposefully in a way that prevents the "systematic use of known facts or accepted beliefs to develop or support other beliefs," there are grounds for ethical criticism. Most such destructive practices obscure issues while apparently attempting to clarify them. The majority of un-ethical misapplications of the methods of language and logic are purposeful diversionary tactics, although well-intentioned but mis-informed individuals may in rare instances serve the same ends accidentally.

The discussant who reasons openly and meticulously, who makes "empirical" contributions in the frame of reference of discussion is more ethical than is the person who conceals his reasoning. Substi-tuting persuasion for critical thinking is usually indefensible, because discussion hypothesizes disinterested investigation and deliberation, and an advocate, particularly one who does not label his interpreta-tions as persuasion, introduces a rhetorical incompatibility and con-fusion among his colleagues who would prefer to continue to pursue the facts and come to understand them.

Logical fallacies persist because they resemble valid forms, and as noted in the chapters on critical thinking, can be highly convinc-ing. Discussion can be led astray by skilled use of the classical fal-lacies, *ad hominem, post hoc,* affirming the consequent, and the like. Thus, an unsound interpretation can be made to appear sound through what often is a carefully developed sequence of reasoning. Fallacies cloaked in colorful language are a most powerful tool for the individual who would predetermine the outcome of discussion.

"Blinding factors," obstacles to critical thinking, are listed in Sattler and Miller [4] to call the attention of the student of discussion to mental habits we all share that affect our learning and interpre-tation of information. These are rigidities, influences which prevent our thinking freely about a problem, and which operate to keep us from following the evidence to whatever interpretation might rea-sonably develop. All contribute something of value to discussion. But each is difficult to keep in perspective. We tend to let these weigh far too heavily and when we start to rely on one or another our mental mobility is sharply reduced. The "blinding factors":

Intuition, the flash of insight that seems to advance our thinking

[4] W. M. Sattler and N. E. Miller, *Discussion and Conference,* New York, Prentice-Hall, Inc., 1954, Chapter 6.

but which needs to be taken apart and studied, to make sure that the gain is not an illusion.

Initial choice, the tendency to adhere to a premature opinion after it becomes shaky or downright foolish. Of what value is being consistent when the facts of the case would convince a wise man to change his mind?

Authority, the opinion we tend to overvalue because of our receptivity to positive prestige suggestion.

Tradition, the patterns we imitate in talking about social issues. What is proper, normal, and regular may not serve the needs of a group with an unusual and urgent problems.

Emotion, getting excited and hence to some degree irrational, but more important, our tendency to let desire determine conviction. We believe what we want to believe, hence a favored solution may or may not represent an impartial review of the available information.

Personal experience, the first-hand observation that makes a discussion lively and concrete, but which is often stretched far beyond its logical limits. A soldier after six weeks in an infantry unit makes confident statements about the army, and the college sophomore feels able to discuss "higher education" in its broad or narrow interpretations. "How much of the whole problem have I experienced?" is a question to help determine how much weight should be assigned to evidence accumulated first hand.

When any of the "blinding factors" are identified in discussion, analysis should take place. Many discussions shift from authority to emotion to intuition to personal experience to tradition and so on, a restricted repertoire of investigative and dialectical resources. Each should be supplemented with other information and reasoning. Any contributor who relies upon intuition, for example, should be willing to produce reasons to support his sudden revelation and should be happy to submit it to critical examination. An unethical manipulator may keep discussion quite largely within the limits of the list of "blinding factors." He finds himself able to influence others more in these relatively undisciplined approaches than in any systematic review of cold facts.

Perhaps the major misuse of language with ethical implications is the failure to use words with the knowledge that listeners supply the meanings from their experience, that *meaning is perception.* A person who uses specialized language and assumes his own or dictionary definitions encourages misunderstandings. The ethical and practical alternative is to be meticulous in clarifying what particular terms mean *in the present discussion*. People not only differ in their interpretations of language, but they tend to shift meanings as discussion advances into new phases. *Stipulating* precise definitions and taking the time to *agree upon* even familiar definitions, also repeating key definitions from time to time, all help to guarantee a meeting of minds. Refusing to cooperate in arbitrary defining of terms is an obstructionist tactic used frequently by the unethical discussant. This takes the forms of protesting at "unwarranted" extension or changes of word meaning, or of apparently going along with the group in stipulating a definition but during the subsequent discussion using the term with other, more general meanings. Because oral communication is a "low fidelity" mechanism at best, intentional attempts to compound confusion frequently succeed.

The best language in discussion is always simple and direct. The introduction of unnecessary complexities is very often a problem, perhaps because we are impressed by big, unusual words. Decorated rhetoric may be used to impress other discussants, a mildly unethical purpose, or to hinder progress while presenting an appearance of profound, sincere deliberation, something that is completely unjustifiable ethically.

Four complexities of language that are unnecessary in discussion and frequently deserve ethical criticism are high-level abstractions, loaded words, figurative definitions, and persuasive definitions. What seems to be a quest for clarification through moving to more abstract concepts may be a masterful attempt to "blunt the point" of a developing issue for a group. Loaded words are a means of stirring emotions to the end that the rational capacities of aroused participants are reduced. Figurative definitions are a special case of flying to higher abstraction through remote analogy. They are a threat to critical thinking because they convey an illusion of understanding and clarification when no real explanation has taken place. Defining "intuition" as "the eye of the mind" has a certain attractiveness, but in bringing people together in an understanding of what intuition is, it is worse than no attempt at definition. Naming is not explaining.

It is possible to define a term or concept in such a way that the listener is prejudiced for or against it. This is done by slanting, a specialty of loaded words. Such definitions mold attitudes more than they clarify. They are conveniently labeled "persuasive definitions." Their purposeful use prevents objective deliberation, hence may be classed as unethical.

SUMMARY

Analysis of ethical issues tends toward negative statements used to describe undesirable conduct. Positive generalizations can be developed by negative instances, however, and the reader will perhaps recall as many "things to do" as "things not to do" in increasing ethical qualities of his performances as leader or participant in discussion. We would stress the following statements summarizing the materials discussed in this chapter in the interest of making the task of being ethical as specific and concrete as possible.

1. The "concealed persuader" is the source of most unethical conduct in discussion. We should avoid playing this role either consciously or unintentionally.

2. It is the responsibility of every participant as well as that of the leader to be alert to, and to expose diversions from, impartial deliberation. The assumption must be made that undesirable manipulations which are thus countered were well-intentioned.

3. Understanding of the many "techniques for manipulating discussion" can protect groups from their most serious detrimental effects as well as prevent individuals from accidentally slowing the thinking of a group by their improper use.

4. Logical fallacies resemble sound reasoning and must be understood to be corrected.

5. "Empirical contributing" in which the contributor takes pains to show each step in his reasoning and the evidence upon which it is based is less deceptive and hence more ethical than are semiconcealed means of contributing.

6. Each discussant must guard against overuse of the "blinding factors," for these are attractive alternatives to the quest for reliable and representative information.

7. Ethical language usage in discussion is that which maintains the lowest possible level of abstraction, rejects figurative definitions, and filters out loaded terms, substituting for them report language.

8. "Persuasive definitions," those designed to mold attitudes rather than to secure impartial understanding of an issue, hinder the process of inquiry and are ethically unjustifiable.

9. Contributions which are designed to produce a maximum of symbol responses and a minimum of signal responses among participants are of higher ethical quality than are contributions which primarily aim at signal responses.

10. In general, ethical practices in discussion are those which promote thoughtful deliberation. A choice of alternatives made upon this criterion is an ethical decision.

APPENDIX

Suggested activities for thirty periods of a beginning college course in discussion.

The following activities are planned with these assumptions: (1) class periods each approximate one hour, and are at least fifty minutes long; (2) students are of college sophomore level or above; (3) not more than twenty-five students (preferably twenty) are admitted to the discussion class; (4) recording equipment capable of making half-hour uninterrupted recordings is available (a separate studio-classroom arrangement is desirable, with facilities for both listening to and recording studio program material in the classroom); (5) chairs are movable to permit rearrangement for practice of different forms of discussion.

No attempt is made to be comprehensive in this period-by-period calendar. Its purpose is simply to suggest ways in which practice in discussion can be carried on throughout the course. Collateral readings, field trips and other observations, term projects, participation in out-of-class discussions, and other learning experiences are available to the instructor at his discretion.

Period 1. Announce text, assign Chapters I, II. Lecture on definition of discussion, introduce concepts of human-relations skills, critical thinking skills, show-type and conference-type discussion.

Period 2. Discuss Chapters I, II. Assign Chapter III, plus one original discussion topic each of fact, policy, and speculation suitable for development as a half-hour radio round-table discussion. In wording topics, students should envisage class members as leader and participants, and the resulting program as broadcast over a local station.

Period 3. Discuss wording of topics for discussion. Select from original topics submitted five to be presented as twenty-eight minute radio round-table discussions. Develop the best possible wording for each. Cast the discussions (maximum, five people per topic) as democratically as possible. Assignment: each student brings a one-page outline of points to be discussed by his group to the next meeting of the class. This necessitates research.

Period 4. Fifteen minutes: discussion of steps in preparing for the radio round table and the application of the Dewey steps in problem solving to making of a discussion outline. Remainder of period: class divides into radio round-table groups. Each group selects its own leader and works on formation of its agenda. Announce: the first radio round table will be heard during period 6. Order of presentation of the programs will be determined by lot at end of period 5. Assignment: research on round-table topic.

Period 5. Forty minutes: small group conferences to complete round-table agendas. Remainder of period: answer questions, draw order for presentation of round-table programs.

Period 6. Radio round table No. 1. Program is tape-recorded when given. Class listens to monitor and takes notes to be used in writing critiques that are due the following class period. We suggest that the recording begin at about fifteen minutes after the beginning of the class to permit the performing group to "warm up"; also that spoken analysis of the program be postponed until critiques are written, to avoid influencing them.

Possible outline for critique of radio round table:

(1) Successful program items (3–5)

(2) Program items to be improved (3–5)

(3) Summary paragraph answering the question, "How successful would this discussion be if broadcast over the local radio station?"

Period 7. Radio round table No. 2. Discuss performance of group No. 1 for first ten minutes. Collect critiques on No. 1. Make appointment with group No. 1 for playback outside of class. Critiques are to be analyzed at time of playback. Assignment: read ahead in part II of text. Apply critical thinking techniques in current radio round tables.

Period 8. Radio round table No. 3. First ten minutes: discussion of No. 2. Collect critiques, make playback appointment with group No. 2.

Period 9. Radio round table No. 4. First ten minutes: discussion of No. 3. Collect critiques, make playback appointment with group No. 3. Announce that period 11 will be devoted to an informal group discussion under a student leader on the topic, "What have we learned about discussion from our experiences with the radio round table?" Appoint or otherwise select a student leader who will make his own agenda.

Period 10. Radio round table No. 5. Discuss No. 4. Collect critiques. Make playback appointment with group No. 4. Announce unit on critical thinking for periods 12, 13, 14. Chapters IV, V, VI, VII are to be thoroughly studied before period 12.

Period 10 and the playback of group No. 5 completes the first performance unit. We suggest that critiques be graded, for student criticism of discussion is a good indicator of the amount of understanding a student has of the process of discussion, and grades will motivate more careful critiques. If a student misses hearing a program, he can make up his missed critique by writing one on a professional radio round-table discussion which he hears on radio or television. This make-up assignment is useful, for it helps him to compare the work done in class with similar efforts on the air.

Period 11. Collect critiques and schedule playback appointment for group No. 5. Informal group discussion under student leader as scheduled. Students can be informed that the final course project will be another radio round-table discussion with different topics and different groups. They should attempt to take notes during today's class discussion which will help them to make the final project better than the first round of radio round tables.

Period 12. Assign Chapter XI to be read by period 13. Periods 12, 13, and 14 may well be devoted to exercises illustrating and applying the critical thinking materials in the chapters on inductive analysis of evidence. We hesitate to recommend methods of doing this because preferences of different teachers differ so widely. We suggest only that we have found contemporary sources of examples, radio, newspapers, and magazines, to be most helpful and productive of student interest in these exercises in reasoning. Examples from the first round of discussion often illustrate desirable and other practices in inductive analysis.

Period 13. Exercises in inductive analysis (continued). Select, word two topics for cooperative investigation. Cast each with six investigators and a leader. Assign Chapters VIII, IX, and X to be read as fast as they can be assimilated.

Period 14. Exercises in inductive analysis (continued). Schedule cooperative investigation No. 1 for periods 15, 16, and No. 2 for periods 17, 18.

Period 15. Cooperative investigation No. 1, first phase, devoted to presentation of information by investigators. Last ten minutes: select, word topic for, and cast a "mock trial." This is scheduled for period 19. Assign Chapters XII, XIII by period 18.

Period 16. Cooperative investigation No. 1, second phase, devoted to questioning of panel, further information, general discussion.

Last ten minutes: select, word topic for debate. Cast two two-man teams. The debate during the twentieth class period will complete a second round of participation for twenty-three people.

Period 17. Cooperative investigation No. 2, first phase.

Period 18. Cooperative investigation No. 2, second phase.

Assign Part Four of text, "The Criteria of Discussion," Chapters XIV, XV, XVI, to be read by period 20.

Period 19. "Mock trial."

Assign 500-word paper (1) analyzing strengths and weaknesses of leadership and participation in the second round of discussions and (2) commenting on particular usefulness or shortcomings of the co-operative investigation and "mock trial" forms of discussion. This paper is to be handed in at the twenty-first class meeting.

Period 20. Debate. Class takes notes on evidence and forms of reasoning used. Audience decision.

Period 21. Teacher-led, informal analysis of previous day's debate and discussion of similarities and differences between debate and discussion. Key controversial discussion topic: "Should debate enter into discussion?"

Assign buzz session on language in discussion for period 22. Students prepare by reviewing Chapters XIII and being able to explain or illustrate all concepts therein. A committee of three students is selected to prepare buzz session questions to pose to the small groups.

Assign each student to bring a well-worded topic for a radio round-table program in the final series to class period 23.

Assign Chapters XVII and XVIII by period 28. Collect papers due today.

Period 22. Buzz sessions on language chapter materials.

Period 23. First half of class: discussion of buzz session method and, if necessary, of language theory. Second half of class: selection of five topics for final radio round-table discussions. Cast each. Designate chairmen. Draw for order of presentation.

These final round-table discussions are to emphasize the processes of generalization and deductive application of generalizations. Period 24 is to be devoted to clearing up any confusions about these operations as presented in Chapters VIII, IX, and X.

It is suggested that the final radio round tables, twenty-eight minutes in length as were the first programs, be recorded outside of class and played back in class. This makes possible substitution of oral comments for written critiques.

Period 24. Informal discussion of generalization, implication, alternation, and the syllogism in discussion.

Period 25. Playback round table No. 1. Class analysis and evaluation.

Period 26. Playback round table No. 2. Class analysis and evaluation.

Period 27. Playback round table No. 3. Class analysis and evaluation.

Period 28. Playback round table No. 4. Class analysis and evaluation.

Period 29. Playback round table No. 5. Class analysis and evaluation.

Period 30. Discussion of ethical problems in discussion, the relationships of inquiry and persuasion in social action, evaluation of the course, review.

INDEX